Items should be returned on or before the date shown below. Items
not already requested by other borrowers may be renewed in person,
in writing or by telephone. To renew, please quote the number on the
barcode label. To renew online a PIN is required. This can be requested
at your local library.
Renew online @ **www.dublincitypubliclibraries.ie**
Fines charged for overdue items will include postage incurred in recovery.
Damage to or loss of items will be charged to the borrower.

Leabharlanna Poiblí Chathair Bhaile Átha Cliath
Dublin City Public Libraries

Marino Branch
Brainse Marino
Tel: 8336297

Comhairle Cathrach
Bhaile Átha Cliath
Dublin City Council

Due Date	Due Date	Due Date

D0540222

GEORGIANA
Duchess of Devonshire

The Face without a Frown

IRIS LEVESON-GOWER

FONTHILL

Devonshire House was built in 1735 and demolished February 1925. These splendid gates, photographed *c.* 1900, survive and are now nearby providing an entrance to Green Park from Piccadilly.

Fonthill Media Limited
Fonthill Media LLC
www.fonthillmedia.com
office@fonthillmedia.com

First published in the United Kingdom
and the United States of America 2018

British Library Cataloguing in Publication Data:
A catalogue record for this book is available from the British Library

Copyright © in this edition Fonthill Media 2018

ISBN 978-1-78155-557-6

Typeset in 10.5pt on 13pt Sabon
Printed and bound in England

Contents

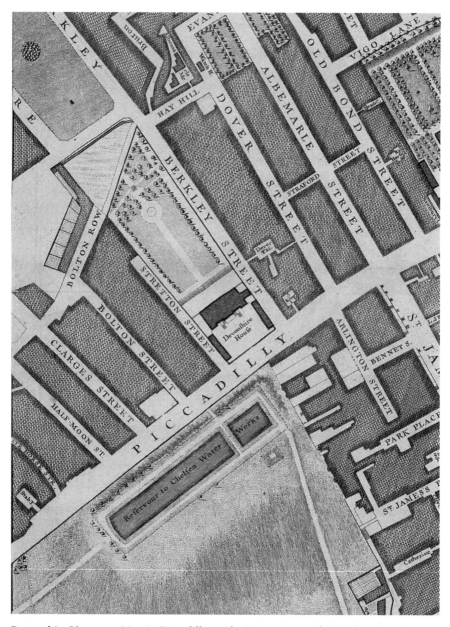

Devonshire House position in Piccadilly on the Rocque map of 1746, between Stretton Street (now Stratton Street) and Berkeley Street. The current lane named Mayfair Lane covers what was the gravelled drive separating the house from the pleasure grounds. The house was virtually opposite what is now the Ritz Hotel.

Publisher's Foreword

Iris Irma Leveson-Gower (1899–1944) was the eldest daughter of Sir George Granville Leveson-Gower, KBE and the Hon. Adelaide Violet Cicely Leveson-Gower, née Monson (1868–1955). She married, 5 January 1922, William Henry Buchanan Mirrlees (1892–1964), but the marriage ended in divorce in 1928. She married secondly, 29 June 1938, Major Richard Lodge Palmer DSO, MC (1892–1956), a First World War officer who had served in the Royal Artillery. There do not appear to have been any children of either marriage.

Iris's suitability to write this book was twofold. First she was extremely competent, even if perhaps a little flowery in her writing. Secondly, and perhaps more importantly, was her ability to open doors through family connections, for she was Georgiana's great-great-granddaughter. Her grandparents were Edward Frederick Leveson-Gower (1819–1907) and Margaret Mary Frances Elizabeth, née Compton (1815–1858); her great-grandparents were Granville Leveson-Gower, First Earl of Granville (1773–1846) and Harriet Elizabeth, née Cavendish (1785–1862), known in the family as Hary-o.

As Iris admits in her 'Apologia', the Trustees of Castle Howard allowed her to loot their gold mine and to carry away much booty. Can one imagine such things being allowed now? Undoubtedly she looked after everything and returned it safely, but this is just one example where she had ease of access to the important documents necessary for this work.

The work has been left exactly as she wrote it, so the reader should be aware that when she refers to 'now' she is referring to her time of writing during the Second World War.

The original illustrations in the book were in black and white, and were not of good quality. New colour versions have been sourced and other illustrations have been added.

Above and below: Chiswick House in Burlington Lane, Chiswick, was designed by Lord Burlington, and completed in 1729. After his death in 1753 and the subsequent deaths of his last surviving daughter, Charlotte Boyle, in 1754 and his widow in 1758, the property was ceded to William Cavendish, 4th Duke of Devonshire, Charlotte's husband. After William's death in 1764, the villa passed to his and Charlotte's orphaned young son, William Cavendish, 5th Duke of Devonshire. Although only 5½ miles from Devonshire House, it was then in virtually rural countryside and was used as a retreat by the Devonshires. It was the place of death of Charles James Fox in 1806. Tory Prime Minister George Canning also died there in 1827.

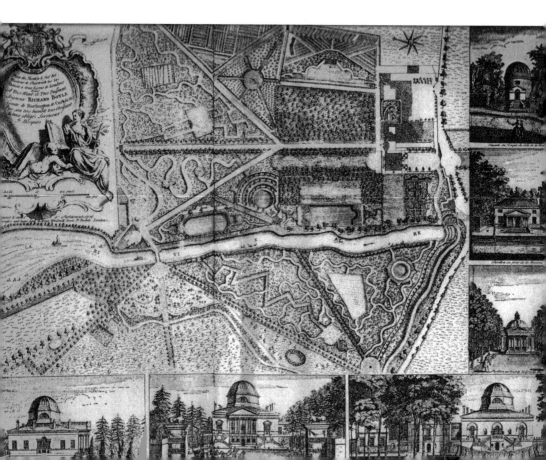

Chronological Chart

1792   (?) Birth of Eliza Courtenay (Georgiana's and Grey's daughter) at Aix between 11 January and 3 February.

1793   18 September , Georgiana's return to England.

1794   Marriage of Charles Grey and Elizabeth Ponsonby.

1801   21 March, Marriage of 'G.' Cavendish to Lord Morpeth.

1806   30 March, Death of Georgiana. 13 September, Death of Fox.

A mid-nineteenth-century view of the north elevation of Devonshire House, viewed from the pleasure grounds.

The south elevation as it was in 1844, viewed from Piccadilly shortly after major changes. Kitchens and other offices are to the right, and behind that east wing is Berkeley Street. Alterations were made to the house over a long period. In 1843, a new portico, entrance hall, and grand stair was built for the 6th Duke. At this time, the external double staircase was swept away, allowing formal entrance to be made to the ground floor through the new portico. Hitherto, the ground floor had contained only secondary rooms, and in eighteenth-century fashion been the domain of servants.

Apologia

This is a book which does not pretend to any historical importance, unless as a kindergarten lesson in how easy it is for mountains to be made out of molehills.

The slender thread on which history is strung is bespangled with tiny highlights which catch our eyes, fix our attention and often obscure the true course of events.

Helen's face launched a thousand ships and burned the topmost towers of Ilion; the debatable length of Cleopatra's nose changed the history of her world; Nell Gwynne sold oranges, called herself the Protestant whore and endeared herself for ever to the English people. Georgiana Devonshire kissed a butcher and wore a large hat; since then she is the beautiful Duchess of a million chocolate boxes.

She is also my ancestress, and I remember being introduced to her through the medium of her picture. 'That's your great-great-grandmother,' I was told, 'the beautiful Duchess who kissed the butcher.' It is true I was told this during a general election, but being very small at the time, that significance escaped me and the hat and the kiss were imprinted on my mind as the important points in the introduction.

Afterwards, when editing her daughter's letters with my father, I came to know her, and found that most of the time she did not wear the hat and that she was not exclusively occupied in kissing tradesmen, or even other men, for that matter.

I found that, contrary to legend, she was a simple woman who was often very unhappy; that the contrasts between her instincts, her upbringing and her surroundings after her marriage had created a conflict and given a purpose to her life. Gradually I found that her story and the development of her character had a meaning of their own, both to her times and, perhaps, to ours.

So I have tried to clear up a misunderstanding. The title of the book is taken from an inscription on her portrait by Downman which reads, 'She seldom wore and never met a frown.'

Everything I have written about her is fact, save where, in one or two instances, when I have been driven to conjecture, I have indicated otherwise. I have preserved her spelling when quoting from her letters, but have put in punctuation which, according to the custom of her day, she omitted. I would like to add that her name was not pronounced euphoniously 'Georgiana' but, more vigorously, 'George-ayna.'

All the material is from contemporary sources, but no book of this kind can be written without much help from others, and I can never express the gratitude I feel for all the generous assistance I have received.

I would like to thank my mother and my father for their patient encouragement and for making the index; Baroness Budberg for all her help; the Staff of the London Library and Mr Cox for their omniscience. To Professor L. B. Namier and Algernon Blackwood I owe a special debt.

To all those descended from, or connected with, Georgiana, I have received unfailing help: Lord Bessborough has most kindly allowed me to reproduce four letters from Georgiana's mother written during the Duchess's last illness; Lord Halifax has contributed Georgiana's epitaph on herself; the Duke of Devonshire allowed me to read the whole of her correspondence and to quote from her letters, Bess Foster's letters, and made full measure with a letter from Mr Adair. The Trustees of Castle Howard allowed me to loot their gold mine and to carry away much booty (all the letters written to her children by the Duchess during her 'exile' come from there).

Finally there are two others without whose help this book could never have been written: they are its godparents—my friend Francis Thompson, who is the Librarian (I almost said the Library) at Chatsworth, and my cousin Christian Howard, who for endless hours would piece together the scraps of evidence with me until we found the puzzle was completed.

WASHINGTON, D.C.
August 10th, 1943.

IRIS LEVESON GOWER

The Duke was called 'Ca' (from Cavendish) or 'Canis'; Georgiana was 'Mrs Rat'; Elizabeth Foster was 'The Racoon' (her pointed face resembling that creature) or 'Mrs Racky'; the Prince of Wales was, of course, 'Prinny' or 'My Brother,' and Fox was 'The Eyebrow.'

Below and over: A letter from Georgiana to her daughter, Georgiana. See pages 170–172.

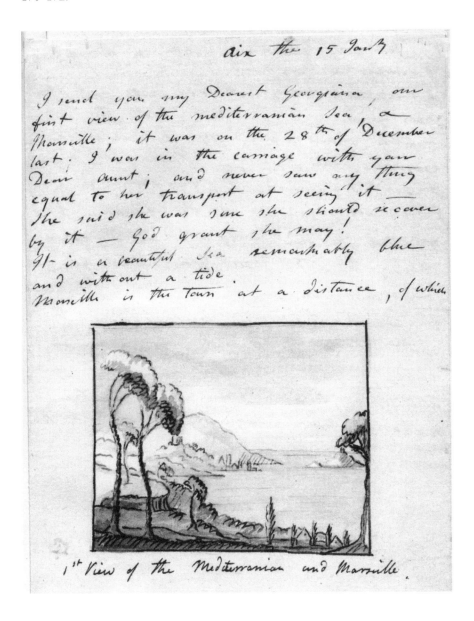

I shall give you an acc't of some
Drawings in my next.

I am very sorry you did not get the
new years gift in time but the
weather has made the post very
very uncertain.

I send you a drawing of Caroline 1st
Jules carrying her child like a
gypsey & a drawing for Hartington
I expect to join you Dear grandmm
& aunt in about 10 days —

How I should like to go to Sir Ashtons
Leavers with you; — I am glad you
like the sparrs & fossals; in
Derbyshire, which is the country for
natural history of that kind you
must have a little museum of
your own.

I cannot tell you how glad I
am y't the French master is
come; pray remember whilst you
are labouring at French I shall
probably have begun Italian at Nice
— addio gioja mia.
                        G D.

Kiss Hartington from me with
his drawing.

1

Spring Morning, 1774

The rough tussocky grass which tripped up Georgiana Spencer was an amusing obstacle to her rather than an irritation. If she could catch the butterfly in spite of the hummocks, in spite of the dew-drenched muslin gown cluttering her ankles, in spite of the sun in her eyes, she felt that it would be a prize worth achieving. As she stumbled, laughing, over the uneven paddocks patched with elm-shade, flecked with flowers, she had no thoughts but of butterflies and a happy consciousness that the morning routine of the Wimbledon villa was behind her.

The routine was indeed strict, for her mother was insistent on order, habit and application. 'Method, you know,' she would say, 'is my hobby-horse.' Up at half-past five with the summer dawn (with a concession in winter of an hour and a half later); down to prayers before sleep had cleared from eyes and brain; revolutionary breakfasts of fruit and milk and eggs; tasks with books, with needles, with churns, with wooden-headed village children; making one's own shoes (more often of serge than of silk), fashioning one's gowns, embroidering flounces, frilling caps, netting gloves; learning Ariosto; classifying fossils.... No wonder that to catch a butterfly was to net a golden fleece.

No wonder that she chose to ignore the half-heard voice calling to her. Routine was supreme; the morning tasks were done; Mama was occupied in answering the letters that had arrived punctually at midday, her beautiful bold writing flowing evenly over the paper; dinner was not till three; she could not possibly be wanted; if it was fussy old Nurse—well, she could shout in vain.

'Milady, milady, come here. Come here at once!'

Bother Nurse. Which way had the butterfly gone now? Georgiana paused for a moment, screening her eyes against the sun. She could hear

Nurse panting behind her, and more to tease than to disobey, she started off in the opposite direction. Nurse's patience and breath were both exhausted.

'Drat the girl!' she thought and wielding the lath with which she had helped herself over the uneven ground, she reached out and brought it down with a sharp whack on Georgiana's auburn head. The girl was so surprised that she stopped dead in her tracks.

'Didn't you hear me hollering after you? You ought to be ashamed of yourself. You're to come in at once. Her Ladyship requires you. And you are to change your gown. Quickly now. Enough time has been wasted as it is.'

'Change my gown? What for? It's not time to dress yet.'

'I can't answer all your questions now. I've told you—her Ladyship is waiting for you. And his Lordship. And there's a visitor.'

'A visitor? Who?'

'Come along now, my poppet.' Nurse had regained her temper and her voice had softened. 'Never mind who—you'll find out soon enough, my lamb.'

So it was to be today.... Georgiana's heart missed a beat and made her catch her breath. The slightly unreal conversation, or rather interview, she had had with her father a few weeks previously was to be translated into reality. When Lord Spencer had sent for her then, and in the presence of her mother had informed her that now she was sixteen years old, she was of marriageable age, and that they, her parents, having given the matter and her interests every consideration, had decided to accept the offer made for her hand by the Duke of Devonshire and that they hoped she would agree with their choice, she had curtsied, thanked them, expressed her duty and been dismissed. She had felt excited, curious, very important and rather alarmed. She had expected to find herself and the course of her life immediately altered by those few words spoken by her father. Instead of which things had gone on just as before—in fact, she had been treated rather more strictly than usual, so that the momentous announcement had gradually dwindled into unreality.

But now ... as Nurse dressed her she did not know whether it was her laces or her heart that made her feel so breathless. Suppose she did not like him? But that would hardly be possible: Mama was such a wonderful judge of character, and from all she had heard he was a most admirable young man. But there was no more time for speculation, for Mama stood beckoning at the door of her room and escorted her downstairs.

Lady Spencer was dressed in her usual plum-coloured riding habit, fine lace at her wrists and throat; she had two early pink roses tucked into the top button-hole of her coat and her hair was unpowdered. She, at least, looked just the same as ever and some of Georgiana's nervousness disappeared.

When they came into the beautiful library, she took a quick look at her father; he too looked no different from when she had seen him at breakfast. Georgiana heard words of presentation and only lifted her eyes as she rose from her curtsy. She was greeted with great courtesy and punctilio by a young man of good looks but of a sulky, spoiled expression, whose bow, she noticed, was rather clumsy. This reassured her, and her relief that the worst of the ordeal had passed so simply made her smile at him happily.

She never could remember what they had talked about then or during dinner. She remembered, with awe, that he had refused the boiled fowl and had seemed quite unimpressed by her formidable parents. Somehow she had expected an elaborate feast on this great occasion, but on thinking it over was not really surprised that dinner was as usual—after all, Lady Spencer inflicted her rather Spartan ideas about food on all their friends. 'Take it or leave it,' she would say, and even Papa's half-hearted protests were of no avail. What was remarkable was that the Duke had knocked over two of the lovely wine glasses that Mama was so fond of, and broken them, and that he had neither apologized nor had Mama even *looked* her disapproval. Yes, that was remarkable from all points of view: a young man who, sober, could break two glasses without noticing his gaucherie or to be called to account for his clumsiness by Lady Spencer—somehow the two-faceted incident made her realize the importance of the occasion. Otherwise it was all rather hazy, even the walk she and the Duke had taken on the lawn afterwards. True they had said very little and that little was confined to remarks about the weather and the view, though she was sure he *had* said something about the great honour she was doing him.

That night Lady Spencer wrote to Sir William Hamilton at Naples, saying that 'Georgiana had several considerable offers made her which she declined without the least hesitation in favour of the Duke of Devonshire. You know Lord Spencer and me well enough to be very sure we avoided saying anything that could bias her in an event so material to her happiness, but it is a great addition to ours that she has made a choice that gives her so fair a prospect of it.'

Upstairs Georgiana could hardly wait till Nurse had brushed her red-gold hair, put away the best dress and carried away the candelabra leaving her with a single taper. Her head was in a whirl: what did she know of him, she thought? That he was William, fifth Duke of Devonshire, aged twenty-four and orphan-heir to the leadership of the Whig party; that old

Horace Walpole had called him 'the first match in England'; that she was suite sure she was in love, that he would love her—probably, certainly, for ever; that, even if it had started by being Mama's idea, it was now hers and that it was all going to be wonderful.

The immense future lay like the Promised Land before her; she seemed to survey it from the peak of her new standing as a bride; over her shoulder lay the past, remote and small and clear. Even the Grand Tour they had taken in France only two years ago seemed far away, and yet how vividly she remembered it.

Papa, Mama, she and her younger sister Harriet, then eleven years old, had set out from Wimbledon on the last day of July, a day so scorching that one of the horses had died of heat. They arrived at St Omer the following day, and immediately wonders and strange people crowded about them. Both the little girls had been told to keep their journals carefully; Harriet still had hers; she wondered what had happened to her own. At Brussels there was a very pretty play which they watched from a fine box all lined with looking-glass and which had a fireplace in it, and, better still, there was 'ice and sweetmeats.' There was Prince Charles of Lorraine, a great, fat, good-humoured man in a brown coat with a great many ribbons and stars; an old, old man called Count Varelst, who always dressed in a nightgown and a green velvet nightcap and who had neither left his house nor had a window opened for twenty-five years; there was the Duchess of Northumberland, who had a beard like a man, and the Comtesse d'Egmont, who wore a great deal of very red rouge on her face. '*I* shall be able to wear rouge now,' she thought. There was Madame Golifet, who had been married almost two years and was not yet fifteen, and a man who had come to teach Papa how he might always win at faro.

In France the two girls, mounted on ponies, had gone boar hunting, and on St Hubert's Day they had seen all the Royal Family of France, who alone had out 1,500 horses. They had visited the famous seminary at St Cyr, where little Harriet, who had had experience of convents, whispered to Mama that she should beg the Reverend Mother to lift the ban of silence, upon which request being granted such a babel of bird-clear noise arose that Mama was quite amazed.

There had been many shocking but salutary sights too—of dead bodies broken upon the wheel and exposed by the road-side: of twenty or more corpses swinging from a great triangular gallows near Toulouse and of a poor young man of eighteen who had robbed his master and was hanged outside their windows, on which occasion Mama pointed the moral by reading them the play of 'George Barnwell.' Worst of all, there were the terrible catacombs into which little Harriet was taken by her father who, when he saw the child was frightened by the dreadful company, made her touch one of the terrifying mummies. Georgiana had been in luck here, for the Friars would not admit females over the age of twelve, but Papa and Mama had considered it was a suitable, even an edifying, sight for a shaking child of eleven. Georgiana remembered how Harriet had clung to her for nights afterwards when they were in bed and how she had whimpered in her sleep.

She remembered, too, how, just before Papa was taken ill and underwent those two dreadful operations without shrinking, he had given a great ball in the empty Government house at Montpellier in honour of the Queen's birthday. Mama had hung the walls with sheets, with festoons of linen, with ribbons and flowers, and it looked excessively pretty. The dancing had started at eight; they had supped at ten with fifty soldiers of the Bourbonnais Regiment handing the dishes, and after supper the fine ladies changed their ball gowns and came back dressed *en paysanne* and danced till six in the morning.

In Paris, old, blind Madame du Deffand ran her fingers over their fresh young faces; called Harriet 'her little religious' and wrote to Mr Walpole to tell him that, in general opinion, Georgiana was found to be quite lovely.

Indeed, they had both excited much admiration, and Georgiana remembered with amusement how pleased Mama had been at their success and how anxious that they should not become conceited; she remembered, too, her first transparent frock, it was a polonaise of white lutestring trimmed with blue and white gauze, and she had rather enjoyed its diaphanous and revealing charms and couldn't imagine why the elders had expected her to feel embarrassed. And how Harriet had called forth shrill cries of admiration from the French ladies, who were enchanted by her unpowdered, uncurled hair—so different from their own poor frizzed and powdered mites.

Of course, most of her life had not been so exciting: the routine of education had pursued its even way, whether the family had been in London, at Althorp, at St Albans or at Wimbledon. At Holywell, the charming sham-Gothic house in St Albans, and at Althorp, Mama had indulged to the full her hobby of educating the children of the poor, together with Georgiana and Harriet. Indeed, lately Georgiana had been promoted to teach in the little schools. ('I'll start a school of my own one day soon,' she resolved.) But at Althorp, among the beautiful pictures and the many books, education had been on a rather higher plane, for there were always so many interesting visitors to talk to—she thought of

Mrs Montague with her jewels and her sharp wit, and decided that she preferred Sir Joshua, who always treated her as though she was a sort of fairy queen, and dear dirty Dr Johnson, who was adored by all of them and who in turn, charmed as he always was by simplicity and youth, behaved towards the girls and their brother as though they were his equals and friends whose company he particularly sought out and enjoyed. And these were actors and statesmen, divines and scholars—not all of them so welcome to the children as Sir Joshua and the Doctor, but all interesting in their way. Indeed, she thought, everybody is interesting in one way or another.

Up in London at beautiful Spencer House, with its painted ceilings, its carved doors and pillars, its statues and, last but not least, its fascinating modern *cabinets de toilette*, education had reached its peak; there the backboard was allowed a rest in favour of the dancing master, who used to bring his fiddler with him—an odd little man like a monkey; and there were fewer lessons on mathematics and syntax and more on painting and music. Lately she had been promoted to her mother's *festinos*, which, to tell the truth, she had found rather dull, and those routs at which her mother's two great friends, Mrs Howe and Miss Lloyd, were always present, and who, with their endless talk of the Navy and the Court, contrived to make the parties even duller.

Still, even routs and Mama's *festinos* were better than endless hours of sewing and reading out loud—and oh! what dull books Mama always chose.

The memories of those moral books, of those unending Penelope-like samplers, stretched farther and farther back into the past, back into the time when she could remember darling Harriet as a baby all swaddled up in stiff embroidered bands, back to the time when she was stood on a table in front of Mama, dressed in her best frock (and very uncomfortable it was too), stiff buckled shoes on her feet and a starched cap on her head, Mama's arm round her and Mama's little dog on the table beside her, to be painted by Sir Joshua. What a long time ago … why, she was a very little girl then, and now she was going to be married and the whole of life was going to be different; except of course one would have to remember one's duties for oneself instead of being always reminded of them.

Suddenly she saw limitless vistas opening before her. Dazed with the vision of constellations of diamonds, guineas pouring forth from Fortunatus-William's purse, Mama's precepts achieved without perplexity, good deeds stretching to infinity, a host of rosy children fluttering around her—she gave herself up to unbridled fancy. She shifted carefully in her narrow bed, for she knew by experience that if one turned too impetuously one displaced the feathers in the mattress so that one felt the cords beneath, and as she turned in the fresh sheets she giggled—no more sleeping hard! She remembered how, only two years ago, when the inn at Saintes had been full, she and her sister had been wrapped in blankets and made to sleep on the floor, for Papa had said that girls of their age should learn not to make a fuss but to sleep anywhere. Well, that was one childhood rule that was going for ever. She thought of the splendid state beds at Spencer House and at Althorp—she would have a finer. It should be the finest bed in all England; a great bed on a dais, hung with brocade, the curtains fringed and tasselled in gold (she pronounced it 'tosselled in goold'), the tester surmounted with great bunches of ostrich feathers, and the colour—the colour? 'Soupir de la Dauphine,' 'Feuille Morte' or 'la Noisette'? 'Cheveux de la Reine,' carmelite or puce? And the canopy should have silver stars on it, or, better still, it should have butterflies, golden butterflies, butterflies that fluttered down from over her sleeping head and flickered away over the fields of Wimbledon.

Devonshire House from Piccadilly, *c.* 1850. The artist has captured more of the rural look of Piccadilly from Green Park as it would have looked, with the Great West Road being narrower, but he has incorrectly shown the window façades on the east and west wings.

2

The Marriage

Only the irresponsible or undistinguished could marry to please themselves, and the Spencer–Devonshire marriage presented all the conventional components of suitability and was typical of its kind.

Firstly it was politically suitable. Politics were then a matter of heredity, and it is only very recently that children of families old in politics can break away from the traditional doctrines without being considered as renegades or traitors.

The Liberalism of the eighteenth century is too often attributed to the influence of Voltaire, Rousseau and the French Revolution, but the Whigs considered themselves the direct descendants and heirs of the pioneer families of the English Revolution. The frequent allusions of the time to 'the Revolution' are sometimes puzzling until it is remembered that the events of 1688 were as portentous to them as the Russian Revolution is to us. For close on a hundred years these families had believed themselves the liberators of the English Constitution, and had come to be regarded, as they regarded themselves, as its champions. To the Whig oligarchs the Constitution and Parliament were of supreme importance, taking precedence over all other rights. The occupier of the Throne was there only by sanction of that Parliament, and not the other way round, as before. Loyalty to the chosen King was right and proper—there was no virtue in choosing a leader whom you did not support; but in turn, let the King remember that he ruled by the right of the People instead of by that right called Divine. It is true that to the King the agreeable light of divinity flickered round his crown, but alas! it was barely visible to his loyal subjects.

Understandably, the powerful Whig families, though their strength derived largely from being the opposition party, came to regard their power as natural and hereditary, and what we would now call favouritism was simply that the children of the families of both parties were educated for the places which they would hold in order to continue the tradition.

Two of these young people were now to marry, and their alliance would be of political as well as personal interest.

Apart from the political aspect, they were of the right age, breeding and position. Nothing else mattered.

The bride was the eldest child of John, first Earl Spencer and of Georgiana Poyntz of Midgham. Her father was an upright, if not noticeable pillar of the Whigs, a man of great taste, kind to his children according to his lights, interested in their education, always ready to inform their minds and to mould their young, soft natures. Georgiana's mother was the first practical democrat in their circle.

Indeed, Lady Spencer was a most remarkable woman; of unbending integrity, liberal ideas and iron discipline, she brought up her three children with an anachronistic ideal of service. She was far-sighted enough to recognize in the stirrings and manifestations of the new Revolution a retribution to the increasing complacency of her class. She wrote that 'if we can stem the torrent, our hearts ought to glow with the warmest gratitude, though it should cost us half we are worth in the world. If we cannot, let us remember life is short, and get through each danger and difficulty with as clear a conscience as we can.' She enjoyed to the supreme degree the English characteristic of 'knowing her place' knowing that station in life to which it had pleased God to call her—and in that knowledge she had educated her three children.

She extended her interest and belief in education beyond her own children towards those others who were generally supposed to be better without any. She herself was never tired of learning: she was proficient in French, Italian, Latin and Greek; at the age of fifty-four she tackled and mastered German, possessing both accuracy and application, which assets she did not transmit to her daughters who, though fluent in French, made the most astonishing mistakes in spelling and grammar. At the same age she also took up botany, which she studied with her usual energy and intelligence.

She did not believe that her children should be seen but not heard, but brought them up to be at their ease with cultured and intellectual people: Georgiana had listened to Garrick reading Shakespeare on his annual visits to Althorp; she had been commended by the great ladies of France; she had gone with her mother, a great admirer of Captain Coram, to inspect his Charity for Foundling Children and many other schools where new-fangled methods of education, such as Miss Hannah More's, were being tried out—visits which made her jaws ache with suppressed yawns and her legs with weariness.

But Lady Spencer was never tired and never bored: she was extremely critical, even censorious, it is true, but she was curious and indefatigable: she longed to see a pair of tame snakes from which Georgiana had shrunk in horror; she dragged her granddaughter to see a crocodile and put her in a twitter lest she should insist on trying a new, and what seemed to the old lady an admirable form of transport—a chair strapped on a wheelbarrow pushed by a footman.

Lady Spencer was one of those enthusiasts who never mind trying out their convictions on others, maybe weaker than themselves: she kept a simple, wholesome table in the days when over-eating and drinking were universal, and indeed her daughter begged her to take an occasional glass of wine, emphasizing the dangers of too low a diet, whilst her simplicity and frugality led her granddaughter to complain of dinners consisting of 'egg-shells and turnip-tops.'

She was equally unconventional in her dress; though she could dress as richly as any when the occasion called for it, and liked to see her girls in pretty clothes, she herself was happiest in the simplest gowns. Indeed, one lady asked permission when she came to dinner if she might 'spencer it,' that is, be dressed in a riding habit.

But the best portraits are painted from life, and here is the picture drawn by the Earl-Bishop, Lord Bristol, who as peer and cleric was considered even more eccentric than his sitter:

> Lady Spencer, you know, is my model of a woman, and having seen her in retirement and in all her domestic employments my admiration and respect of her increases. She has so decided a character that nothing can warp it, and then such a simplicity of manners one would think she had never lived out of the country, with such elegance 'tis as if she had never lived in it—her charitable institutions are worthy of her, both for their object and their direction. She has reclaimed the manners of a most vicious parish, merely by her charitable institutions in it, and is so bent upon having the Parishioners neat, as well as religious and virtuous, that she is paving every path through, and not ostentatiously, but single flagstones, just to give the inhabitants a taste for cleanliness. The old ones who die with a fair character have a gravestone at her expense, and sometimes the Duchess of Devonshire has wrote the epitaph, which I promise you is not spelt by an unlettered muse. Nothing could tempt Lady Spencer to London but the restlessness of her poor husband.

She hated extravagance, ostentation and pretentiousness. Decorum, method, piety and energy were the foundations of her own life and on them she built those of her daughters.

Georgiana's bridegroom had had a very different upbringing. Born in 1748, he had lost his mother when he was six and his father when he was sixteen. The heir to immense estates with all their concomitant obligations, educated in the casual-precise idiom of his time, with no rough-and-tumble, no competition, simply vast privilege and vast opportunity, with censure only possible from his peers; without the taste for licence or the inclination for individualism, he was already, at the age of twenty-four, the armature of the effigy he was to remain.

Naturally lethargic and with no incentive to make any decisions, he early became a creature bound by habit. It was comfortable, and also more convenient, to arrange that his life should conform with the greatest possible ease and the least possible disturbance.

He was not blessed with humour nor passion, and gravely recognizing his duty to his inheritance, he acknowledged the necessity for marriage to one of his own kind, who would act as the first hostess to Society and mother of, it was to be hoped, many children.

It is absurd that it is impossible to write of him without using all these ridiculous and pedantic words, his taciturnity being ill-suited to these polysyllables.

Never mind, let me start again: William, fifth Duke of Devonshire was a dull, worthy, conscientious young man, without humanity, humour or spontaneity, grave in his manners, clumsy in his movements (he brought one lovely crystal lustre crashing to the ground at a rout, and then leaned against its brother with the same deplorable result and only said, 'This is singular enough,' with no further word of distress or apology). He gambled habitually at Brooks's, ate far too much, begat one child by a milliner and disliked moving from one of his palaces to another.

He was not a bad man; he was a shadowy and unambitious man, and had he been born to a lesser state might have been a good and worthy man.

A full-length portrait of him may easily be reconstructed from the many glimpses to be caught of him from the gossips of his time, but he would probably prefer to be remembered in the words of the compiler of an early-nineteenth century peerage. This gentleman says: 'The Duke, who was distinguished by an even temper and retired manner, is said to have 'read well,' and to have had a critical acquaintance with the works of our great dramatic poet, so perfect, that to know his writings as thoroughly as the Duke of Devonshire, was an admitted encomium. Of his Grace's poetical talents, his lines on Lord Nelson's death and his epitaph on Earl Spencer, will afford the reader two very beautiful specimens.' Having read these examples of his Grace's poetical talents, I propose to omit them.

It is important that we should have a clear picture of Georgiana and the Duke as they were at the time of their marriage, for the course of their subsequent lives depends largely on what they were then.

We see therefore a tall girl, just seventeen years old, not strictly beautiful but of so frank a countenance, so full of spontaneity, kindness and impetuosity, so imbued with charm, that she enchanted such divergent characters as Dr Johnson and Horace Walpole. The latter wrote of her in March 1774, 'She is a lovely girl, natural and full of grace.' Fanny. Burney remarked that she was 'quite gay, easy and charming; indeed, the last epithet might have been coined for her.'

She was of a most loving and demonstrative nature; anxious to please, of great vitality, well-educated, well-mannered and, above all, simple in her upbringing, tastes and reactions; of the untried stuff, malleable and docile, which might be moulded into any shape, provided that the shape were lovely and honest. On her marriage, despite her youth and inexperience, she would immediately become the first hostess, not only of Society but of the most vital political party in England.

The Duke was only seven years her senior, but already so set, so cold in his manner, that he was removed from her by a score of years. Slow of speech and thought, accepting his great position as a right rather than an obligation, undemonstrative and extremely selfish.

Yet to the Spencers it was a pre-eminently suitable match; of appropriate rank, of the same political party and of a proper age to breed more of their kind, the marriage was bound to turn out well.

The news that Devonshire House was to have a Duchess for the first time in twenty years spread like wildfire. Innumerable quills were dipped in the brownish ink and scratched across the big square sheets of notepaper with their gilt edges, rough surfaces and elaborate watermarks. The clubs, the drawing-rooms and the alcoves hummed with speculation. What was to come of the marriage of the year? How would it turn out?

The bride was rumoured to be a phenomenon—so charming, unspoiled and, lud! so *natural*! Why, *anything* might happen! Whilst the ladies gossiped together, their silks and whispers making a rustling like the wind through autumn leaves, their powdered heads nodding in agreement, their fans screening their faces so that their slightest words issued as obscurely as oracles, the men straddled in front of the great marble fireplaces in

Brooks's, in Wattier's, as they warmed their silken breeches before the coals blazing in the chased steel grates.

Lady Spencer's cronies, Mrs Howe and Miss Lloyd, were assuring her that the trousseau must contain yet more refulgent satins, finer laces. Sempstresses were embroidering golden corn-stalks on cherry-coloured paduasoy, silver seaweeds on pale green moiré, swathes of flowers on pearly brocades. Gauzes of every hue, glittering with spangles; bales of fine yellow straw to be twisted into hats and bonnets; ribbons of silk, of satin, of velvet; cornflowers, roses and daisies to twist among the ribbons; little pointed satin shoes waiting for great buckles of white, green or amethyst. There were fans of painted chicken-skin and gloves of chicken-skin too to protect delicate hands. Powders and perfumes—

Amber, musk and Bergamot; Eau de Cologne, Eau de Luce, Sans Pareil and Citron Juice, Painted Lawns and chequer'd shades, Crape that's worn by lovelorn maids, Water'd Tabbies, flower'd Brocades.

The shining, costly heaps of folly grew and grew, and with them grew the gossip, the strangest part of which was that the future Duchess was so simple a chit.

On April the 6th, Horace Walpole was writing to Lady Ossory:

... rude and savage as we think our ancestors ... you see they indulged in more delicacies than the Maccoronies do. The future Duchess of Devonshire will have nothing but tea and sack-whey, not gentle pots of ginger green; nor will her head lie soft on a bolster set with diamonds and rubies, unless Miss Lloyd and Mrs Howe hear of this sumptuous description and insist on Lady Georgiana's having a still richer bolster.

Innumerable dependants, too, had their parts to play in the bridal preparations. Each house belonging to the Duke—and there were ten of them—had its own staff of servants, from housekeepers, butlers, grooms-of-the-chambers, to the countless underlings, scurrying like rats, living like rats—sleeping in corners, under eaves, in passages, in great tortuous basements; eating well and wastefully; earning what we should consider very small wages, but proud with the boundless snobbery of those times to be in such high service. At the gates were the gatekeepers, in the halls the porters with their peculiar high-winged chairs, in the courtyards the linkmen; while in every house was the servants' hall, not as we know it, but a place where the running footmen and maids of visitors gathered together to gossip on much the same topics (and probably with a good deal more accuracy) as were being discussed by their masters above-stairs.

Facing the Green Park across cobbled, rutted Piccadilly stood Devonshire House behind its high brick wall, broken by a large pair of double doors surmounted by urns. Behind the wall was a courtyard, where the porter had his lodge, flanked by two pedimented buildings. The house itself, though it had been designed by Kent, was very plain, almost dowdy, with its three stories of unornamented windows, those of the bedroom floor being small and inadequate. Externally it could not compare in elegance and beauty with Georgiana's home, Spencer House, which she could see from the windows overlooking the Park, but the two lower floors were devoted to splendid reception-rooms—vast saloons, richly decorated, leading one from the other. It was, therefore, ideal for entertaining; and as individual comfort went for very little in the eighteenth century when the pleasures of Society outweighed every other attraction, it was perfectly suited for its purpose, especially as its lovely gardens stretched as far as Lansdowne Passage. Quiet and shady, full of bird-song, they contrasted delightfully with the unceasing hubbub of Piccadilly where, in Georgiana's own words:

> there was such a crowd of carriages of all sorts, that I could hardly hear my own voice for the continual rattle of coaches, etc.... but I was still more amazed when he told me they would continue driving with the same vehemence all night.

Not ten miles from Hyde Park Corner was Chiswick, an enchanting village whose glory was the Palladian Villa created by Lord Burlington and which was to become Georgiana's favourite home. The house is so much of its period that it is not difficult to imagine life as it was then. Save for one or two exceptions the rooms are small, but appear even smaller than they are by the profusion of their ornament; ceilings, cornices, friezes, walls and mantels are carved, painted and gilt. Each room opens from the other, and what with staircases, ante-rooms, halls and alcoves, it is as complicated as an eighteenth-century *comédie de mœurs*. Lady Teazle, who was Georgiana's stage portrait, would have no need of a screen here—she would only have to open one of the many carved doors in each room and slip through it. True, she might find herself surprising another tête-à-tête, either in a powder closet or on the steps of a spiral stair, but there would always be another exit to hand. Climbing one of the broad stone staircases, her hand on a wrought-lead balustrade as delicate as lace, she would find herself in a maze of tiny bedrooms, and would very likely be forced to run downstairs again till she came to the ground floor or semi-basement. But that would be no place for her, as it was a warren of corridors, strange, dark, windowless little rooms inhabited by lackeys, polishing silver, decanting wines or snoring on straw pallets. Out into the gardens she would then go, and amidst the statues, under the great cedars, by the ornamental waters and across the velvety lawns, she would run till she found refuge in a temple or grotto. The whole place is as elegant and dream-like as a painting by Boucher or Watteau, and though now it wears the same nostalgia as the pictures of those times, then it must have been a gay and perfect setting for the young bride.

In Yorkshire, lovely romantic Bolton was lapped by a ripple of the further waves of preparation, and older Hardwick was more indifferent—the red velvet hangings and panelled walls were so much a part of the place that no one thought of refurbishing them. But at Chatsworth the tide of preparation was at its height.

There in the golden palace, surrounded by the sharp blue Derbyshire hills, saloons were being stripped of their holland covers, the great brocaded curtains rehung and their carved pelmets dusted; feather mattresses were being plumped up, piles of exquisite bed-linen being aired and the tufts of ostrich feathers on the tester of the state bed shaken and reaffixed, for it was at Chatsworth that the honeymoon was to be spent. The park emerging from the high wooded hill behind the house sloped towards the bright river, old trees shaded the Hunting Tower and Queen Mary's Bower; the waters tumbled from the mouths of dolphins and from the triton's horns; they spouted from sea-monsters and dripped from the leaves of the copper tree. All shone and sang waiting for the bride.

They were married on her seventeenth birthday, the 7th of June, and for a while everything seemed as rosy as she had planned: her husband was courteous and kind, and every day she wrote to her mother. From 'Fryday Sepr the 23' to 'Sunday the 11 of Dec.,' she records the little rippling days. The copy-book handwriting that starts so tidily for the first few lines betrays the touching immaturity towards the end of the page. Each day resembles its neighbours: the young bride records a walk so long that she limps home; a visit from Sir Harry Hunloke, 'half grown doating, a worthy antiquated prig'—one of whose nephews has a wife just as tall as his knee; a day in Matlock, another in Buxton; a day with the shooters and poor old Lord George falling into a ditch; the inevitable game of whist. She wanders round the great house where she found so much to learn. Perhaps old Shinwell (whose name she learned was pronounced Shimmell) accompanied her on her voyages of exploration—or was it his descendant who displayed the treasures to us with proud and insistent inaccuracy—for such as they are of all time? He, or another, would show her the great state rooms, hanging above the world like the splendid palaces painted on their ceilings, for to reach them she must climb the wide shallow stairs with their fairy-like gilt balusters. She would gaze at their chestnut-coloured walls, their lacy swags of wooden fruit, flowers and birds, their pictures in the frames that Kent had made for them. The tapestries and the hangings would hardly stir in the golden autumn air, while in the huge painted hall Caesar was murdered all unconscious of the pity in her eyes.

Or, to find comfort, she would descend to the one small room on the ground floor that was cosy and intimate, and here she would arrange her books—Blair's 'Sermons' and Rapin's 'History'—standing on a pair of library steps. Or she would visit the almshouses at Londesborough, where six old women and six old men in blue gowns and cloaks greeted her with blessings.

In the gardens she would ask the sphinxes their secret, and she delighted in the elegant chinoiserie of the willow tree, all made of copper, from whose pointed spear-like leaves showers of diamond-bright needles of water were released on the unsuspecting by the boy, concealed for that purpose, among the moss-grown rocks.

She decided to make a grotto, and with her let us stoop beneath the heavy rock mouth of the cave, part the obscuring curtains of ivy, and pause till the density of the darkness thins to reveal a door. Painfully, with our nails, we ease open the hinged and rusted panels and peer within. Strange morbid icicles compose a cavern, dusted over with the dancing motes of air, with the dust of gold, they glimmer forebodingly. The light filters from above and with it descends a strange artificial peace. Georgiana, you and I are in her grotto made of Derbyshire spars.

But she must hurry back to the house, for it is the Public Day. Every Monday the Duke and Duchess received the visits of the county gentlefolk, the doctors, attorneys and clergymen. These worthies will stay for dinner, compensated by their young hostess's fresh, unaffected hospitality for the Duke's silence as he sits mute and inattentive to his neighbours. At first she found these formal receptions really trying, but later on she could laugh them off in verse:

> *If out of sorts & out of Fancy*
> *When all things seem to turn astray,*
> *A toil no mortal ever can see*
> *So irksome as a Publick Day.*

The Captains, Squires & Clergy drinking,
Whilst toasts & noise their powers display
Are all united, to my thinking,
The horrors of a Publick Day.

She preferred to take a poor local bookseller a 'little en protection,' and settled down to serious reading, beginning with Goldsmith's *History of Greece* and *The Siècle de Louis 14*, and continuing with Vertot's *Révolutions Romaines* and Robertson's *History of Scotland*. Besides these employments, she had a music master in the house, the great violinist Giardini, with whom she practised the minuets he composed for her, the thin noise of her harpsichord mingling with the tenuous strings.

Lady Spencer showed her approval of so sober and useful an existence, and Georgiana, fired with emulation, decided to copy her husband's kinsman, Henry Cavendish, the great scientist whom she had visited at Clapham, and fitted up a small laboratory of her own where she could study geology and experiment in chemistry to her heart's content. When it was ready she called her husband and showed it to him with shining eyes.

The Duke surveyed it coldly and told her that he did not find such occupations suitable for his wife.

'But, but,' she stammered, 'Mama always encouraged me to learn the natural sciences, and indeed, Mr Cavendish himself has promised to help me with my experiments.'

'My dear,' replied the Duke, 'now that you have performed your duty in waiting upon Mr Cavendish, I would prefer for you not to visit him again.'

'Why ever not? He is so charming ... so learned....' The Duke held up his hand with a gesture of finality. 'He is not a gentleman,' he said; 'he works.'

Georgiana felt her world reeling round her: all her life she had been brought up to consider all kinds of work admirable and necessary—idleness was the sin, not employment—but another of Mama's lessons had been of obedience to one's husband; so, puzzled and disheartened, she shut the door of the laboratory behind her.

With a sigh she took up her pen and wrote again to Mama—another letter—(or was it the same?) expressing her love and duty, that her greatest happiness is that she may address Mama as her 'dearest Friend,' her '*tendre Amie,*' and each day Georgiana wrote her some pretty, conventional lines of verse. Lady Spencer was becoming anxious: all these poems from a bride, full of dying roses, filial gratitude and devotion, falling leaves and the sorrows of separation and with never a word of the bridegroom. At last, after six months; she wrote tactfully to inquire if Georgiana had written any verses to the Duke.

By a coincidence her letter crossed with one from Chatsworth in which her daughter made her first reference to her marriage. She remarked naïvely that even those who before had been indifferent to the Duke must now feel affection for him when they noted his attention and good nature towards her. If others felt so, then Mama could judge of hers.

'Judge of hers' indeed: Lady Spencer waited with some nervousness for the reply to her inquiry. It was written two days afterwards on December the 11th. She assures Mama, in stilted, formal language, of her happiness in being with, one to whom she is so sincerely attached; that when every action, every word of such a Man is of so much consequence to her, what need, what possibility could exist of describing it? Surely Mama must have realized from the tenor of her letters the feelings of her Heart? Her only wish is to deserve the mutual happiness Mama speaks of and to promote His happiness in any way. 'The Duke,' she adds, 'is going to put a postscript to my letter....'

The Duke, needless to say, put no 'postscript' to the letter and Lady Spencer was scarcely reassured by it: it was suspiciously tidy, with none of the usual blots or erasures and bore every evidence of being the fair copy made from a careful and deliberate draft.

But on the whole she had been telling the truth when she said she was happy with him: her dream was already fading and when they were alone together the Duke was flattering and kind. Indeed he was stirred as never before by this quicksilver girl and was as demonstrative towards her as his nature would allow.

This led Georgiana to make a fatal mistake. One day (some say it was on the wedding day itself), encouraged by a belief in his affection, secure in her own, excited and happy, she subsided on to her husband's knee, putting her arms round his neck in front of her mother and sister. Quickly and roughly the Duke pushed her off his knee and rose to his feet, leaving the room without a word. Georgiana felt as though she had been stabbed; though the pain was numb and icy, no tears could thaw that ice nor words dispel her hurt bewilderment. With that one rough gesture she felt that he had killed her childhood.

About eight years later she was to record a similar incident on paper and to publish it to the world in the form of her highly successful novel *The Sylph*, and as this novel, like every first novel ever written, was largely autobiographical, we may just as well take her word for what had happened rather than indulge in conjecture. In *The Sylph* Georgiana portrays herself as an entirely ignorant and innocent country girl married to a man of the first fashion and transplanted, without preparation, from the depths of the country straight into the hot-house atmosphere of 'ton.' The husband is shown as perfidious, vicious and even, to our eyes, cruel. Naturally Georgiana heightened and exaggerated the characters and situations in her story for the sake of drama: she was not ignorant, though she preserved throughout her life a quality of innocence; the Duke was neglectful and cold, but he was not vicious nor dissipated.

On her heroine's, 'Lady Stanley's,' arriving in town the first great event is her presentation at Court, for 'no married lady can appear in public till she has been properly introduced to their majesties.' In the book the preparation for this presentation plays a large part, and much of it may indeed be true.

After a detailed description of the lengthy toilet, the hairdressing, the exaggerated fashions against which she protests in vain, she was ready, though already late. Finally she arrived at Court where their Majesties received her with great kindness, though she was in an agony that she was not meeting with her husband's approval, for he neither cast a glance at her nor whispered a word of encouragement. On her return home she asked him how she had acquitted herself.

'Like an angel, by heaven! Upon my soul, I never was so charmed with you in all my life.'

'And upon my honour,' I said, 'I could not discover the least symptom of tenderness in your regards. I dreaded all the while that you were thinking I should disgrace you.'

'You was never more mistaken,' he replied. The circle rang with your praises. But you must not expect tenderness in public, my love. If you meet with it in private you will have no cause for complaint.'

If she met with tenderness … ah, if … In the great house, as still as a tomb, made more sinister by the rustling and scratching of the horde of servants, the young Duchess was emerging from her dreams into reality.

3

Faster, Faster

... Tho' foremost in this giddy train
By fashion led I tread the plain
Tho' evr'y Folly soon must see
It finds a votery in me
Yet is my heart unsullied still—
Sincere it shuns the ways of ill ...

Georgiana Devonshire, 1775

The leap from the routine and the gardens of Wimbledon to the complicated life of Devonshire House was too much for any girl to accomplish in one bound. Though to the world she turned the loyal smiling face of a happy bride, her husband's callousness had wounded her irreparably, but she bore her pain with courage, realizing that in the future she alone must be the guardian of their fragile relationship. Afterwards when she wrote *The Sylph*, she expressed this realization when her disillusioned heroine, placed in the same situation as herself, resolved that 'if he is indifferent to my morals and well-being in life, it will more absolutely become my business to take care of myself—an arduous task for a young girl surrounded by so many inducements to suit the straight paths and so many examples of those who do.' But it was not easy: she was told that 'custom justifies everything'; that fashion made it not decent to appear together, for nothing was indecent or otherwise but as it was the '*ton*'; that it was so immensely 'boar' to blush. She began to feel self-conscious and '*gauche*' for the first time in her life and, determined to adopt the way of living expected of her, so different from that in which she had been brought up, she threw herself into it with a kind of self-immolation so fierce that she was soon caught inextricably in its toils.

Somehow, for the first time, she found herself in debt; how, she could not imagine, but we can guess that it was not difficult to the seventeen-year-old girl, suddenly a Duchess, rich and charitable, to believe her new wealth inexhaustible. It could not have been for very much but she was afraid to tell the Duke, and in April 1775 she took her courage in both hands and confessed to Lady Spencer, asking for her help as she was fearful of her husband whose family would be furious if they knew of her scrape. Lady Spencer behaved admirably, as might have been expected: she told the Duke, the debt was settled and she read Georgiana a lecture. The penitent Duchess poured out her thanks to her mother in a letter, as her heart was too full of gratitude to speak of half she felt. She wished she could show the Duke her gratitude, too, but he had had the delicacy not to mention it to her, and she could not bring herself to do so, though surely he could see her feelings in her looks. She asked Mama to consider how all these marks of his goodness must attach her to him.

Lady Spencer considered and found that, in her opinion, the Duke had not succeeded as well as some others who were only too anxious for Georgiana to be attached to them.

Till the Duchess's marriage her closest companion had been her little sister Harriet, but June the 7th had set a frontier between them. Her mother's friends, the renowned Mrs Montague, perplexed Mrs Hervey, royal Mrs Howe and her shadow Miss Lloyd, were all anxious to help the young bride with their friendship and advice, to which she listened with civil gravity but with stifled yawns. It is true she delighted in witty, worldly Lady Clermont, but she was really so *very* much older that one could not confide in her about everything. Lady Spencer, who neither approved nor understood this strange new life, listened to her daughter's perplexities and counselled her thus:

'Suffer no one,' she said, 'to lessen your husband in your esteem ... speak of your confidence in him. But if he may not pay that strict obedience to his part of the marriage contract as he ought, remember, my dear, his conduct can never exculpate any breech in yours. Gentleness and complacency on your part are your only weapons.'

These were wise words, and Georgiana tried to live up to them and long remembered them (for she put them into the mouth of her mother's prototype in *The Sylph*), but she felt that Lady Spencer's weapons were inadequate and soon took those offered to her by other willing hands. Chief among these new allies was Elizabeth, Lady Melbourne.

Lady Melbourne was a woman of great shrewdness and unbounded ambition. The Melbournes' position was largely due to acquired wealth rather than to the prerogative of birth, and unfortunately the great Whig ladies looked slightly askance at these newcomers: the Tory ladies would have nothing to do with them though they were sponsored by Lords Egremont and Salisbury. But opposition was a spur to Elizabeth Melbourne; if she was not acceptable as a part of the Milky Way she would harness her wagon to other stars, and she preferred masculine planets. At the time of Georgiana's marriage her position in Society was still very insecure. There were recurrent scandalous murmurs around her name, which is not surprising, as she was essentially a man's woman.

But if the men of her acquaintance were satisfied with the situation, she was not—'all or nothing' for Elizabeth Melbourne. The great house in Piccadilly, though embellished by the foremost decorators of the time— Cipriani, Wheatley, Mortimer and Mrs Damer—though its doors stood open and its tables were laden with a profusion of food and wine; though the candles shone on the green cloth of the card tables, did not echo to the high, well-bred laughter and endless chatter of the wives of its male visitors. Something must be done.

Not a quarter of a mile away lay the solution. In Devonshire House there was a puzzled girl, with more time and, apparently, more money than she knew what to do with. Into this vacuum of boredom and perplexity swept Lady Melbourne, feathers nodding, silks rustling, full of energy, flattery and advice. Would her Grace cast her glance over the new ceiling in the saloon? Her taste was impeccable. Was her Grace disappointed with her new gowns? Lady Melbourne knew of the first mantua-maker in London—straight from Paris. A man? La! your Grace, that don't signify! He's no more a man than a monkey. Was her Grace disengaged? Lady Melbourne was receiving a few friends to play at brag that night, and, strangely enough, the Duke was delighted to come too, though for three days he and his wife had not met save at meals. But why should the Duchess mind this? Did not she know that it was the vulgarest thing in the world to be seen with a husband?

No wonder that Georgiana was to write that 'the most unsafe and critical situation for a woman is to be young, handsome and married to a man of fashion.' Rousseau was responsible for much of the distance between husbands and wives, for he wrote that 'la femme et le mari sont bien destinés à vivre ensemble mais non de la même manière.' This suited both wives and husbands, leaving the men free for their endless politics, endless cards and ever-flowing wine, while the women could occupy themselves with gossip, shopping and the gallantries that were *de rigueur*.

Georgiana was amused by the men who flocked round her, but her upbringing and her mother's influence were still too strong for her to take their protestations seriously. One of them wrote to her that 'he had no right to flatter himself on being excluded from the general combination against husbands,' and though they were singing at Vauxhall a song entitled 'Female Liberty Regained,' of which the refrain urged the women to

> '... *stand to your charter and let the world see Tho' husbands are tyrants, their wives will be free,*'

Georgiana still hankered for the bonds of marriage rather than the liberties thrust upon her. So clear was her conscience that she asked her mother jokingly how she was to know if one of these courtiers was in earnest, as she was afraid of being like the Dowager Lady Carlisle, who agitated herself by thinking the postilion was in love with her from his frequent backward glances, while all the time the poor boy was only watching the wheels. She also copied a poem written to her by an unknown admirer and sent it to Mama. Of course, he was unknown, so Mama could not complain, and the poem was really very touching and pretty. It ran as follows:

> *'Enchanteresse que vous êtes,*
> *Nymphe et Sylphyde tour-à-tour,*
> *Dites-moi, donc, comment vous faites*
> *Pour peindre & pour braver l'amour?*
> *Tout en vous l'annonce et l'inspire.*
>
> *Quand vous marchez, dans vos habits,*
> *C'est lui qui murmure et se joue;*
> *Vos Rubans, c'est lui qui les noue;*
> *Il se cache dans tous leurs plis:*
> *Il se compose un daïs flottant,*
> *De ces Jeux Emblême fragile,*
> *Qu'il embellit en l'agitant.*
>
> *C'est là qu'il aiguise ses traits,*
> *Dont vous avez su vous défendre.*

Fier et jaloux de vos attraits,
Par tout on le voit sur vos traces,
Il y folàtre avec les Graces,
Il y sourit à votre Succes.
Vôtre caprice est'il d'écrire?
L'enfant est la, prêt à dicter,
Et dès qu'on vous entend chanter,
On croit que c'est lui qui soupire,
Il est dans vos yeux, à vos pieds:
Les Talens qu'en vous on admire
Sont-des amours multipliés.'

'Deign, Madam,' wrote the author, 'to accept the wretched Attempts of a very young Poet and young Soldier, who has no other Excuse to offer for his Impertinence than this—He has seen you.'

Evidently she was the fashion, perhaps even something more, for less than a year after her marriage Horace Walpole, that reliable weather-vane, was recording that at the 'Ladys Club there were all Goddesses, instead of matrons as usual. The Duchess of Devonshire effaces all without being a beauty; but her youth, figure, flowing good nature, sense and lively modesty and modest familiarity make her a phenomenon.' She had achieved the pinnacle of '*ton*,' but by how boring and exacting a road.

The very process of dressing for these empty triumphs was painful and long. Listen to her description in *The Sylph* of her heroine's toilet before her presentation at Court.

Lady Stanley's hair was to be dressed by the most fashionable *coiffeur* who, having enveloped her in an immense *peignoir*, immediately overwhelmed her by a great cloud of powder.

'What are you doing?' I said, 'I do not mean to be powdered.' 'Not powdered' said Sir William [her husband), why you would not be so barbarous as to appear without it—it positively is not decent.'

I submitted, wondering what should be my metamorphosis and impatient, it took so long a time, to say nothing of the pain I felt under the pulling, frizzing and rubbing in of the exquisitely scented *pomade de Venus.*

At length the words,' Vous êtes finie, madame, au dernier goût' were pronounced.

I rose with precaution and looked in the glass. Never shall I find words to express the astonishment at the figure I saw. What with curls, flowers, ribbands, feathers, lace, jewels, fruit and ten thousand other things, my head was at least an ell wide and from the lowest curl that laid on my shoulder, up to the top, I am sure not less than three-quarters of a yard high, besides six enormous feathers, black, white and pink.

'Good God!' I exclaimed, 'I can never bear this!'

'I assure you, your Ladyship is dressed quite in taste.'

'Let me be dressed as I will,' I answered, I must and will be altered and would not thus expose myself to the universe.'

Saying so I began to pull down some of the prodigious and monstrous fabric.

A general hubbub ensued, but Lady Stanley had her way and finally asked how much she owed the hairdresser.

'Half a guinea for the dressing and for the feathers, pins, wool, false curls, chignon, toque, pomades, wax fruits, ribbands, etc., about four guineas, not to mention the finest bunches of radishes straight from Paris.'

The hairdresser departed and, among lamentations that she would be the jest of the whole Court, the toilet proceeded.

'I was late already and to add to my misfortunes, my maid broke two laces endeavouring to draw my new French stays close. You know I am naturally small at bottom. But now you might literally span me. You never saw such a doll. Then they are so intolerably wide across the breast that my arms are absolutely sore with them and my sides are so pinched! But it is the '*ton*'! And pride feels no pain!'

To Georgiana's surprise these extravagant and ridiculous fashions called forth cries of admiration from all sides, and soon, from being 'immensely boar,' it became immensely amusing to out-Herod Herod. This was no mean achievement when even postilions wore white jackets trimmed with muslin, new every other day, and had to be provided with nosegays; when men's coats had button-holes edged with fur or gilded leather; when in the House of Commons the 'Maccoronies' voted against their opinions rather than risk their rouge melting or their posies wilting on their white satin muffs. The monstrous headdresses towered higher and higher; they were satirized in cartoons; at the pantomime Harlequin climbed a ladder to the top of these 'cloud-capp'd belles,' but Georgiana was determined that she would out-reach them all, and at the production of Sheridan's *Trip to Scarborough* in 1777 she appeared in the Royal Box at Drury Lane with gargantuan plumes of pink ostrich feathers, 'to convince the world, we suppose, notwithstanding what was advanced in the humorous prologue, that her Grace's head-dress was the true *bon ton*.' And she wore her prodigious feathers with such a gay air of mischief and defiance that even that dull dog, Lord Carlisle, was captivated and moved to commendation. He sang:

> *When on your head I see those fluttering things,*
> *I think that Love is there, and claps his wings.*
> *Feathers helped Jove to fan his amorous flames,*
> *Cupid has feathers, angels wear the same.*
> *Since then from Heaven their origin we trace,*
> *Preserve the fashion—it becomes your Grace.*

Her feathers became almost an obsession; she even brought them into a poem she wrote to David Garrick, comparing him to a blackbird and herself to a sparrow who dared outstrip him in flight and plumage.

> *Forgive, the timid bird replied,*
> *for I, with pleasure too*
> *Would give my plumes and airy pride*
> *to sing and charm like you.*

However much she adorned her person with these extravagances, she was delighted to strip them from her in the country, where she was never bored and found it hard to understand how others found time heavy on their hands away from the dissipations of the town. For her high spirits found outlets in healthy pursuits; playing with her curly dogs, Pierrot and Mouton; learning to drive, the coachman being her tutor, though he 'held her very cheap'; riding in the company of the gentlemen, when Lord Carlisle's restraining hand on her bridle did not prevent her snatching her hat from her head in order 'to *flap* it and let go of the reins.' Her hat frightened her horse, which bolted, and though she was thrown she was the only one of the party who was not frightened. She was more prudent, however, when she went out coursing, as Fanny Burney tells us in a conversation with Mr Crutchley.

'Among other folks,' says Miss Burney, 'we discussed the two rival duchesses, Rutland and Devonshire. 'The former,' said Mr Crutchley, must, he fancied, be very weak and silly, as he knew that she endured being admired to her face, and complimented perpetually, both upon her beauty and her dress.' And when I asked whether *he* was one who joined in trying her——

'Me!' cried he, 'no, indeed! I never complimented anybody; that is, I never said to anybody a thing I did not think, unless I was openly laughing at them, and making sport for other people.'

'Oh!' cried I, if everybody went by this rule, what a world of conversation would be curtailed! The Duchess of Devonshire, I fancy, has better parts.'

'Oh yes, and a fine, pleasant, open countenance. She came to my sister's once, in Lincolnshire, when I was there, in order to see hare-hunting, which was then quite new to her.'

'She is very amiable, I believe,' said I, 'for all her friends love and speak highly of her.'

'Oh yes, very much so; perfectly good-humoured and unaffected. And her horse was led and she was frightened; and we told her *that* was the hare, and *that* was the dog; and the dog pointed at the hare and the hare ran away from the dog; and then she took courage and then she was timid; and, upon my word, she did it all very prettily! For my part I liked it so well that in half an hour I took to my own horse and rode away!'

But ungallant Mr Crutchley would not have been able to poke fun at her twice, for she soon overcame her timidity and coursing became her favourite sport.

It was not only in the country that she could throw off her splendours, which to her were always in the nature of 'dressing up,' and one day on her husband suggesting a walk in the Green Park, she hurried to accept so rare an invitation so that it was observed that one of her curls had come unpinned, the heels of her shoes were trodden over and one of her ruffles torn. Had it not been for the footman stalking decorously behind them, the Duke and Duchess might have been taken for any commoners! But what did she care? For once she was squired by her husband, her arm in his and he was in a good humour, listening to her chatter, and neither of them noticed the disorder in her dress.

She was so anxious to please him that she encouraged him in his interest in the Militia and accompanied him to Camp, playing at simplicity in palatial tents, paying calls on the other military ladies, drinking tea and taking salutes with the General, dressed in her dashing Derbyshire uniform. She was delighted that the Duke was pronounced to 'salute really vastly well, though he has but just learnt.' She even 'shot off two or three Guns, but as they were Wind Guns there was no fear of their recoiling.'

But it seemed there was no pleasing everybody: if she was simple, Lady Frances Marsham, 'an odious mixture of notable ill-nature,' put her 'into ten thousand passions because she always talks to me as if she thought I had not my five senses like other people, you cannot conceive the astonishment she exprest on my saying I walked very often in the garden at D. House; I am sure you know the kind of person I mean, who because I was dissipated and what they call the *ton* imagine that I can scarcely breathe like other people....'

And here was Mama upbraiding her for being both too friendly and too distant in one breath. 'You should,' wrote Lady Spencer, 'especially at such a place as Tunbridge keep up a Civility and dignity in your behaviour to the Men of your own Set—& Courteous good humour'd affability to the Company in general whom you are little acquainted with, whereas I suspect if you will examine your own Conduct, you put on that killing Cold look you sometimes have to those you should be prévenante to, & a great deal more familiarity & ease than is either necessary or proper to the Men about you....'

Her display of military ardour inspired an 'Ode to the Warlike Genius of Britain' whose author showed it to Doctor Johnson who rumbled 'Here is an error, sir; you have made Genius feminine.' 'Palpable, sir,' admitted the unabashed author, 'I know it. But it was to pay a compliment to the Duchess of Devonshire, with which her Grace was pleased. She is walking across Coxheath in the military uniform and I suppose her to be the Genius of Britain.' The Doctor, who knew and loved his Georgiana, let it go at that and was pleased when 'his good Duchess' made the acquaintance of Mrs Thrale, who was delighted with her.

Perhaps it was Lady Spencer's criticisms that led Georgiana to cultivate more feminine society and such society as would not meet with her mother's disapproval, for spare, active Mrs Montague, Mrs Thrale and Miss Gregory were blue-stockings and stood high in Lady Spencer's esteem. They discussed books, disputed about *Evelina* and played cards, but even these formidable ladies could not damp Georgiana's spirits nor 'their talking Latin and quoting verses' intimidate her, for she scribbles these lines about them to her mother:

> *When Madam Thrale was prest to play at Whist*
> *Her love of learning warn'd her to desist—*
> *At last the Dame gave way, the table came*
> *She own'd she was a novice at the game.*
> *No sooner seated, than the Lady saw*
> *That Madam Montague began to jaw;*
> *She could not bear to lose the palm of wit*

And turning on her chair uneasy sit—
'That line is Gray's—pray was it I that won—
Te duce Cæsar—who that trick begun.'
The game and learning trying to pursue
She lost her money and her reason too.

'This is poetical licence,' adds Georgiana truthfully, 'for she won the Rhuber.'

She enjoyed everything and wrote about it all to Mama, though she admits that

Our amusements in this place [Tunbridge, September 1778] and, I suppose, our minds have degenerated into infancy. In the beginning of the Summer our evenings were past in conversation and singing of fine songs, we then got by degrees to Macao, cribbage, whist and catches, and now we are come down to the point of diverting ourselves with 'Laugh and lay down' and 'I'm come a lusty wooer, my dildin my doldin, I'm come a lusty wooer, lilly bright and shinee,' and dittys of that kind.

I am sorry to tell you that Mrs Greville's head is in great danger, not the inside, but the out, for last night as I was going to perform that wondrous feit of touching a red hot poker, she turned her head round suddenly and set it on fire, and afterwards Mr Grenville in lifting a chair over the table was within a hair of dropping the bottom on Mrs Greville's head, but luckily it only frizée'd her arm—upon these occasions I always think it right to go into something like an hysteric—I really must do something to brace up my nerves, or else I shall be going about the world, like Winifred Jenkins in Humphrey Clinker, who you know on every event is in *high sterics*, and is oblig'd to have *burnt feathers* and *Asses fetida* to smell....

She would dance with zest, and four months after her marriage went over to a ball at Derby from Hardwick where, dressed in a 'pink demi-saison silk trimmed with Gauze and Green Ribbons' she was partnered by Mr Coke of Norfolk, who was also Squire of Longford in Derbyshire, in the country dances. This was a very democratic affair given for the Duke's constituents, for as 'nobody was refus'd at the door, the Ball Room was quite full of the Daughters and Wives of all the Voters, in check'd aprons, etc.' She enjoyed this kind of entertainment just as much as the splendid formal balls in London, or a morning spent in learning the *minuet de la cour* from her cousin Lord Edward Bentinck. It must have been a pretty sight, for she says it was 'quite luxury dancing to Giardini's playing as every tone encourages one to dance gracefully and to make one's steps imitate the softeness of the musick.'

While she was learning the *minuet de la cour*, Marie Antoinette was equally anxious to learn the English country dances, and sent her a request to buy three or four books of these, particularly 'Over the hills and far away,' adding a message that she was much flattered at hearing that she was thought to resemble Georgiana. Indeed, there was more than a superficial likeness between the two young women who already knew and admired each other. They were both lovely; both had been married very young to lethargic husbands who left their ardent natures unsatisfied; both were childless and both longed for children. Georgiana was already miserably unhappy at her barrenness, though she confided to her mother her belief that it was not irremediable or her fault as she knew two or three friends of her own age and equally healthy who were in a like case. Perhaps if she were circumspect and less foolish God would reward her.... Both she and the Queen were rebels against convention, and unfortunately for them their only outlet for such rebellion lay in frivolous and futile amusements, so that they would spend an afternoon throwing their large straw hats into a pool at the Trianon, sending the young men after them like retrievers, which seemed to them the greatest fun, or the Queen would summon Georgiana to join her at the horse races in her pavilion, 'vulgarly call'd a Stand,' where she was very good humour'd and pleasing and talked a great deal about you [Lady Spencer] and said a thousand pretty things.'

All that was of most value in their characters was frustrated by their circumstances, and their strong energies were therefore forced into narrow and sterile channels. Had it been possible for them to choose the expression of these energies or had they been directed by necessity or custom to other uses, both of them would have been spared much unhappiness and, better still, would have brought strength to others as well as to themselves. The Queen's natural impulse to do good and to assuage her aching, empty life made her snatch a child from the gutter and adopt it, but even this innocent gesture was to recoil on her. They were inescapably caught in the narrow confines of their rank and time, and driven by these, one to utter ruin and the other to its brink.

But luckily for Georgiana help lay at hand, though the two men who were to give her mental purpose in her life also encouraged her to share in their wild and reckless pursuit of pleasure.

Charles James Fox did not require the finery or the high red heels he affected in his youth to raise him to the height of a colossus, and as his character gained in stature so he discarded these embellishments for the buff and blue uniform of the American insurgents. Bushy-browed and blue-chinned, he was so imbued with vitality that all his actions had something seismic in them, and he was able to impart something of his stature and fire to the girl who might otherwise have remained the puppet of fashion. Her natural energy and enthusiasm, and above all her integrity, appealed to him, and what had probably started by being amused tutelage on his part was to develop into an alliance. He sensed qualities in her that he fostered, so that she became more and more his female counterpart.

They shared the defects of their qualities. They were both a 'little larger than life-size': when they gambled they were reckless to a degree that, though their friends saved them from irretrievable ruin, wrecked both their lives. They both read everything they could lay hands on; their natures were such that he, having been brought up as a Tory, and she, as a conventional lukewarm Whig, were to become more and more liberal-minded: rebelling against restraint they were fired with the ideals of freedom; both were insatiable in their curiosity.

Georgiana crammed her days with cards, reading, writing poetry, composing music, devising both fantastic and simple costumes (for she was so much the leader of fashion that she succeeded in abolishing the cumbersome 'hoops' which in future were worn only on State occasions). Everything new was of interest to her; she took up the craze for freak parties, regattas, electrical experiments and ballooning, and her patronage of this new sport led Lunardi, the Balloonist, to give a ball for her at the Pantheon; she sat up all night in Mrs Montague's Cupidon saloon talking Shakespeare with Doctor Johnson and was the first by whom the new was tried.

Fox would drink, study politics, race, devour books and gamble with the same unabated zest. He would play faro for eighteen hours on end, keeping his gloves on in order that the guttering candles should not smear his hands, and then go off to a debate as fresh as a daisy. He would travel down to Chatsworth at night and ride races the following morning, and 'won 1 or 2 races which considering his not having been a-bed and his size, is doing a great deal.'

Three years after her marriage Georgiana describes a gathering at Chatsworth which was typical of many. It is in August and she is writing to her mother.

Mr Townshend and Mr Fox came this evening from town—*Charles Fox is à l'ordinaire*, Jack Townshend is really a very amiable young man, he has great parts though not such brilliant ones as Charles Fox's, and I dare say he will make a very good figure hereafter—he is just twenty now, though he has the appearance of being older. I have always thought that the great merit of C. Fox is his amazing quickness in seizing any subject —he seems to have the particular talent of knowing more about what he is saying and with less pains than anybody else—his conversation is like a brilliant player at billiards, the strokes follow one another, piff paff—and what makes him more entertaining now is his being here with Mr Townshend and the D. of Devonshire, for their living so much in town together makes them shew off one another. Their chief topic is Politicks and Shakespear. As for the latter they all seem to have the most astonishing memorys for it—and I suppose I shall be able in time to go through a play as they do....

Fox and Georgiana shared unbounded enthusiasms, throwing themselves into any and every occupation that caught their fancy; they had a talent for friendships and their friends repaid them with the loyalty and devotion that they gave with both hands. The Duchess, having inherited her mother's energy, used it unsparingly; night after night she threw open the doors of Devonshire House, cramming it with people, burning the countless candles at both ends. During the weekends she would jump into her coach and drive to Chiswick, not to rest but to entertain as many friends as she could collect.

Fuel seemed added to her fire, and though it was said that she turned days into nights and did not rise till the late afternoon—a failing she shared with the Duke who hated to be waked before four—she found time to sit to the artists who swarmed around her. She was painted standing in a park, holding a rose and crowned with an immense hat; or with one hand on a balustrade and one foot on a marble step, light as a butterfly; or flying through the night sky with a crescent in her hair; or there is the portrait in which her smile is the only decoration. She was painted in miniature, and her profile was snipped out of black paper or modelled in wax. She was sketched in crayon, in pastel, in oils—at an assembly, at Vauxhall or at a military review. A caricature of her was handed round at the Opera, Mrs Crewe protesting loudly that the face and figure were libellous though the Parasol and the Derbyshire uniform were like. There is even a self-portrait 'with my hair very rough and my handkerchief up to my chin.' She was painted as Pharaoh's daughter by the river and as the Goddess of Liberty hanging trophies on a column, but always her likeness was hard to catch. She laughed at this, but unwittingly hit on the reason:

I've oft puzzled to find, why hard 'tis to trace
The Features and looks of my comical face,
Since a moderate drawing might surely comprize
A snub nose, a wide mouth and a pair of grey eyes.

And thus 'tis my Vanity tries to explain
Why all Painters have try'd at my likeness in vain,
I fancy their Genius their Pencil forsook
When a heart that's uncommon, distributes each look.

No talents it boasts and no worth it can prove
But that true 'tis to friendship's affection and Love.
To those 'tis attached to, its praises are due
And its merits thus owing to Canis and you.

But for eight long years the canvas for her picture with her child upon her knee was to lean its blank face to the wall.

It was through her old friend, Sir Joshua Reynolds, that she made two new friends, the Sheridans. She was bewitched by Elizabeth Sheridan's loveliness and gentle manner, by Sherry's wit and charm, by his marvellous smile that lit up his half-heavy face and dark hazel eyes, and above all, by their being so openly in love. It was less than a year since they had been married, and she remembered that the Sheridans' romance had rivalled her own wedding in the public interest. One marriage, she thought, had been talked of because it was blessed by the world, the other because it had been achieved in face of much opposition; for Sheridan had defied Mr Linley, the father of the lovely singing 'Linnet,' had fought two duels for her, had eloped with her to France, hidden her in a convent, married her under the rose, re-married her in England, and here they were, almost unknown in London, with little money and few prospects, radiantly happy and gorgeously in love.

She threw open her house and her heart to them, and for thirty years the doors stood open.

The Sheridans were an immediate success; Elizabeth's perfect voice and beauty became the rage, and no one could resist her sweetness or her devotion to 'Chéri.' Sherry himself was instantly at home in Devonshire House, where he made friends with Irish ease, his wit and intelligence soon binding him and Fox together. Some of the older members of that society thought it unconventional and in rather poor taste for the Duchess to become so intimate with what were, after all, only stage folk; but if neither the Duke nor Lady Spencer disapproved, it was obviously impossible to restrain the young Duchess's patronage. But patronage never entered Georgiana's thoughts; she, like Fox and Elizabeth Sheridan, believed in Cheri's genius, and their belief was more than vindicated when, in January 1775, *The Rivals* took the world by storm.

They were carefree days. The whirlpool of success had caught both Sheridan and the Duchess; faster and faster it swirled round them. Like children they delighted in its dizzy speed, catching glimpses of Lady Melbourne as she rushed past, splashing Fox with its diamonds, and they laughed gaily at the Duke as he stood, gravely aloof and indifferent, on the solid banks.

But often in the midst of the vortex, Georgiana would give a sharp gasp of remorse: she would compare her present self with the carefree girl of so short a time ago, who neither knew of debt nor the fruits of thoughtlessness. Then she would confess to her mother that without real cause for remorse, and though she had only to look into her soul to find thoughts that should make her overwhelmingly happy, yet she was saddened by many memories, for though she had never really sinned, she believed no one could have been more imprudent than herself. At the same time she had the consolation of knowing that these same errors, of which she now repented, had sprung from the best intentions in the world.

She could unburden herself thus to her mother, for among all these new friends there was none so close or so dear, as she realized when Lady Spencer was tossing on the packet bound for Spa. Then the lonely girl could pretend no longer. She cried across the sea that she could not bear to think that one little weak ship bore in it almost everything that was dearest to her.

4

The Larger Stage

In the midst of this bewildering new life Georgiana found time for two new occupations: she wrote her novel *The Sylph*, which met with terrific success, first from being attributed to the author of *Evelina* and then, when its authorship was discovered, as being unequivocally autobiographical; and next she found the new craze for speculation as exciting as gambling— besides, she needed the money badly to meet the interest on loans she had already raised to meet her gambling debts. She was a little nervous of this new venture at first, but was reassured by Lady Melbourne, who took it so lightly that she would discuss the markets whilst she arranged her feathers in front of the looking-glass. 'Lord,' she said, 'they say the stocks will blow up—that will be very comical.' If speculation could be described as comical, there could be no harm in it.

Lady Spencer strongly disapproved of both these activities, but for once she was forced to turn to Georgiana for help and advice. Her second daughter, Harriet, was proving something of a problem, a situation so foreign to Lady Spencer that she felt she could not deal with it.

Anyone reading the journal kept by Harriet when she was eleven years old during the Spencers' tour in France will be struck by the strength of her character. Despite the dutiful respect with which she notes her parents' exordiums, the child forms her own opinions as to what is good or bad for her and her sister. Though Georgiana was three years her senior, there was a narrower gulf between them than is usual at their age; sometimes one almost feels Georgiana to be the younger of the two. That state of things was soon to be altered by Georgiana's marriage, and Harriet was left behind in the schoolroom to the company of tutors, Lady Spencer and her serious friends. She would have been quite content to stay there except that she missed the companionship of her sister badly. She had grown very tall, danced to perfection, was already showing a remarkable gift for expression both in her conversation and her letters, being incisive, witty and, without being in the least self-opinionated, she was sure of herself.

But she did not want to marry. The Spencers had received offers for her hand from the Duke of Roxburghe and Lord Trentham, which she had rejected; she was now eighteen and continued in this unheard-of attitude. Something must be done, and Lady Spencer confided her worries to Georgiana, who was as much perplexed as her mother by this inexplicable conduct of Harriet's. Finally they decided that perhaps if she shared more of her sister's life at Devonshire House she would alter her resolution. After all, Harriet enjoyed parties and society as much as any girl, and possibly when she was with Georgiana she would realize the advantages of marriage and cease this celibate obstinacy.

So with delight Georgiana took on the new role of chaperone, and not only was she amused by arranging entertainments for her sister, but all at once they rediscovered that companionship they had missed so sorely and which was to endure, becoming stronger and stronger, all their lives.

Harriet was not in the least reluctant to enjoy this worldly life, but she was more eclectic in her tastes than her sister, and her considered judgments sometimes made Georgiana wonder at their maturity.

At the same time that Harriet was taking her place in the world, the young Prince of Wales burst upon it like a brilliant firework. He was one year younger than Harriet Spencer and, in the tradition of his family, his thwarted, misunderstood childhood turned him instantly, on his attaining even a small degree of independence, into the leading rebel against his parents. As heir to the throne, his rank combined with his striking good looks, his unsurpassed charm and perfect manner, all united to make him the inevitable focus of the younger members of the opposition. No wonder he was popular, for he was the epitome of his age, combining the extremes of refinement and coarseness that are the hall-mark of his century. He became a star overnight, and what untried human being has come unscathed through such an experience?

In September 1782, Georgiana amused herself by writing some *Anecdotes concerning his R.H. the P. of Wales*, as in the eight years since her marriage she had seen parties rise and fall, the 'ties of Love give way to caprice,' and the likelihood of the Prince being soon at the head of a faction opposing the King would render every early recollection of him interesting. After a preamble praising freedom at the expense of royal favour, and regarding homage paid to the throne as a due to the subject rather than to the King, she proceeds to describe the Prince's appearance: rather tall, his figure was too fat and womanish, but his graceful movements and extremely handsome face counteracted these defects. He loved to attend masquerades in disguise, and his tawdry taste in dress and the admiration he met with, especially from women, which he magnified hugely to himself, were his chief interests, though he had a shrewd, precocious grasp of affairs. He was known to have behaved on occasion with generosity towards his friends when in distress, though the instances she quotes are not more than we should expect from anyone with a sense of good fellowship. He was less scrupulous towards his mistresses and played them some very shabby tricks.

Georgiana describes his seeing the actress Mrs Robinson, a natural daughter of Lord Northington's, from the Royal Box in company with his parents, how he fell passionately in love with 'Perdita's' beauty and how he, though she was married to a man who lived on her stage earnings and the money provided by her young lover, Lord Malden, believed her to be both a miracle of loveliness and virtue. So closely supervised was he that while he sat for his miniature in his bedroom at Windsor, a page was posted at the door and the artist was told that the picture was destined for a relation in Germany, though 'Florizel' had promised it to 'Perdita.' This was the miniature she had framed in diamonds, inscribed 'Gage de mon amour,' and which she wore long after she had fallen from favour.

She was succeeded by Mrs Armistead, then the mistress of the Duke's brother, Lord George Cavendish, who, visiting her one night, found the Prince hiding behind her door. Lord George, though drunk, luckily preserved enough humour to retire with a laugh and a bow, leaving his Highness in possession.

The Prince was much attached to Colonel Lake and Lord Spencer Hamilton, both upright men from whose influence he would have greatly benefited. However, his jealous parents surrounded him by dull, censorious gentlemen, whose uncongenial society forced the Prince to seek friends outside his own strictly supervised establishment.

His official début was on New Year's Day, 1781, when he was almost mobbed by Society. Georgiana danced with him that night and was struck by his ease and grace. From the other Court balls that year she, and all other ladies of the opposition, were excluded, and he was so closely chaperoned by his parents that the only women with whom he became acquainted were met in secret and were of ill repute. He was already drinking so heavily that for some time he was quite disfigured.

But his men connexions counteracted in some part these undesirable influences, for he began to frequent Brooks's, where he joined the younger set of men whose opposition to the Court party was sympathetic to the rebellious Prince. These young men, among whom were the Duke of Devonshire, Fox, Fitzpatrick, Hare, Grenville and Fawkener, combined wit, wonderful quickness and good sense, though their biting tongues made them redoubtable. The eldest of them was but thirty; even so their worldly wisdom made them too old for the boy of eighteen, and he turned to his coevals, a society of young men who, strangely enough, were all followers of Lord North, belonging to that very party so distasteful to the unfilial Prince.

At this point the manuscript breaks off, just at the time when the Prince was finding his way from Brooks's to two great Whig houses in Piccadilly. Lady Melbourne cultivated him shamelessly, overwhelming him with flattery and attentions. He was lost in gratitude and slightly surprised delight at finding he was so important a person after all. At Devonshire House his welcome was as warm, though less fulsome. It was the gayest time in Georgiana's life, and the Prince and she were soon calling each other 'Brother' and 'Sister.' He was enchanted with her and Harriet; so happy was he in their laughing company that from the windows of Devonshire House he would observe without regret 'Perdita' driving past in her light blue carriage, on the panels of which were little bunches of flowers which she, who had hoped for the rank of Duchess, had had painted so skilfully that they looked like armorial bearings.

Flowers, jewels and bright lights were indeed the armorial bearings most suited to these refulgent children: he in the 'splendour of his youth and the manliness of his beauty'; the Spencer sisters, equal in their charm, glittered like stars embowered in flowers.

But these children of fortune acknowledged their responsibilities as well, accepting their political influence as their *raison d'être*, for as Georgiana said, 'politicks appear to be approaching to a crisis and some great crash will happen soon.'

She became involved in political life at one of the crucial moments in English constitutional history. At the time of her marriage the Whigs were split into three factions. Her husband was, by inclination and family connexions, associated with the section led by Lord Rockingham and his cousins, the Dukes of Portland and Richmond. They were the upholders of tradition, and Rockingham was to prove this on his deathbed, when he told Fox that his 'Whiggism is founded on the Constitution and not on two or three great families; my Whiggism is not confin'd to the Peak of Derbyshire.'

The oligarchs of the party, led by the Bedfords and Grenvilles, were concerned with the preservation of their own vast interests; whilst the third faction, under the aegis of the elder Chatham, introduced the first tentatives towards reform.

Burke, who always insisted that the control of America should rest with Parliament, was instrumental in the repeal of the Stamp Act of 1765, reserving Parliament's right of legislation and taxation, and it was the monopolists whom he supported who crushed him eventually. In 1773 the levy of certain taxes in America was so strongly opposed there that the question became the dominating interest in both countries. It seemed to liberal minds on both sides of the water to be a flagrant injustice infringing the liberties of a people: to George III, whose natural obstinacy insisted more on the obedience of his loyal subjects, it appeared rebellion pure and simple, to be annihilated by any and every means. Obedience to the throne was his watchword, and therefore negotiation was not to be considered. The question resolved itself into Repeal or War. To the King repeal was weakness, a very assault upon the strength of the Crown, so he persisted rigidly until it came to war, supported unwillingly by his Prime Minister Lord North, whose loyalty to the King was stronger than his political convictions.

Rockingham, Richmond and Burke, the champion of all that was finest in their party, whose blazing conviction in 'common opinions, common affections and common interests' was to scare even Burke's supporters as something foreign to the English character and therefore something to be mistrusted, were in opposition.

We must consider the extraordinary exclusiveness in the ruling ranks of the time, the compact, sealed hierarchy in whose hands lay the reins of power, and to remember that Burke was, to them, an outsider, an interloper, if we are to comprehend why he fought a losing battle and why he was cold-shouldered by even his own party. The governing class had something in the nature of a secret society, from whose freemasonry the leaders of both sides were drawn. Burke, with his hatred of injustice, his worship of liberty, had no social powers or graces and had stormed the political ranks and, without the least concessions to the political shibboleths of the time, presumed to teach his betters their place.

Fox, who had no need of a social passport and who possessed all the advantages that Burke lacked, did not hesitate, when he joined the Rockingham–Devonshire faction in 1774—an action which strengthened their political position and assured his own—to elect Georgiana as his pupil-patroness.

It did not occur to the already middle-aged Burke to cultivate his acquaintance with Georgiana; but had he used Devonshire House as his extra-political rostrum he might have achieved the great position as leader of his party, for which he was so eminently fitted. But he was too single-minded, too consumed with the integrity of his own passion, even to consider burning with a gentler flame, and so he remained 'very civil and strange,' and their friendship was to wither from inanition.

The Duke's position, and especially his having married, was to make Devonshire House the obvious private focus for his party. Fox took his place in it naturally and as by right, and his friends and the Duke's left their clubs and followed suit. They came to discuss politics, to be amused, because their young hostess was the fashion; they stayed because her fervour, her desire to learn, the pleasure she showed in pleasing and her gay charm, bound them to her in devoted and admiring friendship.

Chief among these were Fox and Sheridan, whose dramatic ventures came tumbling after each other with bewildering speed and increasing success. 7 January 1775, saw the production of *The Rivals*, the first performance of which was severely criticized, but in ten days' time Sheridan offered an amended version which was instantly acclaimed. In May the short farce, *St Patrick's Day*, followed it lightly and successfully, and in November he produced *The Duenna*, that 'new sing-song thing,' which immediately leapt into popularity such as no English musical play since *The Beggar's Opera* had enjoyed. The following year he became manager and part-owner of Drury Lane, and despite the incredibly complicated negotiations and heavy responsibilities connected with it, he found time to write both the *Trip to Scarborough* and *The School for Scandal*, which was met with applause that confirmed him as the foremost playwright of his time.

It is my conviction that Sheridan's 'Lady Teazle' was a much closer portrait of Georgiana than is generally recognized now, though the likeness was commented on at the time. But the contemporary fashionable audience pounced upon the unflattering side of the picture—the frivolousness, the deliberate casual flirtation, the aversion from her unsympathetic husband—and shut their eyes to the true Lady Teazle, whose character, as well as her person, is revealed by the fall of the screen when she exposes Joseph Surface, denounces herself, and begs her husband to recognize that her wrong had lain in folly and not in vice, and with magnanimity gives him the credit of having shown her the danger of her ways.

Perhaps Sheridan hoped that others would see the Duchess in the light that he and Fox saw her, but they were blind or worse and with cynical pity he wrote:

See yonder in the thickest throng
Designing Envy stalks along
By co-malicious Laughter;
Fiction and Cunning swell her train,
While stretching far behind—in vain—
Poor Truth comes panting after!

But while he was engaged in the composition of his plays, their production and the affairs of Drury Lane, his political instincts had been aroused and fostered by Fox who was the first to recognize that Sheridan's talents were those of a statesman as well as a dramatist and who listened with approval to the paper which Sheridan had written, attacking Lord George Germaine, and which was read by John Townshend to Gibbon one evening at Devonshire House.

In February 1780, Burke made 'an elaborate and judicious speech to promote petitions to Parliament for retrenching sinecures, superfluous places and pensions.' This was also the occasion of the Duke's maiden speech, and Burke's half-ironic, wholly disinterested attitude towards what he may have suspected as irresponsible zeal in the Duchess, combined with a genuine desire that the Duke should make his mark politically, is clearly shown in his letter to Georgiana written on March the 7th.

Madam,

I am much flattered by your Grace's extraordinary condescension in defrauding your Toilet of an hour or two, in the reading of a long, and, I fear, rather dull discourse on Cooks, Upholsterers, Contractors and jobbing Members of Parliament. I had directed one to be sent to Lady Spencer: But I find, that I have not been better obeyed than if I were a great Man....

I never was more angry with myself, than for having quitted the House of Lords early yesterday. If I had received the very best *Bonus* in Lord North's Budget, if I had swallow'd the highest morsel of *scrip*, reserved for the Lickerish Mouths of the most gluttonous contractors, it would not have made me amends for attending the Nonsense, of long and short annuities, and of three per cents. and four per cents., whilst I lost my share of the pleasure of the Duke of Devonshire's first speech in the House of Lords. I find on all hands, that this beginning had all the dignity, spirit and propriety, that would naturally have been expected by all that know him. It is, I find, and I am happy beyond measure to find, the universal opinion. I sincerely congratulate all friends to this Country upon his taking an active and forward part in publick business. He, and the business will be both the better for it. But, as you know that people grow more importunate as they are more gratified, I must be one amongst many Sollicitors, to your Grace, that since this very happy, and very much applauded beginning, is made, that the Duke of Devonshire will push his first advantage; until, it will become, by habit, more disagreeable to him to continue silent on an interesting occasion, than hitherto it has been to him, to speak upon it. I hope your Grace, in addition to your other instances of goodness and partiality to me, will be so kind as to forgive this intrusion. I have the honour to be with the greatest possible sense of Obligation and Respect

Madam Your Grace's Most Obedt and humble Servt

Edm Burke.

So the Duke, 'dear Canis,' 'dear Ca,' might be about to have a real career in politics after all—how proud and pleased she would be and how good it was of Mr Burke to take so much trouble in writing to her about it; she would preserve his letter carefully. And he had even asked her to encourage the Duke—why, that was what she would do the most readily in the world. But why did he want to drag in that part about her toilet? Would they never realize how she was 'bored and hacked to death' by the expectation of amusement;

In one continual round to see
The same dull figures roll along,
That void of pleasure life and glee
Are pushed and pushing midst the throng

That she was far more interested in their new 'Westminster Association for Reform' than in anything else?

The Mass Meeting held in Westminster Hall, sponsored by the Dukes of Portland and Richmond, at which Fox and Sheridan had pressed for 'Constitutional Information' and advocated the revolutionary measures of universal suffrage and annual parliaments, had been the annealing of the chain which was to bind Fox, Sheridan and Pitt together for a short time.

But there were to be stranger alliances brought about by a general feeling that the time had come to abolish the old Penal Laws afflicting the Catholics. The Whigs espoused this cause from a sense of the crippling injustice which these laws inflicted; Burke and Fox were the champions of the outcasts, the Duchess and her friends following them wholeheartedly. The Tories took their lead from the King, many of whose most loyal supporters were Catholics. None of these Catholics were allowed to be educated either at public schools or universities; they could not sit in the House nor serve in the Forces.

Their plight enlisted the strangest sympathisers, one of the oddest of whom was the Anglican Bishop of Derry, who, though his own religious beliefs were singularly vague, fought with conviction for the Catholics, especially in Ireland. Such a state of things, whilst manifestly unjust, had long been tolerated and encouraged by Church and State, but now feelings were veering towards 'freedom of faith,' and obviously it was to His Majesty's interest to reward the loyalty of his Catholic supporters by lifting their shackles. There appeared to be every reason why the reform should be brought about without opposition. But the incalculable human factor, in the shape of Lord George Gordon, the spark of whose fanaticism lit a forest fire of 'No Popery' among the people, wrecked the reform, nearly burned the whole of London and almost brought about a general rebellion. The chapels of the Embassies, the houses of Catholics and those of their Whig supporters were sacked, burned or plundered. Naturally Devonshire House was in great peril, but Georgiana kept her head.

On June the 5th she makes the first mention of the Riots, saying that 'Ld. George Gordon's people continue to make a great fracas, there is a violent mob in Moor fields & I have heard that five hundred of the guards are gone down there.'

Evidently the gravity of the situation was not recognized by her till two days later, when the seriousness was apparent, though she concealed her alarm from her mother.

I shall go to Chiswick tomorrow, for tho' there would be no kind of danger for me, yet a woman is only troublesome. I hope and think it will be all over tonight, as the Council has issued orders that the Soldiers may fire. The kings bench is burnt down and I suppose you know that Lord Mansfield's was burnt this morning, the mob is a strange set and some of it compos'd of meer boys.

I was very much frighten'd yesterday but I keep very quiet and preach quiet to everybody—the night before last the Duke was in Garrison at Lord Rockinghams till five which alarm'd me not a little but now Lord Rs is the safest place, as he has plenty of guards, a justice of the Peace, and a hundred tradesmen arm'd, besides servants and friends.

All our houses are quite safe.

There is Minchin's Hampshire regiment, and the Queens are encamp'd in Hyde Park, but till today the sloth and irresolution of the Government has been inconceivable. Even now the Kings bench might have been sav'd had not Lord Amherst prevented the soldiers from firing.

Amidst the felons let out from Newgate yesterday there was a poor devil who was to have been hung today, the poor wretch fainted away at his reprieve, one cannot but be sorry for him. It is reckon'd right or I must own that I am very sorry to go out of town as I shall be anxious to a degree, I wish I could take yᵉ Duke with me, yet I comfort myself with his being quite safe, and everybody says the worst is past....

The next day she continues to reassure her mother. She says:

I am sure you will be delighted to hear that everything bears a more favourable aspect—I saw Lord Melbourne and Mr Grenville just now return'd from the borough, where the mob is very small and the military will keep it in that part of the town without letting it come near this and the inhabitants of the different streets are preparing to defend themselves.

She enumerates the various regiments encamped in the Parks and says that

two troups of Mr Fitzroys are to patrole up and down Piccadilly, and as the Duke don't like having the soldiers here again (as there is no need) the depôt of guards for this part of the town will be at Lord Melbourne's, so you see that Piccadilly is the safest place in the world—I stay in town as there is no manner of danger ... I should have gone to Wimbledon, but I wished to stay to hear the news....

My brother is station'd at Hammersmith and that division are not to come to London, but to stay there, I own I am glad he's there tho' evry body says it is the finest thing for a soldier to see something a little like fighting without danger and the Duke does nothing but regret his regiments being gone to Portsmouth.

Adieu my dearest Mama, I really am assur'd that the mischief is over.

On Friday, June the 9th, she writes her last letter about the Riots.

... My confusion was so great on the 7th that I totally forgot it was my birthday till late in the day, thank God all is over now, and I am quite easy about my brother, ... I went to see him with Miss Shipley this morning (but I don't come near him by a mile), he look'd vastly well in his red jacket, Lord Westmorland is a very strict commander, they were all dying when I was there to see some blue cockades go by that they might pull them out.

You will know probably that Lord Geo. Gordon is taken and at the tower, my pity now begins to be mov'd for him, but two days ago I believe I could have kill'd him myself—I now begin to hope he won't be hang'd, but banishment by all means, surely if he has any feeling he must be enough punished by the confusion he has occasion'd.

... I feel mad with spirits at alls being over, it seems like a dream. We had a guard last night tho' we did not ask for it but tonight ye Duke has desir'd not as it is absolutely useless. There was a report yesterday that Mr Alman and a Roman Catholick next door to him would be attacked and as that is near Mrs Garners[1] I despatch'd her and Charlotte to Brocket Hall [Lord Melbourne's country house]; Lady M[elbourne] thinks she is a relation of mine, I was in a great hurry and fright about it or I should have sent her to Wimbledon but I thought the Shipleys might be going ... and that it might occasion enquirys.

There is a council sitting tonight on Lord G. I suppose...

For the girl who had said that on alarming occasions she always thought it right to go into something like an hysteric, she had not done badly; she had minimised her fear to her mother, written daily to reassure her, thought about everybody's safety except her own and even found it in her heart to pity the villain of the piece.

The outcome of these dangerous days, during which nearly everybody had lost their heads, except the King, who had behaved with the greatest personal courage, was his insistence that the Relief Act should not be shelved. The Government had not come out of the affair with any credit but with much loss of confidence. A General Election was inevitable.

About this time the Duchess introduced Sheridan to Lady Cork, whose brother John Monckton was one of the two members for Stafford, thereby bringing him into one of those close family nuclei of the party, for the Moncktons, Devonshires and Spencers were all Whigs and all related. Through this connexion Sheridan was elected as the second member for Stafford on September the 12th, which constituency he was to represent without a break for twenty-seven years.

Georgiana's excitement and gratification knew no bounds; at last she had been of real use; it was almost as though she had been elected to Parliament herself, though that, of course, was manifestly impossible.

Sheridan, too, felt how instrumental she had been to his election, for on September the 19th he wrote her a most grateful letter. He said that he was

... entirely at a loss how to thank your Grace for the Honor and Service which your Grace's condescending to interest yourself in my election at Stafford has been to me.... I profited by the Permission allowed to me to make use of your Grace's letter as my first and best introduction to Lord Spencer's Interest in the Town. I assure your Grace that I found good effects from it even out of the circle of influence which Lord Spencer's Property and Character so justly maintain in Stafford. It is no Flattery to say that the Duchess of Devonshire's name commands an implicit admiration whenever it is mentioned, and I found some that had opportunities of often seeing and of hearing more of your Grace, who were so proud of the distinction as to require no other motive to support anyone who appear'd honor'd with your Grace's commendation.... I have avoided asking Mr Fox to thank your Grace on my account, because I am perhaps even unfairly ambitious to owe all the gratitude myself.

The result of the General Election was disappointing; the Whigs had sustained some bad defeats, and both Burke and Pitt lost their seats, but were returned through two convenient pocket boroughs. Georgiana, however, knew that her first practical venture into politics had been crowned with success and turned to more domestic preoccupations.

Lady Spencer and she had been right in their handling of Harriet who at last, they sighed thankfully, was behaving like a normal young woman.

Surrounded by a crowd of suitors, instead of becoming more undecided as to which one to choose, she had become attracted to 'Ca's' first cousin, Lord Duncannon, the only son of the Earl of Bessborough. They had known each other all their lives and Harriet wondered why she had never appreciated him before. Perhaps it was the contrast between the life she had been living at Devonshire House and the life that he preferred to live that made her regard him with particular attention; perhaps it was the very differences between them that drew her towards him. She had become even more politically minded than her sister—he detested politics, though, naturally, as his father's son, he was found a seat in the House which he regarded with distaste, saying, 'however convenient a place may be, independence is much pleasanter.' She was sociable—he solitary in his tastes. Her strong sense of individualism respected his studious desires, which were to collect books and prints and to make charming sketches; though like all his kind he was not without a sense of public duty. Contrasting the noisy hyperbolic protestations of her many other admirers with his quiet intense devotion, she was convinced where her happiness lay, and she joined her hand trustfully with his.

Both families were delighted—here was another match that was perfectly suitable in every way. Lord Bessborough gave them his blessing and a charming rural villa at Roehampton, in which idyllic retreat they spent a happy honeymoon after their marriage on November the 23rd.

Georgiana was filled with content: Fox was her friend, Sherry too, and though she would miss her constant companionship, her darling Harriet was perfectly matched and in love. There were only two clouds in her sunny sky; she was still childless and she owed a great deal of money. Otherwise things were going very well indeed.

The saloon, Devonshire House.

5

Enter Elizabeth Foster

Georgiana's life was now as full as only an empty life can be. There was a constant preoccupation with politics; Devonshire House hummed with schemes for reform, the chief of which was the introduction of the Bill for the Revision of the Civil List, which was sponsored with brilliance by the younger Pitt and Sheridan. The 'present distressful war in America' was becoming increasingly distressful and its prolongation clearly impossible. Obviously its mismanagement by the Tories would force Lord North to resign before peace could be made, and then—ah! then the young men of Devonshire House would convert their Utopian schemes into realities. But this, like countless other inevitabilities, was not to be.

Meanwhile, as one could not talk politics all the time, there were other delights, the most outstanding being the revival of Faro, as the new spelling had it, for as the fever for the game grew, so they spelt it in fewer letters. From its original stately 'Pharaoh' it had degenerated phonetically to 'Pharo,' and now they were in such a hurry to play it that it was 'Faro' *tout court*. It possessed them all, except Harriet Duncannon who, pregnant and contented, stayed at Roehampton playing chess or cribbage with her bridegroom.

The others flung themselves into the pit of gaming without a vestige of restraint, with a veritable madness, ruining each other, ruining themselves, plunging deeper and deeper into the Hell whose furnaces were fed by I.O.U.s and whose stokers were the money-lending Jews. Everything went to feed the flames: jewels, houses, horses, all were fuel, and men married girls in order to throw their brides' dowries into the fire. Fox ran a table, and as banker was solvent for the first time for years; Georgiana, who followed him in everything, plunged deeper and deeper, but losing, not gaining, money, and soon her debts were of such dimensions she did not dare confess them to the Duke. She resorted to crippling and underhand agreements with the usurers in order to obtain money without his knowledge; she borrowed from bankers, friends, tradespeople and servants, and once the precious guineas were in her hands, she would give them to others who applied to her for help, believing that her means were inexhaustible, making her position worse than ever. These subterfuges were agonizing to her open nature, and she suffered tortures wondering how to pay the interest to the money-lenders and her debts of honour and yet keep her straits from her husband, in terror lest he should learn of the blackmailing terms she had been forced to accept.

A typical agreement is dated London, 18 December, 1779, and runs as follows:

> Mr D—ll having lent me two thousand six hundred and fifty pounds, I do hereby promise to pay him two hundred and fifty pounds every three months, at the usual quarter days, and continue to pay that sum quarterly to him or his heirs (allowing five per cent. interest and five per cent. for insurance of my life per annum) until principal, interest and insurance shall fully be paid. G. D.

Mr D.'s agreement is

> that in case the Duchess does not pay me two hundred and fifty pounds quarterly that I shall acquaint the Duke of D. with this transaction; and her Grace has promised, in case of her death or other accidents, to leave in writing a request that I may be paid, as I have lent her the money to relieve her from play debts, under a solemn promise that she will not play in future. J. D.

Unhappily she could not keep her promise to Mr J. D., for how was she to pay him more than half her income (for the Duke allowed her £2,000 a year), and his fellows unless she made money at the tables?

She and her friends raised the stakes privately, so that a guinea would represent a hundred, then a thousand, and so the wild perdition went on till the vicious circle of debt, half-confession, repentance and broken resolutions destroyed her peace of mind, her health and, she believed, the remnants of her unstable marriage. But in this she was to be mistaken, for the Duke, though unimaginative, was honourable, and was moved to pity for her sufferings and wonder that she had been so afraid of him. It was this fear that was the rock on which the unseaworthy bark of their marriage was wrecked. Meanwhile she saw no way out.

In August 1781 she escaped with 'Ca' to Devonshire, where they saw 'Tinmouth' and Torbay and visited the Parkers at Saltram. The Duke played at soldiering and she bathed and got tanned as brown as a berry 'car on ne suit pas un soldat pour rien.' In one day she would bathe early and so miss her breakfast, then drive off to see the fishing nets hauled in, clambering in and out of the boats up to her 'knees in mud and water and jaded to death,' hurrying back to dress before going out to dinner and then to play at whist till she fell, tired out, into bed.

Then she would accompany the Duke on a field day, starting at eight in the morning and still be able to admire the beauties of Mount Edgcumbe, likening it to her rival the Duchess of Rutland and declaring with her usual lack of vanity that 'it makes other places look as little (always excepting Wimbledon) when compar'd to it, as the Duchess of Rutland does little beautys when she comes into the room.'

The following day she would write a description to her mother in verse whilst she was dressing—pen, ink, paper and powder all mixed up together—of 'Judges, circuits, camps and fleets, Of Edgcumbe's Mount, of Parker's Place, Of Marystowe's more placid Grace, Of Gen'rals, Admirals, Ships-masters, Of Lady Cork and her disasters,' ending with an assurance that despite all these, her thoughts were for her mother only.

Two days after there was a water party to Plymouth Sound, for which they had to rise at seven in order to be ready in time. But the Duke's brother, Lord George Cavendish, who had been drunk the night before, kept them waiting till nine. They were to have landed at the 'Eddy Stone, a Light House built on a Rock ... but the wind was too high for us to think of it. What passed afterward I don't know.

> *Soon as the ship began to roll*
> *away went all delight,*
> *down to the Cabbins furthest hole*
> *I shrunk from ev'ry sight....'*

She was not alone in her suffering, for the entire party succumbed except the phlegmatic Duke.

Then followed an alarm that the English fleet was driven in and that the French might attack when they chose. 'I shall be frighten'd out of my sences,' she confessed, 'but I vow I won't say so.'

The next day an immense naval review revived her courage (though she could have beaten Lady Cork for thinking a fleet twice the size of ours a laughing subject), and her old friend, Mr Bastard, complimented her, calling the sea her element and comparing her, amongst numberless other fine things, to Venus.

All these junketings were very fine, no doubt, but what would she not have given to be in Harriet Duncannon's place that last week in August, agonizing in her child-bed. Lucky Harriet—she whose reluctance to wed had been rewarded in nine months' time, while Georgiana, who had married when she was bid, was still barren seven years after.

She had a makeshift compensation however, for with the honesty of the time, her husband had told her of his daughter by a milliner and Georgiana's wide heart of pity had opened to her. 'Miss William' (the name they decided on if Mama did not think it conspicuously odd) was a very healthy, good-humoured child, not very tall and so amazingly like the Duke that Lady Spencer would have recognized her anywhere. She was very active and lively and she seemed very affectionate. Her teeth were bad and she often had the toothache, but as they were her milk-teeth perhaps her second growth would be better.

Evidently Lady Spencer did not like the surname 'William,' for the Duchess said that she would discuss the subject with the Duke, but as the little girl was remarkably intelligent and inquisitive, to change her name again might have a bad effect upon her.

The Duke, who on being introduced to his progeny, was 'vastly pleased with her,' had thankfully accepted his wife's offer to look after the child, a charge she must have undertaken previously, for we have witnessed her concern for Charlotte's safety during the Gordon Riots. This had been perfectly easy whilst the child was of age to be 'at nurse.' This was the usual procedure, not only with the many love-children of the time, but also with their equally numerous legitimate half-brothers and sisters, whose fashionable mothers salved their easy consciences with the narcotics of country air and salubrious diet. A healthy countrywoman, wife of some reputable small farmer or labourer on one of the feudal estates, would be chosen; the baby, still in its swaddling clothes, would be installed; small but adequate monthly payments made, and if one of the hedgerows fledglings went hungry for the sake of the cuckoo in its nest or was less finely feathered, well, that was admirable too, as it might teach these poorer folk not to breed so incontinently and to realize the proper distance between them and their betters.

Then four or five years later, when the nursling had reached a more interesting age, Mr Morland would set up his easel in front of the pretty thatched cottage, in summer, of course, and sketch in the charming scene. The cottage has a background of great shady trees, and in the foreground are some very clean ducks and hens. Presently the wheels of a cabriolet are heard and, before they stop, a buxom, kindly-looking woman, dressed in the cleanest of print gowns with snowy cap and apron, comes out of the cottage door. Clinging to her skirts and tumbling round her are a whole bevy of children, as rosy and buxom as their mother, though their equally clean clothes are perhaps more picturesque than they would have been when quite new. In her arms is a lovely baby in a long lace gown and cobwebby lace cap, and she leads by the hand a most delightful little girl dressed in a fine white frock tied with a wide blue satin sash, her hair falling in glistening chestnut curls round her shoulders. There is a little boy, too; he wears a frilled shirt, with high-waisted trousers buttoned on to it, a costume forced by modern brides upon their unwilling pages, and his hair also is neat and shiny. The carriage has stopped and through the rustic gate comes a magnificent figure. Heedless of her sweeping skirts trailing in the dust, the lady stretches her mittened arms towards those two children who, perhaps, Mr Morland has painted with a little more care than the others. The baby crows with delight at the sight of her huge plumed hat—it would never be so tactless as to bawl with fright at so alarming a stranger—and the little girl runs forward and is clasped in the lady's arms. Mr Morland has painted a very pretty picture.

A few years later Mr Morland would set up his easel again, but this time indoors. The room is elegant, washed in pale colour, and it has a classic mantelpiece. A blackboard indicates that it is a schoolroom. The buxom country wife is replaced by a wholly admirable gentlewoman (is her name Mrs Garner?), whose neat and simple dress is in the best of taste, and who clearly is well fitted to educate the children of gentry. The little girl, slightly subdued, is still there, and the lady who visits her is still as lovely and well dressed. Mr Morland has painted a delightful pendant to his first picture.

But can he paint a third? Has not the awkward age by now been reached? The Duchess rather thought it had and the next stage was definitely perplexing. But the problem was soon to be solved.

Among Lady Spencer's friends she numbered, it will be remembered, the Bishop of Derry—soon to succeed his brother as Earl of Bristol, and his wife, Mrs Hervey. This prelate was as eccentric a Hervey as any of his family that ever lived, and more eccentric it was therefore impossible to be. He patronized the fine arts, spending his money like water—naturally, in Italy, the fountain-head of taste—he elaborated incredible financial schemes as intricate as spiders' webs: to build churches, chapels and cathedrals for the Catholics in Ireland, guaranteeing the Bill, if it should pass, with £60,000 sterling of his own, whipping up the Pope, the Empress of Germany and an ex-Governor of Peru for subscriptions; or to marry off his son to the King of Prussia's daughter, by which scheme his family would benefit by £10,000 a year and an English Dukedom for himself; and finally, a transcendent plan to divide France into a Northern Republic and a Southern Monarchy, milking both to the advantage of England. But he was forced to recognize with regret that it was unlikely that the English Minister for Foreign Affairs would have vision enough to listen to his plan. He treated his family, which was a large one, in the most arbitrary fashion, dragging his wife and unmarried daughters ruthlessly through Europe, unheeding of their faint complaints, their ceaseless fevers and fears. He would lavish presents with a princely hand and quibble at farthing expenses, and his name is emblazoned on a thousand European hotels to this day. One day he went driving with his wife, apparently on as good terms as usual; on their return they never spoke to one another again, Lady Bristol deploring his conduct to the end.

In 1776 he married off his two elder daughters, Mary to Lord Erne and Elizabeth, the younger, rather against her will, to John Thomas Foster, an Irish squire. The Bishop then set off on one of his prolonged tramontane tours, his wife writing plaintive letters to her girls at home. Soon the unsatisfactory answers began to arrive—neither marriage was going well.

The Bishop and Mrs Hervey returned to England in 1779, and soon they were visiting Lady Spencer, whom they both held in the highest esteem. They confided their doubts and fears to this understanding and broadminded friend: all had gone well with Elizabeth at first; she had borne one son, Augustus, quite easily, and though her health had not been very good afterwards, the Bishop had reassured her regarding a second pregnancy, telling her never to fear honest childbearing, since for one mother that grew thin with this work there were five hundred old maids that grew more thin for want of it. His words proved true and a second son, Frederick, was born soon afterwards. Meanwhile, they told Lady Spencer they had sent and received very civil messages from their son-in-law, whom they had nicknamed 'Slimness.' But Elizabeth continued to throw out hints that all was not well, and soon 'Slimness' became just little 'f' or 'our philosopher,' for it really was ridiculous to listen to the whims and fancies of these girls—whoever heard of taking the seduction of a waiting maid seriously? But by the time they had returned to England and seen their daughters, they found that things had got beyond their control:

indulging in two of her periodical rages for drawing and reading history, and wrote to her mother

> that I devour what I read and feel about it as one does about a novel—I should prefer Rapin to 'Cecilia' and I believe I should even delight in a long dissertation upon the feudal laws. It is my misfortune that every turn I take towards anything like study is by such starts that it is of no use to me—I am too eager at the moment and too easily disgusted, and you may observe I only succeed in what is to be obtained in a short time....

If anybody ever succeeded in painting a self-portrait it was Georgiana on that summer's afternoon.

Not all Georgiana's reading was on so elevated a plane as Rapin's History, for she had just got into trouble with her mother for reading that licentious and influential best-seller, *Les Liaisons Dangereuses*, the success of the year.

> As to the 'Liaisons,' it was the noise the book made that tempted me to read it—I plead guilty, but I am going to defend the reading of 'Mes Confessions.'
>
> I think the private history of a Man like Rousseau in which one may trace the wonderful progress of his great and burning genius, may excuse some indecency which is of a kind that cannot hurt—and except in a very young unmarried person I really think it is a book to be read. If Rousseau had lived when a Horace or a Catullus did, no scruple would have been made to it ... the odd principles of a Mad^me de Warens can surprise, and strike one as odious and ridiculous but cannot entice or mislead. In Rousseau who is of course the Character that interests one, one observes a romantick sincerity and candour in allowing every fault, and with the highest ideal of honour, a horror of deviating from them yet a steadiness in confessing any deviation. In the second volume one finds a very useful and easily adopted course of study (for Rousseau's erudition was not very deep) and the whole interspers'd with language and sentiments that inchant. All this therefore must render it an interesting and surely not an useless book.
>
> Another reason for reading it, is that every body I saw was talking of it, the Duke especially who has read it with the greatest pleasure and mark'd it all through—but I am going to astonish you for I know another who will read it whose authority will be best of all and that is You. Indeed I shall make you, my Dst. M.

Poor Lady Spencer, what was she to make of her chameleon child? This sinful gambling, late hours, dissipation and eccentricity in dress (who ever heard of wearing gold bracelets like dog collars with 'The Duke of Devonshire, Devonshire House' engraved on them? It was in downright bad taste). And then the next minute she would be writing these charming letters, showing her pursuit of knowledge, much fun and sometimes her good sense, and she was so kind to her less-well-off sister, too, always giving her new gowns, and she was an angel to the Bristols' girl, Lady Liz. Though Lady Spencer was uncertain whether she quite approved of her daughter's absorption in Lady Elizabeth; sympathetic hospitality was commendable but this 'engouement' quite another thing; besides there were things about that young woman that Lady Spencer did not quite care for. But Georgiana was always headstrong—if only she had a child....

The foundations of the incredible relationship between 'Canis,' Georgiana and Bess were laid during this visit to Plympton. Throughout the lifelong correspondence of Bess and Georgiana run references to that summer which appeared to them in the golden light of an idyll. The Duke and Duchess decided that Bess, 'their Angelick Angel,' 'their loveliest Friend,' was to be their Sister: they were both infatuated with her.

Obviously the Bristols regarded this visit as but a temporary solution, and so eventually it was arranged that Lady Elizabeth and her sister Lady Erne were to retire to Bath, where they could live cheaply, without scandal under the chaperonage of a Mrs Gordon, each paying the cook 14s. a week for themselves and 7s. a week for servants, each person to breakfast alone and at no time to be a clog on each other. Lady Bristol, who had evolved this scheme, adds that she is afraid that her daughter will not 'look favourably on such a party' and that she is aware it will be a dull one, but that the advantages would be in 'a kind relation, an appearance of protection, retirement, a good air and lovely scenery.'

But even as she wrote of these unattractive plans a letter arrived from Lady Elizabeth enclosing letters from the Duke of Devonshire and his wife. Lady Elizabeth was to be rescued from the tedious company of the respectable relation, for the Devonshires were also going to Bath and she would spend most of her time with them. The Duchess had marked with delight how fond dear 'Ca' had become of her angelic friend; she herself dreaded the boredom of Bath—but with Bess in their party it would become heaven itself.

Heaven it did indeed prove, a strange Christmas-like heaven, the clear frosty air echoing to the sound of bells and the thin singing sound of skates. It was a picture that would remain for ever in their minds, small and distinct as a picture by Breughel: the classic houses, frozen in their perfection under the star-bright winter sky, harboured leaping fires so that in the warm high rooms the cards fell softly as leaves from the jewelled fingers, the leaping flames and myriad candles picking high-lights from the embroidered silks. They were small intimate card parties with Bishops and their domineering wives, whom the Duchess delighted to relieve of a few guineas.

During the day they would sip the nauseous waters and then go skating, the ladies seated in chairs pushed across the ice by their cavaliers. Georgiana laughed when she 'fell upon her bum-fiddle,' legs in the air—but Bess saw nothing funny in this tumble.

The strange trio, the heavy Duke with his ponderous jokes, the gay Duchess and the lovely grass-widow, were cosy and happy together, bound by the spell of intimacy woven by the icy outer air and the warmth within.

The visit to Bath was to be the turning-point in all three lives.

So much has been written, so many conjectures made, in the attempt to solve the problem of one of the strangest *ménages à trois* ever known, that it was almost a shock to stumble on the solution. It is a simple sentence in a letter of Georgiana's to Bess after the birth of her first child: 'You have saved your Brother Canis.' This cryptic remark is gradually explained as the drama of the friendship is revealed.

The Duchess had been married seven years. Save for an early miscarriage, there had been no sign of a child. She was almost in despair. Only the year before, she wrote to her mother of her desire to have children which she believed were denied to her till she deserved them. She was openly reproached by the Duke's relations, who attributed her barrenness to her mode of life. They therefore arranged that the Duke's brother and heir, Lord George Cavendish, should marry Lady Elizabeth Compton, for, as George Selwyn maliciously wrote to Lord Carlisle, it was 'agreed that the Cavendish family should be continued from his loins' as 'Mme. la Duchesse fait des paroles mais non pas des enfans.'

Soon Lady George declared her pregnancy. The Duchess confided to her mother that, to her horror, she felt an ungenerous sentiment at the approaching event, something like envy and uneasiness that she could not understand, for she wished her sister-in-law well from the depths of her heart. At first she had not minded the news, but as the time for the birth drew near her feelings increased in intensity. She was convinced that she would not feel as she did if it were not for her belief that she, too, *could* bear a child if only she could bring herself to lead a rational life and have a calm heart and mind. Yet despite her desires, she yielded to things which she believed to be antagonistic to her wish with open eyes. 'You must direct and save me, Dearest M., for you only can.'

But Lady Spencer, loving and wise as she was, could only direct her daughter and not save her.

Then came Bess: in Bess's company, Canis, usually so remote, became human. Georgiana, who was convinced that she had failed him, saw his new happiness with infinite thankfulness—they both felt happy and content, for Bess provided the background to their marriage, so that the darkened, shadowy stage was lightened, throwing the players into relief and reality.

And the coming of Bess coincided with the coming of Georgiana's child. On December the 2nd she was in an almost hysterical state of hope: there were signs that she might be pregnant. She wrote hourly bulletins to her mother—'I think … I hope … I believe …' In each one she bravely and superstitiously included an assurance that she would not be disappointed 'if the worst were to happen.' She vows she would bear disillusion with fortitude—that she is sure it cannot really be true.

But true it was, and in her mind, crazed with joy, she identifies Bess's influence, Bess's love, with the fulfilment of her heart's desire. From that day the baby was 'their child,' shared by all three, and nothing that the world, Canis or Bess could do would ever shake her almost fanatical love and gratitude.

Naturally the ill-natured world did not take her point of view; there was much gossip about the extraordinary new friendship of the Devonshires. Whatever happened, the Duke and Duchess were determined to retain that friendship and to shield their beloved Bess from harm.

Providentially, as it turned out, poor little Bess had a bad cough and a pain in her side. She was obviously consumptive, and must spend the rest of the winter abroad. In her unfortunate situation of wife-and-not-a-wife she could not go alone, but the Duchess found the inspired solution—Lady Elizabeth Foster should receive her expenses, and in return, the world was informed, she would very kindly take charge of a poor little orphan, whose father was dead and whose mother was a distant relation. The little girl was called Charlotte William, whose education the Devonshires had undertaken. On Christmas Day, 1782, Lady Elizabeth and Charlotte William sailed for the south of France.

Georgiana's adoration of her friend was peculiar to herself. Why were the other two attracted to each other?

If Georgiana was the prototype of 'Lady Teazle,' Lady Elizabeth Foster was the original, if unrecognized, 'Becky Sharp'; a better-looking, better-bred, more successful Becky, but precisely similar in character and conduct. She was an adept at turning her woes into assets.

She pleased the Duke, who, if not indifferent to his wife, did not attempt to understand her. We know him to have been lethargic and reluctant to make any plan, unable to take any action without much deliberation and many hesitations. Georgiana did not know what deliberation or hesitation meant. She invariably leaped before she looked, which alarmed and irritated the Duke, which in turn made her shy and almost frightened of him. Lady Liz, on the contrary, was a creature of calculation; she never made a spontaneous gesture or uttered an unpremeditated word. She was soft, ingratiating and humble in her approach. Georgiana never thought about herself. Elizabeth never thought of anything else; she planned her campaigns and, having thought out her strategy, pursued it ruthlessly; but she would endlessly discuss these plans with her friends, going over every point time and time again, asking advice, appearing thunderstruck by the wisdom of the advice given, exclaiming at her blindness and stupidity in not having thought of such excellent solutions herself—but then, of course, she was but a poor weak woman, abandoned to misery and incapable of looking after herself and helpless without her dearest, kindest friends.

Both the Duke and Georgiana were completely hoodwinked by this procedure—Georgiana because her greatest delight was to be of help to others; the Duke because, like every man that has ever lived, he could not resist the role of champion to a distressed female, especially when it entailed no effort. Here was a woman after his own heart: he would find her, smiling bravely through her tears, and ask, rather half-heartedly it must be admitted, what was wrong. Elizabeth would reply that she could not think of bothering him with her foolish troubles, but really she was so perplexed, so distraught—she had no one to turn to—if the Duke would really condescend.... Of course the Duke condescended, and they would then discuss for hours the advantages and disadvantages of this or that plan for her future, the Duchess agreeing with everything they said.

When it was all over the Duke would rise and take himself off to Brooks's, warmed with the glow of knight-errantry, delighted that there was at least one woman who had the sense to know that deliberation and a man's advice were best. The Duchess, equally delighted, would embrace her dearest Bess; it was such happiness to know that she was assisted by dear Ca's wisdom, she herself would never have seen half the points that seemed so clear to them, but then, perhaps, it was because she did not think enough. Bess would try to express her gratitude, but really words were inadequate, and having dried her very becoming tears, proceeded serenely with her original plan which both her benefactors were convinced had been suggested by them.

Her plan was simple enough; she had found a perfect harbour and she had no intention of weighing her anchor. It suited her in every way—she could live in the height of luxury and fashion without it costing her a penny; meet the world and his wife and ingratiate herself with them without the slightest effort; the interests of her entire family, parents, brothers and sisters, in-laws and eventually her own sons, were considered as much as her own, for if Georgiana opened her heart to a friend she never shut it to the rest of the tribe.

How could she show her gratitude in return? Why, the only return they wanted was for her to take care of her dear health so as to preserve to them the joy of her companionship and love. If, at the same time, she would do them the favour of taking Charlotte William abroad, they would be doubly in her debt, besides it would be so good for her after the terrible trials she had been through, and meanwhile would she amuse Canis? Georgiana confessed sadly that she herself seemed to fail in this, but Bess was so clever and so amusing. And this indeed was true, for Bess studied how to please.

Georgiana's charm lay in her openness, her frank spontaneity; Lady Elizabeth's in her considered approach. We have only to lay their portraits side by side for their characters to be made manifest; take as many as you will—half a dozen of each—and the characteristics are only accentuated. Georgiana's face is round and composed of curves, her eye-sockets large, the eyes round and laughing, her nose is deplorable, for it turns up unashamedly and her nostrils are wide and winged, it has no kind of dignity—nothing but impertinence and zest: her mouth is curved, generous and irrepressible, and her abundant hair is uncontrolled.

Lady Elizabeth's more beautiful face is oval and subtle, pointed and vixen-like. Her fine eyes are set in almond-shaped sockets, her nose is narrow at the bridge and her mouth smiling and sensual. The two faces epitomize impulse and calculation. Yet Georgiana was considered the paramount beauty of her time, though we might consider her a 'jolie-laide'; but the eighteenth century detested subterfuge, and it was probably the shining honesty of her face, 'that seldom wore and never met a frown,' that made her seem so lovely to them. Lady Elizabeth never had the reputation for beauty that was enjoyed by the Duchess, though Miss Burney tells us that she had the character of being so alluring that it was the opinion of Mr Gibbon that no man could withstand her, and that, if she chose to beckon the Lord Chancellor from his woolsack, in full sight of the world, he could not resist obedience. In the same passage, written at Bath in June

1791 when Lady Duncannon was thought to be dying, she describes the Duchess as follows:

> I did not find so much beauty in her as I expected, notwithstanding the variation of accounts; but I found far more of manner, politeness and gentle quiet.... There is in her face, especially when she speaks, a sweetness of good-humour and obligingness, that seem to be the natural and instinctive qualities of her disposition; joined to an openness of countenance that announces her endowed, by nature, with a character intended wholly for honesty, fairness and good purposes.

Even their voices were characteristic—the Duchess speaking with an infectious lazy drawl which she shared with her sister and passed on to her children so that the 'Devonshire House Drawl' became as well known as the 'Hervey Whine,' which persists to the present day.

The fact of Georgiana's pregnancy and of the Duke's 'brotherly' devotion to Bess reacted on her in an obvious way—she no longer felt herself to be a failure; her wifehood had been justified, her sins forgiven, and her thankfulness and sense of redress were joined with gratitude to Bess who had so humanized the Duke. At the same time she no longer had the effort of constantly trying to please him and of, as constantly—so she believed—failing in the attempt. Her relief made her fond of him for the first time in her life, and from the summer of 1782 her attitude towards him is one of deep affection and trust.

Back in London, though she grieved over the absence of Bess, she was transcendent with joy—nothing was of consequence except the miracle of the coming child that bound her, Canis and Bess together. She could not understand the attitude of the world; instead of criticism and slander, surely the unique beauty of the friendship must strike all hearts? The ideal purity of a relationship between a man and woman, both endowed with all that was amiable, who loved each other as brother and sister, watching over the woman they both adored, united by that woman's coming child, must surely be apparent to all? With starry eyes and a look of rapt preoccupation, she made the most fantastic plans for the layette, had the most Utopian ideas for the future, and even insisted that she was going to nurse the baby herself. They all, except Lady Spencer, thought she was mad and that soon her rage for gambling would oust this new interest, but her happiness increased instead of lessening.

Bess meanwhile was not enjoying herself abroad: she found the society of Charlotte William an indescribable bore and tie, as she confessed to her mother but concealed from the Devonshires. The very necessity for circumspection irked her, but on the other hand the exile was beneficial to her health, and the Duchess provided her liberally with money, over and above the sums allotted by Ca, sending her whatever winnings she made, the proceeds of the sale of a pianoforte and *douceurs* from her own sadly depleted purse. There *were* compensations, not the least of which being a certain Chevalier who was evidently deeply in love with her. In May she wrote that the prospect of her impending departure from Nice had reduced everybody round her to tears. As to the Chevalier, his melancholy silence, his unavowed love, had made her feel quite 'gulchy,' for he persisted in referring to the *last* walk, the *last* ride he would take with her. Even her singing had so moved him that he had to beg her to desist. They made a romantic expedition to La Napoule, where she fancied herself desolate and abandoned, even hearing dismal sounds and hollow groans. Finally they walked back to the house, and there, at the door, were all her poor crowding round her with tears and blessings, hanging on her hand, some holding out their little infants to her. It was too much—she could scarcely support herself.

Luckily the Chevalier was at hand to support her, and he escorted her to the boat, where she embarked amid sobs, prayers, blessings, kisses and nosegays. The voyage to Toulon was not uneventful, for she was obliged to sleep on board the ship, and by unselfishly sharing the inconvenience with the rest, none could complain. And though she had suffered from fever she revived sufficiently to enjoy a moonlight supper of tea, bread, eggs and fruit. It is gratifying to learn that Charlotte, too, enjoyed the supper and had her egg.

Sleeping on board was not Lady Elizabeth's only unselfish action. Finding herself in need of more money, she begged for a loan—for it *must* be regarded as a debt—and to discipline herself to that economy to which Georgiana's tender friendship had made her insensible, she would begin by sending away her horse.

But soon she was to receive a letter of such importance from England that the news it contained would require more than an equine sacrifice if she was to retain her supremacy. It was from Georgiana, who wrote:

I was laid on a couch in the middle of the room—my Mother & Dennis [her maid] supported me—Canis was at the door & the Dss. of Portland sometimes bending on me & screaming with me & sometimes running to the end of the room & to him. I thought the pain I suffer'd was so great from being unusual to me—but I find since I had a very bad time.

Towards the end some symptoms made me think the child was dead—I sd. so & Dr Denman only sd. there is no reason to think so but we must submit to providence. I had then no doubt & by watching my mother's eyes ... I saw she thought it dead, which they all did except Denman who dared not say too much—when it came into the world I sd. only let it be alive—the little child seemed to move as it lay by me but I was not sure when all at once it cry'd. Oh God! I cry'd & was quite Hysterical. The Dss. & my Mother was overcome & they cry'd & all kiss'd me. They took away the child & when they brought her back again I fainted. I would not change her for ten sons nor Canis either, nor you either, I whope,' my Bess.

Bess's reply is written at Geneva on July the 20th.

My wish, my fondest wish, is thus accomplished. You are a Mother! Yes, my beloved Angel, you are then a Mother! God, oh God bless you! Oh may this dear Infant be like you; 'tis the greatest Blessing that Heaven can grant you, dearest Georgiana. 'Tis still almost as a dream to me & so difficult is it for a heart oppressed & long acustomed to sorrow to bear up under Joy that I quite sank away at the news I have been pining for—but no matter of this; it is over & I am better today, well enough to feel all the gratitude to God that this his wondrous goodness demands, for oh my best Love, my heart since I have known you has formed no wish but for your happiness, no prayer but for blessings on you & to deserve your Lover. This was the event I most earnestly, most fondly desired; you will know how anxiously my heart watched over you in the first moments of your being with child & when others more fortunate than me cd. attend you in yr. progress, I did not less solicitously attend you in imagination—I am feeling you as my greatest good, as my all in the world; my grief oppressed mind made present to itself the ultimate misfortune it cd. experience, my fears I dared not express to you; wd. not to those around me, penetrated so into my Heart that I lost all Health & strength, so that when hopes of change of air might relieve me I came here; the arrival of your Courrier an hour after me was as much as I could support; there was a moment of silence after I had rushed to the door to seek him; my troubled imagination conceived every thing that was most horrid & the rapid revolution when he spoke overcame me; my tearless brain grew hot; & I really thought for some time that I should have gone mad. Your all-powerful influence saved me, the Courrier seized an interval to speak to me of you; your wonderful letter too, writing to me in the last moments and referring me to Canis for the event; I bid him speak on & at last tears came to my relief; I blest God that you was well & today I feel the full extent of *our* happiness.

Kiss *our* Child for me: how happy are those who have a right to be its god-mother, but I am to be its little mama; Canis said so. Adieu my angel for a little while.

Becky Sharp herself could not have done better.

The library, Devonshire House.

6

Personal and Political

A christening then was a matter of some import: it was the occasion for ceremony and rejoicing; god parents were chosen after much deliberation, for their spiritual, as well as their social qualifications, were considered. A week before the arrival of Georgiana's baby, Harriet Duncannon had given birth to her second son, and the baby cousins had a joint baptism at Wimbledon.

It was a very fine, pretty affair: Lord and Lady Spencer and Ca's sister, the Duchess of Portland, stood for Georgiana Dorothy, while the Devonshires and Lord Bessborough acted for Frederick Cavendish Ponsonby. Everybody wore their best clothes: Canis, dear dog, was dressed in a 'very pretty grey frock,' the Duchess all in Brussels lace—a snowy mist over a cloud of pink. The Duke gave a new frock to the Duncannon's eldest son, and the baby Georgiana was identified with her mother not only by name but in her apparel, as a robe of lace, all of one piece, had been woven for her in Brussels, the finest ever seen. The whole villa was decked with summer flowers, and baskets, foaming with lace and lilac ribbons, displayed tiny G.'s finery.

This was a family event; next came the public ceremony.

A great cortège rumbled up through England to the Duke's domain of Derbyshire. Here at Chatsworth and again at Buxton, the lace robes were brought out and worn at the ceremonial presentation of the baby to the ducal subjects and neighbours, her parents dining in public with the people crowding round to admire the tiny heiress.

Debarred from the joys of official god-motherhood or from being a witness of these rites, Lady Elizabeth indulged in a nervous breakdown brought about by the strain of spiritual motherhood.

Apparently this did not cause as much distress as she hoped, but she succeeded in focusing the limelight on herself all the same. The Duchess, to her infinite distress, heard reports that Lady Liz had been behaving indiscreetly. Of course, it was all nonsense and her dearest friend was as innocent as driven snow, but would she not herself have judged a beautiful, solitary young woman imprudent if she had invariably appeared in public accompanied by a couple of young men, both of whom were known to be in love with her? For Lady Liz's own sake, the Duchess implored her to exercise more caution. Lady Liz hastened to thank her beloved Angel for the friendly reproof, and proceeded through two pages of foolscap to explain and excuse herself. Surely as Charlotte was always with her; as there were two gentlemen; as she was indifferent to the ardours of both her admirers (for did she not live to please her dearest Canis and Georgiana?), and as, after all, it was but a trip across the Lake of Geneva, was it not prudent rather than imprudent for a lonely, helpless woman to accept an escort? But of course in future she would live entirely alone: she would leave Geneva (where she was having an unprecedented success at the Court of the Prince of Parma) and retire to Rome, where she would employ a music master and desire nobody to be let in. She believed that there was an English gentleman there with his two daughters from whom she hoped to get real comfort: in all cases she would find *serious* occupations and proper amusements enough.

Georgiana's two little anxious pages, protecting the reputation of her friend, are swamped by Lady Liz's courageous self-martyrdom.

From Rome Lady Liz, reluctantly dragging the burdensome Charlotte with her, made her way to Naples, whence she overwhelmed the Devonshires with romantic descriptions of its classic beauties and of yet another equally romantic love-affair, in the course of which her gentle denial and deep melancholy reduced her lover to tears, which he scattered on her hands as he kissed them respectfully but with passion. But this was by the way; what are important are her sorrows, her ill-treatment by her family, her shrinking from the world, that only with Georgiana and Canis can she be happy. There are bright spots, of course, and she is glad that dearest Canis still loves his little Bess and mimics her, for though it makes Georgiana gulchy, yet it makes her more present to their minds.

For the whole year and a half she was to remain away she practises her moral blackmail, bearing up under adversity, threatening, should she forfeit Georgiana's friendship, never to return to England, lamenting the, hardly surprising, disimprovement in Charlotte. Only once does she express a generous sentiment; let us record it to her honour. She says 'the more I think, the less I can guess what you mean in yr. letter by yr. obligation to me: I only know you can have none to such a bankrupt as me—I owe you everything & can repay you nothing.'

Though Georgiana's heart was full of her friend and her little daughter, with whom she spent every possible moment, brooding over her with adoration, the world soon reclaimed her. The coil in which she soon found herself had had its beginnings in the spring of 1782 when the Prince of Wales, whose career of pleasure now resembled a runaway horse that he could not stop even had he desired to do so, was always present either at Devonshire or Melbourne House. He, the Duchess and Lady Melbourne were inseparable. The usual scandalous rumours started running like evil weeds through London, and the betting was evenly divided between Georgiana and Lady Melbourne.

Should we wish to join in the speculations, we can be morally certain that if either of the women were his mistress it was Lady Melbourne, for the very good reason, apart from internal evidence, that Georgiana had not yet borne her husband an heir. At that time when marital infidelities were two a penny and fidelity regarded as a comic idiosyncrasy, save with such as Lady Spencer, there was one very strong unwritten law made to safeguard inheritance: this was that until a woman had borne her husband an heir she should remain faithful to him. In Georgiana's novel *The Sylph*, 'Lady Besford' (generally accepted as a portrait of Lady Melbourne) gives the bride some specific advice, which amounts to 'you can do what you please once you have done your duty by your husband, *but not till then.*'

The reasons for this rather cynical code of honour were two: the eternal philoprogenitiveness of man, ever desirous to perpetuate himself, and the risks run of illegitimate conception due to the lack of any safeguards. It is rare to find a man who does not want and talk of '*his*' son, it is his nature to want to reproduce *himself*, to hand on *his* name, *his* estates, whilst a woman wants a child as a love token and not as a second self. In the essentially male eighteenth century this was especially true, and men generally married for money and for an heir; hence the recurring excitements and scandals over 'love matches' and elopements such as the Sheridans'. The code endures, and for the same reasons, in the Catholic and 'Faubourg' society of Latin countries to this day. Lady Melbourne, who offered Georgiana this advice, had practised it herself, for it is generally accepted that only her eldest son, Peniston, was by her husband, who recognized this with bitterness, since he only cared for this one child which he knew to be his. Lady Melbourne, having already 'done her duty,' had therefore every reason to encourage chastity in Georgiana, by which she eliminated a rival more attractive than herself, whilst apparently acting in the interests of morality, and strengthened her own position by becoming the Prince's mistress.

There is strong evidence to believe this actually was the case; meantime Society found it amusing to speculate on the chances of the two rivals. Both women had many enemies—Lady Melbourne because she was a dangerously successful parvenue, and Georgiana simply because she was beautiful and the most fashionable woman of her day.

Harriet, the more level-headed of the sisters, realized that her presence, if it could not stop Georgiana's insensate indulgence in a life of pleasure, which had become an anodyne essential to her, could at least check its impetus a little and perhaps save her sister from some fatal mistake. So she spent more and more time with her, and as she could only be of use if she were by Georgiana's side, she too was swept into the vortex. Not that she was unwilling, for she had nearly as keen a sense of enjoyment as Georgiana, and her distinct personality, which had developed and increased in charm and poise since her marriage, brought her almost as many admirers as the Duchess.

Meantime the whole country was sick to satiation of the war; there was not an individual or a party, whatever had been their original opinions, who did not realize that it was time to acknowledge that an appalling mistake had been made, the whole campaign mismanaged, and that the time had come to make peace with as little loss of dignity as possible. Only the King, obstinate as ever, disagreed.

The Whigs opened the attack with a strong measure that the war be abandoned and, so generally was their feeling shared, that it was defeated by only one vote. This infinitesimal margin of success satisfied the King who, to mark his displeasure with the Whigs, elevated the discredited Lord George Germaine, then under sentence of court-martial, to the Peerage. Even Lord North's long-tried loyalty broke down, and in March he resigned.

Never had there been such excitement at Devonshire House—the millennium was at hand. But like a long-awaited, much-discussed theatrical masterpiece whose production has been deferred time and time again, the players had been cast and recast so often that not only were the principal roles duplicated, but the supernumeraries tumbled over each other in their desire to say their promised line, to occupy their little place upon the stage on the opening night. Lord Rockingham, the producer, was at his wits' end; deafened by the clamour of so huge a cast, he lost his head, distributed the principal parts to the Devonshire House quarter whence came the loudest voices, included a sly Tory professional, Lord Thurlow, and committed the incredible blunder of refusing a part to the prodigy of the day, for he was too flustered to give young Mr Pitt an audition.

The first act of the badly produced, badly rehearsed masterpiece was a Bill for Electoral Reform on which the company had to ring down the curtain, as they could not agree upon their lines, though Burke had a personal triumph in his Bill abolishing many sinecures.

Behind the scenes the company were quarrelling over Foreign Policy. Fox and Shelburne, sharing the rôle of Foreign Secretary, each had individual ideas of how it should be played. Fox was pledged to support American Independence, but not to knuckle under to her ally, France. No one knew Shelburne's conception of the part. The Foreign Secretaries' representatives were quarrelling in America; Fox's deputy sending home a rumour that his rival (who should have been his co-operator) was bribing America with Canada as the price of peace.

The Devonshire House company were horror-struck at this 'betrayal'; their chief supporting members, Sheridan and the Prince of Wales and the two leading ladies, Georgiana and Elizabeth Melbourne, all urging Fox to resign. Rockingham, they argued, could never continue in office without Fox, 'the Man of the People'; if he was firm, he was bound to be allowed to pursue his own policy.

Fox listened to their advice, threw in his hand, and Lord Rockingham incontinently and dramatically died. The second act had ended in a chaos worse than the first. There was no applause, but a hideous, ominous silence from the pit.

The King appointed Lord Shelburne, the rebel Fox's colleague-opponent. There was a hasty consultation as to whether the Devonshire House faction should resign *en masse* or accept the new direction. They decided to dissociate themselves, especially as Fox's part had been given to that mere boy, Master Pitt.

But though Pitt proved a young Roscius, the barracking of the Devonshire House set, especially the loud interpolations from Fox, now an on-looker, so held up action that Shelburne sent for Mr Pitt to invite him back. They were snubbed for their pains, and Fox, with an undignified display of temperament, severed his connexions and joined Lord North's rival production across the way.

The English audience is a long-suffering one, but this action, which they were undecided whether to call treachery or conceited folly, combined with the Prince of Wales openly running with 'the Fox hounds,' an 'ill-starred alliance of the party of progress with the extravagances of a royal rake,' was too much for them, and Fox lost much of his popularity. However, his arguments were so plausible and his charm so great that he persuaded his friends at Devonshire House that he was justified in his new alliance with North, and they continued to support him, especially Prinny, Fox having promised to obtain £100,000 a year for him as soon as the Heir to the Throne came of age.

The confusion caused by Fox's *volte-face* was indescribable: Shelburne, disgusted with the whole affair, wished to resign; the King refused to allow him to do so; Shelburne insisted and the King sent for Pitt, offering him the ungrateful task of managing what had become an out-of-hand circus. Pitt wisely refused. There was nobody to take the vacant place except that amateur politician, the Duke of Portland. Unwillingly, the King appointed him, and amid catcalls from both the Tory and Whig factions, whose idols North and Fox had betrayed them by their unnatural alliance, the curtain rose upon the fourth and last act, which was to prove the most interesting of all.

It opened on November the 11th (an ominous date) with the King's reading the declaration of Peace with America, France, Spain and the United Provinces, and asking for fiscal reform.

Meanwhile Burke, whose great stature would have outweighed the rest of the players and so had not been included in the cast, produced a soliloquy of his own. For some time he had been studying the administration of India under the Chartered Company, and had found gross abuses at the expense of India, whose development was now too far advanced to be left in private hands. He brought forward a scheme for reform, and Fox showed his first glimmering of sense in the whole deplorable production by joining hands with Burke in the name of Liberty and Justice, presenting the Bill to the House on November the 18th. But this could not redeem his prestige, which had suffered yet another blow by the refusal of the House to grant the £100,000 a year which he had promised to obtain for Prinny. The India Company Reform Bill was killed by a small margin by vested interest, represented, I regret to say, by another ancestor of mine, Earl Gower, its noble death redeeming to some degree an ignoble session. Portland fell with the Bill and, after his previous refusal, young Mr Pitt consented to take his place.

So strong was Fox's jealousy of Pitt that when the latter reintroduced the Bill on January the 16th with some slight amendments Fox, that large man, was small enough to oppose it.

The situation was hopeless: from January the 26th to February the 3rd desperate efforts were made to effect a coalition between Pitt and

Portland, but Pitt determined to preserve his integrity and Parliament was dissolved on March the 25th.

The long-desired and prayed-for Whig administration, which had been going to reform the world, had crumbled upon itself; its own discordant trumpets had brought its bastions to the ground. The tragic farce was over. Dismayed, bewildered and angry, the audience streamed into the political night.

During all this while Georgiana had had little time for politics, disastrous or otherwise. She had been wholly occupied with her pregnancy, though on one occasion the world intruded on her, threatening her peace. This was in the spring of 1783, when the crisis in Ireland, which was on the verge of rebellion, the Protestant Bishop of Derry fanning the flames, reached its height. It was suggested that the Duke of Devonshire should be appointed Lord-Lieutenant, perhaps in the hope that his cold phlegmatic nature would extinguish any sparks of revolt. The Duchess was in despair—to be exiled to Ireland, to bear her child in that barbarous country, the one country where Bess could not join her—for was not Mr Foster there?— was more than she could bear. She was incoherent with fear, but finding it so much the wish of the Duke of Portland that Canis should go, she went to her husband and told him that she not only advised him to accept but wished it. She was sure she had done right, but the feeling that her fate was probably deciding contrary to all her desires, but because of her advice, was almost too much for her. Having put her interests second to those of her husband, for once his lethargy, which made him refuse the appointment, brought her a reward.

One of the reasons why she had been so reluctant to go to Ireland was that for a long time she had been secretly much worried about her debts, and feared that if she left England they would be exposed. Her letters to her mother abound with hints: that she is in 'a scrape' but that it don't signify; that it does signify after all, but that she can't bring herself to confess it; that she would have confessed but that she was too busy, and so she goes on, putting off the evil day. The truth of the matter was that she did not know where to turn for the money: the Duke had several times before settled her debts with great generosity and no reproaches, but now she was afraid to tell him of them, for the simple reason that she thought his affairs were in jeopardy and they were in the hands of a man whom she feared and mistrusted, his agent, Mr Heaton.

She was suspicious of him on two accounts, the chief of which arose from his having suggested to the Duke that he had heard some kind of scandal connecting her with the Prince of Wales. She was not afraid of the Duke's reaction to these hints, for she asserted that her husband had implicit faith in her which only she herself could destroy, but she was angry and suspicious of Mr Heaton's motives. Had he accused her of extravagance she could have understood his action, though regarding it as an impertinence, but the other must have arisen from other causes—did he wish to protect himself from the suspicion of peculation, the idea of which had been firmly implanted in Georgiana's mind by the Duchess of Portland? At all events, she was sure he would prove no ally if her financial distress was disclosed. She justified herself for these accusations by saying she had neither shrewdness nor ill-nature enough to have formed these prejudices on her own accord but for the Duchess of Portland's warnings.

Mustering her small stock of moral courage, she confessed her debts to the Duke, saying she had not done so whilst she was pregnant or nursing her baby as it would have been taking an unfair advantage of her situation, and at the same time she cautioned him against Heaton, imploring him to verify the truth of her assertions. This, he replied, would be difficult, as he was disinclined to look closely into his own affairs, and that even if he found Heaton to be the greatest rascal, his exposure would mean their ruin.

Mr Heaton, contrary to her expectations, proved her ally, and found the necessary money to settle those debts to which she had confessed. She was moved by this further instance of the Duke's forbearance and generosity— she was the vilest of beings—he the noblest of men. She believed she had brought him to the brink of ruin.

The truth was that the Ducal expenditure had been enormous, that Heaton knew the Duke was too lazy ever to look into his affairs, and that the only way he could keep a semblance of control was by painting in the darkest colours. The easy-going Duke, provided money was forthcoming for his needs, neither chose nor cared to ascertain the extent of his resources, so that for the rest of her life Georgiana suffered needless agonies, always believing that her debts would ruin her husband and, rather than bring this about, plunging deeper and deeper, ever hoping that some stroke of good fortune would free her from her creditors.

Long afterwards when Mr Heaton handed over the estates to her son, his faithful stewardship was recognized by the new Duke, who was alike astounded by the extent of his inheritance and by pity for his mother. 'If only she had known …' he said. But she was never to know, and now, racked with anxiety both on her own and her husband's behalf, she knew not where to turn, for as usual she had made but a half-confession, so that, despite the Duke's and Heaton's exertions, she was still in debt. What was she to do? What she did was to send £600 to Lady Liz who she heard was forced to remain at Turin for lack of money.

The only solution she could find was to give up gaming; but this resolution she had often made, only to break it again; for one thing she always hoped to win back what she had lost, and then gaming was in her blood. Even Lady Spencer, who alternately railed against her daughters' propensity to gambling and blamed herself for having passed on to them the fatal love of play, enjoyed a game herself, and Georgiana, rather illogically, tried to exculpate her mother, reminding her that her own damning weakness was innate, for even when she was nine years old, in quarantine for measles, she had played at Lansquenet from seven in the morning till eight at night with old Mrs Newton.

> *The truth is, since first I a thought understood*
> *From You I derived ev'ry worth I e'en had—*
> *Of your Character then, if I share half the good*
> *I, into the bargain, will take all the Bad.*

She confessed her predicaments to Bess, whilst imploring *her* not to curtail expenditure, for her expenses were but as a drop in the ocean and her comfort was of paramount importance to her friends. She suggested to the Duke that they should retrench and winter abroad; but this meant that the world would know they were in financial difficulties, and he would not agree to this plan.

There seemed to be no way out. Like Georgiana, let us take refuge in the nursery. Even this quiet haven was troubled by storms. There was the affair of 'the Rocker.' This minor cog in the complicated machinery of the nursery caused the Duchess much distress and alarm. One of her duties was 'to turn the baby dry and lay her down to sleep,' but when she approached the bed the baby shared with her mother, the Duchess noticed that she stank of wine and strong drink whenever she came near it. Then Mrs Smith, the head nurse, told the horrified Duchess that not only had 'the Rocker' been so drunk as to fall down, but that when bidden to blow out a tallow candle she had melted it in the fire, and last of all that she had pinned up Mrs Smith's bed-curtains under pretext of sheltering her from the cold, but really so that her intoxication might be unperceived. Georgiana's reaction was typical—'the Rocker' must be kept from the baby at all costs, but if left idle she would be drinking all day, so the Duchess gave her ten guineas and paid her journey up to town, saying she needed her no longer. To her surprise 'the Rocker' was quite contented, and only desired time in which to wash her clothes before she left.

Next came the great bathing schism. Mrs Smith suggesting bathing G. as she had always done with Lord Gower's children, whose doctor had advised this as a strengthening preventive against colds and infections. So a little tub was ordered which put the whole household in alarm; they said the child was very well without such contraptions, which would kill her. The Duchess was so frightened that she called in Dr Denman who said that he saw no necessity for the bath, as the little girl was quite well, but that it could do her no harm. Mrs Smith gave in very quietly, though she remarked that it seemed an odd thing to say that something was harmless and yet not let it do good. This led to a further consultation between Dr Denman and two other physicians, but their final decision is unknown to this day.

But worst of all were the plaguings of her brothers- and sister-in-law, which, though she denied it, tormented her with misgivings. For instance, Lord John saw the baby at an unfortunate moment when she was throwing up her milk, which made her look ill, and he terrified the Duchess by saying that a dairymaid was a better nurse than a fine lady. She would not have minded this very much, but the Duchess of Portland advised her to drink porter and Lady Sefton and the Duchess of Rutland told her that Lady Lincoln's little girl was fatter than G. Even though she learnt that these criticisms arose from the family's desire for an heir which they believed she would not have while she was nursing G., they continued to worry and distress her.

Still, after they had all gone, after she had said good night to her guests, after she had left the great state-rooms and shut the door of her silk-hung, delicately medallioned room behind her, a sense of peace stole over her and, taking her pen in hand, she wrote:

> *Second November eighty four*
> *And two o'clock at night*
> *The gentle Muses I implore*
> *To you, Dear M. to write.*
>
> *All in my little room I bide*
> *My little fire half gone,*
> *My little table by my side,*
> *A little light thereon.*
>
> *All blooming in her little bed*
> *My little child's asleep,*

May Angels guard her little head,
My little darling keep.

Adieu—and tho' my little skull
But little wit can prove,
For you 'tis not a little full
Of not a little Love.

In October Lady Spencer had taken her husband to Bath, for he had been ailing, and on the 19th Georgiana was able to write to her that she had fulfilled one of her earliest vows.

Today was the Commencement of my Charity in honour of Georgiana. You know I give too a year—to cloathe to boys and to girls and school them and the surplus is laid out with an attorney at Chesterfield who will always deliver it with 2 and ½ per cent. interest, and is to be employed in apprenticing or marrying them or fitting them for service.

They dined here today—my girls have dark blue jackets, long sleeves white aprons and handkerchiefs and black silk hats—the boys blue coats silver buttons and buff waistcoats and breeches and round hats.

The School Mistress is a very ingenious as well as industrious Woman for she understands fine needlework as well as plain—the schoolmaster is a vastly handsome young man but has lost an arm. They eat their roast beef and plum pudding very comfortably and walked back in procession—the age in general is 9 or 10....

Lady Spencer was much pleased with her daughter's charitable action, but there was room for improvement. In reply she wrote:

I am delighted with your school—the boys buff waistcoats and breeches will I fear soon get dirty, perhaps all blue will hereafter be found better— and the Girls hats should have been the Leghorn or straw hats which are cheap strong and pretty, and if the Boys buff waistcoats are to continue would suit them better than black hats and make a little Correspondence between the dresses of the Boys and the Girls.

Exactly a week after she had written this sensible letter, Lord Spencer, whose health had not improved as it was hoped, died quite quietly and suddenly, and for once Lady Spencer could find nothing but good in her daughters; they comforted her, looked after her, were as gentle and tactful as could be. They were good girls, after all.

Lady Spencer paid Georgiana the highest compliment in her power by asking her to write her father's epitaph. Georgiana was much touched with this sign of her mother's affection, and also she had been genuinely devoted to her father, though his personality had been overshadowed by that of her mother. All day she strove to produce something fitting the great honour paid her and which she wished to repay to his memory, but for once her fluent pen failed her. Once, long before, she had told her mother that some feelings lay too deep for expression. Then it had been untrue, but it was true enough now—she could only produce two little verses whose loving simplicity showed clearly the depth of her emotion. She showed them to the Duke, who though he was very kind about them, thought that something a little more carefully composed would better suit the occasion. He asked if he might attempt such a composition; Georgiana was overcome—this was more than she could have hoped for, and she felt sure that her mother would be much touched by her son-in-law's thought. The Duke sat up all night and produced a splendid effusion, which, after a few suggested amendments, Lady Spencer accepted with gratitude. It quite eclipsed Georgiana's two short verses, especially the end which ran thus:

All posterity should know
How pure a spirit warmed the dust below!

Though she grieved sincerely over her father's death, the weaning of her baby was a greater loss to Georgiana, for she felt she had lost the first human being who had ever been completely dependent on her. For some time the horrid separation had been imminent, but she had always found some good excuse for postponing it, until finally the baby herself decided the question. Poor Georgiana was really heartbroken:

Oh, how weary are my spirits.... I do miss my Dear little girl so I do not know what to do—I have been twenty times going to take [her] up in my Arms & run away and suckle her—I would give the world for her dear little eager mouth at my breast. This is the first night of my sleeping away from her for months & my room looks so dreary—oh dear, dear, but it is for her good....

The loss of her father, her anxiety over her debts, the weaning of her baby, all combined to make her feel desperately lonely, and she began to plan how she could contrive to bring Bess back to England. She had now been away over a year, and it was time to consider Charlotte William's future. The Duchess hoped to prevail on the Duke to give Charlotte the name of Cavendish; then she would prepare the way for introducing her to the county, and she was sure there would be no difficulty in finding a husband for her therein—either Sir Harry Hunloke's son or Mr Gisburne would be suitable. This marriage would have the double advantage of placing Charlotte in a happy situation under the Devonshires' own eyes, whilst, in some strange way known only to the Duchess, it would increase Canis's connexions and power in his own little kingdom of Derbyshire.

Apparently Lady Elizabeth was not so eager to return to England as had previously appeared; she was having far too interesting and romantic a time with her Neapolitan lover, so she fell back upon the plea that her delicate health would suffer from the English climate.

Having pleaded her loneliness and Charlotte's future in vain, Georgiana urged Bess to return for Canis's sake. She was sure his health and spirits depended on Bess's soothing friendship; even now he had asked Georgiana why he never heard from her, why wouldn't she come back? She should return to Italy for the winter, but the Duchess must write and persuade her to spend the summer with them at Chatsworth.

After this Lady Elizabeth agreed to return, but before she was to arrive, bringing with her Charlotte who proved to be the cleverest little witch, speaking perfect French and Italian, there were greater happenings in Devonshire House.

Devonshire House from Piccadilly, *c*. 1900.

7

The Great Westminster Election

And now behold in those days, being the eighteenth century, an idol was adored in the land of Albion, and a new religion established; the people of that land being governed by the moon and the tides and the following after novelties, and hankering after strange gods.

The idol was black, and fearful to behold; and therefore he pleased the lower sort, who delight in being terrified; and the higher order were charmed with his ill example, which destroyed all decorum and distinctions, and left them at liberty to follow their own inclinations, which were none of the best.

And now the women of the land rose up and they said one unto another, let us raise the idol on high, and make the men fall down and worship him; and they did so; and every living thing, which had folly in it, worshipped the idol; and the geese and the ganders lifted up their silly heads, and cried long live the Fox; may the Fox live for ever.

Now behold a woman, fairer than wise, and more wily than discreet, said, let us take the Fox's tail for our type and symbol; let us bear it aloft, and run about the streets, and the squares, and the lanes, and the blind alleys, and make proselytes to the new religion.

The matrons and maidens, widows and widows bewitched, were seized with religious fury, and ran wild through the streets, crying Fox! Fox! and they kissed the Fox's tail and put it in their hats.

The idol raised upon the shoulders of the women, was adored by the men; and so the woman of Piccadilly carried him up to the Temple, ... and thereby hangs a tail.

Thereby hangs a tale indeed indeed. The above extract from the propaganda of Fox's opponents puts the whole notoriety of the

Westminster Election in a nutshell, that election which is important to us because it was the climax of Georgiana's political career; because it was the first time in English history that a woman had influenced so direct a political issue and because of the immense stir the election caused at the time.

To understand why the election appeared of such significance in 1784, when a quarto volume of 600 pages was devoted to this one contest alone, is difficult to a modern reader until the reasons for its fame are considered and the contrast between the times appreciated.

Let us anticipate the General Election after the present war: the whole of the world will be war-sick; Labour will make a great bid for power, crying for and promising reform; the diehards will still protect their vested interests. So far the comparison is parallel. Gigantic, formless London alone will have over sixty contests; all over England similar contests will be fought, many of greater significance and import than those in the capital. The election will be fought passionately and seriously. There will be outstanding contests, undignified or notorious contests; the countless daily newspapers with their multiple editions will print full reports of all these elections; they will also contain a great deal of news from all over the globe. The majority of men and women will already have their personal convictions as to how they will vote; many of them will attend one or two either dull or inspired party meetings in dreary halls; most of them will record their votes for their chosen male or *female* candidate (though the sex of their representative is of no particular interest to them) on the polling day, entering the booths soberly, conscientiously and anonymously before or after their day's work. Human nature, being immutable, they will then seek their relaxation according to their tastes; the theatres, cinemas, dog-racing tracks, dancing halls will all be filled by patrons from every walk of life, whilst those who prefer to stay at home will read, smoke or knit to the accompaniment of their wireless. From the suburbs, the slums, the flats and the individual houses, the same programme of canned music and canned opinions will float through the steel-framed windows into the brightly lighted streets where, though it is still late at night, the pavement crowds will be gazing into the brilliantly lit shop windows, whilst the great noisy river of traffic bellows and roars in the roadway.

Wind the hands of the clock back till it stops 150 years ago, and what do we find?

We recognize the names of the streets from Covent Garden to Hyde Park Corner, where the houses stop abruptly; but surely it is all very small? The steel and concrete houses have shrunk into little brick dwellings, huddled and close, and above their uneven roofs Carlton House, Devonshire House and a dozen others, also built of brick, stand out as conspicuously as Broadcasting and Transport Houses do today. We feel like Gulliver in Lilliput. The streets, too, appear in a deplorable condition; the narrow ones are cobbled, the broader ones paved. But though they are cleaned by scavengers in winter and water-carts in summer, they are all pitted and rutted, they have no kerbs, only posts sometimes linked with chains to keep the grating iron-shod wheels from crushing pedestrians to the walls. Down the majority of them runs a foul open kennel, black and oily with effluvia. The neat, busy taxis have gone, and the small bobbing sedan chairs carried by Irish porters have taken their place; instead of bright red buses there are clumsy hackney coaches. After dark the flickering lights from the open shops make a 'fine illumination' till eight or nine at night; but in the residential quarters, inhabited by the 'ton,' the flambeaux of their lackeys and the torches at their doors give a flaring uncertain light.

The sounds and smells of the two Londons are different too, for by the time of our modern post-war election we suppose the roar and stench of petrol-driven traffic will have flooded back, drowning all human sounds save the man-machine noise of the radio; the peppery ammoniac smell of horse manure being replaced by the fumes of Castrol and Shell. In our earlier London the unceasing iron-sound of hooves and wheels pounding and grating on stone forms a background to the shrill human accompaniment: year in and year, out the vendors cry their wares; there are the apple women who, according to the season, sell their fruit raw or roast; men crying baskets, bandboxes, brickdust, bellows, cat's-meat, cherries, cress, hot loaves, hot gingerbread and pale muffins. Milk, matches, mackerel, potatoes, rabbits, lavender and strawberries are all hawked in the streets. There are dustmen, bear-wards, knife-grinders, tumblers, sweeps and sand carters. Punch and Judy shout down a red-breeched and turbaned Turk selling medicinal rhubarb. The sellers of lace, ribbons, almanacs, sealing-wax, shrimps and spigots make as much noise as the vendors of brooms, doormats and old clothes, and over all, night and day, the shop signs creak and moan and sigh.

These innumerable street sellers, who knew not the protective letters T.U.C. and who had but their poor wares and wits to keep them from the river, would cry their goods and creep back to the unimaginable hovels that they called their homes; for them, the Irish chairmen, the swarms of beggars, porters, discharged soldiers and sailors there would be none of the social amenities their modern counterparts would enjoy. They died unnoticed and without pity of horrible diseases, their bones and teeth rotting, eyes sightless, their bodies ravaged by hunger; they knew no redress, no sanitation and, above all, no recreation, save when they could afford the gin or beer shop. A cockfight was their cinema, a street brawl their boxing match, their drunken Saturday night chorus their broadcast symphony.

The better-off tradespeople and professional folk had no holiday resorts; the many 'Spaws' from the Five Fields of Belgravia to those of Marylebone and Islington were their watering-places, and the grave their only sanctuary. London was an over-populated, teeming, dirty, vigorous parish.

These then were the Electors of Westminster, the men who had to choose two representatives out of three—Hood, Fox and Wray. What had this triumvirate to offer them? Not education nor medical services, relief whilst unemployed nor pensions when they reached old age. Hood, in the most gentlemanlike fashion, offered them what they had endured before; Wray offered them the abolition of their only asylum, the Chelsea Pensioners' Hospital, and a Tax on Maidservants; Fox, 'the Man of the People,' offered a vague, amorphous thing called Liberty and a staggering, dazzling novelty—a glimpse, perhaps even a touch, of beauty's robe; presenting to them a woman, a Duchess, who stepped down from her pedestal among them uniting the romance of royalty with the glamour of a screen star. For forty glorious days all three candidates offered them unlimited beer and, with any luck, money.

An election therefore meant to the voters that for forty days they, the under-dogs, were more important than the upper-dogs; the tables were turned with a vengeance. They could defer their decisions forty times, for forty days they were courted, bribed, fed, plied with drink, cajoled and condescended to by those remote and shining beings whose futures were now placed in their omnipotent hands. It was a heaven-sent 'free for all.'

The three candidates are now to be considered: Admiral Lord Hood was an upright Tory, enjoying such popularity as might Admiral Cunningham should he stand in our modern post-war election. The English are fond and proud of their Navy, and Hood was above suspicion. His election was never in doubt.

Sir Cecil Wray had originally been sponsored for election to Parliament by Fox himself, but had gone over to the other side. This 'treachery,' as it was to be labelled, was much less grave than had been Fox's alliance with North, but in political accusations what is sauce for the goose is hardly ever sauce for the gander. His 'treachery' (or his loyalty, according as to how you regard it) was to cost him dearly in votes, but it was in no way as disastrous to him as was the fatal mistake he had made on March the 17th in the House of Commons when the sum of £17,001 15s. 5d. had been tabled as the estimated cost for the support of the Chelsea Hospital for old soldiers during the coming year. Wray had jumped to his feet, remarking that 'according to the number of men then in Chelsea Hospital, the above sum amounted to an average of £51 5s. per man, which, in his opinion, was too enormous; but how to remedy the evil he knew not, *unless it was by pulling the Hospital down, which in his heart he wished to see speedily done*.' This was bad enough, but not content with having jeopardized his chances badly, he proposed to introduce a Tax on Maidservants.

Fox, 'the Man of the People,' had three things to offer his people: he promised to 'Stem the torrent of corruption, to Reform the abuses of the Constitution and to Oppose the destructive principle of Court Influence.' These three pledges sound vague and Utopian to us, but when translated into the language of his opponents, his purpose becomes more clear. Hood and Wray asserted that he proposed to 'Null Charters, to invade Rights and seize on Property,' which interpreted meant that he intended to bring in his India Reform Bill, to abolish sinecures and do away with place-hunting. Whatever else was certain, Fox, Sheridan and Pitt were unbribable in a corrupt age, and his programme was an integral part of the man himself. But unfortunately his people had lost much faith in him: first of all his ill-starred alliances with North and the Prince of Wales had cost him a great deal of his previous popularity. The franchized majority are always suspicious of a turned coat, and North was unpopular enough as it was for his support for the war with America, against which Fox had fought long and bitterly. And whilst the Prince was popular with the masses, who admired his looks, his free and easy ways and open detestation of the Court Party, they knew Fox was pledged to procure a huge annual income for the royal spendthrift and they were nervous for their pockets. His chances looked very poor indeed, but unbeknown to his opponents he had the Ace of Hearts in his gambler's sleeve.

What plan of campaign and what ammunition would the three candidates choose with which to fight their coming battle? The usual scattering of largess, the distribution of free food and drink were *sine qua non*, the remaining weapon was propaganda. The extent, mass and scope of the printed 'advertisements,' squibs, libels, cartoons, poems, songs and handbills are, quite simply, staggering. Every conceivable missile was pressed into service: personalities, obscenities and rhodomontade were the order of the day; the lower you hit below the belt, the more effective your blow. The only way to appreciate the compass of this mass of material is to wade through the 'Westminster Election,' a pro-Fox production published in 1785; but I will try to give the most typical examples when we follow the course of the election from day to day.

The propaganda in the high places was of course a little more dignified; the following letter, written as early as February the 8th, shows that Georgiana had already learned her piece glibly. Writing to her mother she says:

I give you I think a little political lesson ev'ry day—here is one now. If Mr Pitt succeeds—he will have brought about an event that he himself as well as ev'ry Englishman will repent ever after—for if the King and the H. of Lords [which on the next day passed resolutions by a majority of nearly two to one censuring the House of Commons for attempting on their own authority to suspend the law, and interfering with the royal prerogative in the appointment of ministers], conquer the H. of Commons he will destroy the consequence of that house and make the government quite absolute, for a majority in the H. of Lords is always in the King's power by creating new Peers—now there are people and (though we never hear them mentioned without horror) well meaning people perhaps, who are call'd King's friends who from being shock'd at the personal violence that has been sometimes us'd against the K—and from having a Love of Kings and an awe at the idea of them—that would not think this absolute power a bad thing—but the proof that it is, and that the constitution we have hitherto enjoy'd is a good one, is, that spite of ev'ry publick Misfortune and of a ruinous War England is still a flourishing and glorious Country and bore her losses better than any other country could do. You see then that those who are interested in the Wellfare of their Country, for I declare that I believe the D. of P[ortland] & Lord Fitz[william] to be as honest and independant disinterested Men as ever breath'd—cannot without some degree of Warmth and disdain see a Young Man take upon him—and rest upon its being his opinion, the entirely changing the happy constitution of his country. This is an odious subject and yet considering all things do what one will it is a subject one must think and feel about.

Lady Spencer received such political lessons with a placidity she would have been far from feeling had she known the active part her daughter was about to play.

Even the Prince of Wales seemed to realize the gravity of the 'odious subject,' for he gave a series of weekly parties, very different from his usual flamboyant entertainments; for the Duchess reports that they were rather formal and dull.

The election really started, before the dissolution of Parliament, when Fox's party held a mass meeting at Westminster Hall on February the 14th. Fox and his supporters, the chief of whom were Byng, Burke, Sheridan, General Burgoyne, Colonel Fitzpatrick and Lords Derby, Surrey and Foley, met to draw up an address to the King. This was not accomplished without much noise and brawling, the opposition being present in force. The meeting culminated in a scuffle wherein Fox was cast to the ground and a leather bag of 'asses fœtida' thrown at him. Finally the address to the King was drawn up and copies circulated for the collection of signatures. The address is significant, for, after assuring His Majesty of their loyalty, the petitioners state that 'as we have always regarded the Commons House of Parliament as the natural guardian of our unalienable rights, we humbly hope that whatever Ministers your Majesty may in your wisdom call to the high posts of government, they will hold the sense of the House in the *same respect as their predecessors in office have done from the æra of the glorious Revolution to the present period.*' Fox and his friends then got into their carriages, from which the crowd took the horses, dragging them up Whitehall to Devonshire House, the mob booing the Treasury and Lord Temple's house and huzzaing as they came to Carlton House. At Devonshire House Fox 'alighted and harrangued them from the Portico, they gave the Duchess three Cheers also.' That evening at Devonshire House numerous gentlemen cautiously sniffed at the sinister leather bag from a safe distance and even so 'were seized with violent coughing and sickness, some of the Gentlemen being affected thereby for the remaining part of the evening.' The bag was submitted to an eminent chemist for analysis, and found to contain not 'asses fœtida' as suspected, but capsicum and euphorbium, the chemist reporting so gravely upon the possibly fatal effects of the contents that a reward of £100 was offered for the discovery of the culprits. The fight was on.

The battle was even carried into the Opera House, where the *Reine de Golconde*, for which Georgiana had composed some of the music, was the favourite piece. On March the 20th it was particularly full, and Georgiana says she had 'several good Political fights—Lady Sefton says it is a great *Aria* in the History of England. The Duchess of Rutland said D— Fox, upon which Colonel St Leger with great difficulty spirited up Lady Maria Waldegrave to say D— Pitt.'

On March the 25th Parliament was to be dissolved and hostilities opened in a most exciting and mysterious manner, for on the night of the 24th the Great Seal of England was stolen!

Lord Chancellor Thurlow—'the man who had the King's ear,' who was variously painted as the greatest jurist and most brilliant of men, or by his enemies as a scheming 'morose man, surly and a great wine bibber,' and who was generally referred to as 'old Hurlo Thrumbo'—lived in Great Ormond Street, where he slept in the best front bedroom. In a lone unguarded back-room on the ground floor, exposed to the open fields, were the Insignia of England. There, deposited in a drawer, were the Great Seal, the Mace and the Purse, quite unprotected, for no person slept on that floor 'or near so great and valuable a treasure, although his Lordship's private property was cautiously lodged below stairs.' Into this room crept a thief or thieves who removed the booty, whose value lay in its significance rather than its intrinsic worth, and of which they evidently had foreknowledge. Immediately the theft became known there was a terrific hum and stir; there had been no such daring a robbery since Colonel Blood stole the Crown Jewels from the Tower and was surprisingly rewarded by a pension from Charles II. Instantly there was talk of connivance; the Chancellor's flippant remark to his confidential man, Macklin, sounded very odd indeed.

'By God,' said Lord Thurlow, 'I have long ceased to make the impression I wished.'

What did it all mean? The significant date on the very eve of the dissolution caused talk. Georgiana wrote to her mother:

> … the great seals were stole this morning—the King declared he would dissolve the Parliament and it will be tomorrow—I hope the D[uke] will bring in another member—I am dressing and the D. of Portland & C. Fox are writing in my room.

Various unanswerable questions arose: could Parliament be dissolved when the Great Seal necessary to the Proclamation was missing? Could the King use any seal, say the Head of Caesar or a Maid of Honour's thimble? Was there at the instant any Lord Chancellor at all?—apparently if there was no seal there could be no Chancellor. Fox, the Duke of Portland, and for some obscure reason, the French King were all suspected of the theft. Only the King and Hurlo Thrumbo were unmoved; the former had a new Seal made by the same evening and Lord Thurlow wrote to a friend saying 'a gang of scoundrels broke into my house last night, robbed me of some money and several things of value, amongst which was the Seal and be damned to them.' It was a nine minutes' wonder and an indication of excitements yet to come.

Now came a week when the Electors of Westminster were almost snowed under with notices and advertisements. Many meetings were held, gargantuan feasts eaten, interminable songs sung and the usual twenty toasts per dinner drunk. Fox's friends would drink to 'Lord Derby and Liberty Hall,' to 'the Prince of Wales and may the Princes of the House of Brunswick ever countenance those principles that seated their family on the throne of England.' Or to the 'Cause for which Hampden bled in the field and Sidney and Russell on the scaffold,' or they hoped that 'the County of Stafford may ever return Whig members and the Town of Stafford persons of equal virtues and abilities of Mr Sheridan and Mr Monckton.' Or more simply to 'the Duke of Devonshire and the whole House of Cavendish.'

The Duke approved of the drinking to his health, but was it quite necessary that the whole of the House of Cavendish should be included? It flattered and amused him to see the deference with which Fox treated the Duchess; it was pretty to observe at the supper table how eagerly she emulated his political friends, and it was entertaining to listen to her partisanship. There was some talk of the Duchess and his sister-in-law actually canvassing, and if Fox thought it would help his cause, the Duke saw no harm in their driving to the poll, though he hoped Georgiana would not forget the dignity due to the name of Devonshire.

The opposition would drink to 'The Royal Family,' the 'Constitution and Prerogative,' to 'Mr Pitt, Earls Chatham and Temple' and to the 'Invincible Preservation of their Chartered Rights.'

Sir Cecil Wray found that his unfortunate wish to raze Chelsea Hospital to the ground stuck in many gullets and tried to extract the fish-bone. He maintained that he had been misrepresented, 'that he did not wish to close down institutions for retired and loyal soldiers—in fact, he thought there were too few, but he did want to point out that the expenditure per pensioner came to £51 5s. He therefore thought that if each man in the hospital was allowed £20 p.a. and to live where his connections and friendships led him to, that he would live more happily—and an overplus remaining which would provide for a 1,000 out-pensioners as letter-men; a charity more extensive and devoutly to be wished for.' It was no good— he only made things worse, his excuses rang false in every ear.

Hood and Wray attacked Fox on the grounds of changing his politics, of robbing the public (through the India Bill), of accusing Parliament of corruption. They accused him on the grounds of drunkenness, loose-living and gambling. They called him the Hon. Cogdie Shufflecard Reynardine, or the Regicide, or Oliver Cromwell II, or just Carlo Khan. Things looked very bad for Mr Fox indeed. What could he do? The poll would open on April the 1st, and he was not as sanguine of his success as were his immediate supporters.

The two processions having met, there was instantly a mêlée, Hood's sailors attacking Fox's supporters and being beaten off by the crowd.

The procedure of the times was then for the various candidates to be introduced by the High Bailiff for election by the crowd, each (apparently simultaneously) shouting out his programme as loudly as possible, the electors signifying their choice by a show of hands. Should the High Bailiff be in doubt as to the winner, election by a poll would then be decided upon. Needless to say, the turmoil was such that not one word of the candidates could be heard, and though Fox's party asserted that the show of hands was twenty to one in his favour, the expected course of a poll was chosen. The over-excited, uncontrolled crowd shouted and voted its way through the day, Fox scoring a majority with 302 votes to his favour, Hood and Wray having 264 and 238 votes respectively.

It is interesting to note how the populace were determined to 'have their money's worth' and not to be hustled, for the total number of votes recorded during the election was 18,926, only 804 being registered on the opening day. Still there was cause for rejoicing at Devonshire House, and the Foxites faced the next day with justifiable confidence, as he again beat Wray by 75 votes; but Hood was head of the poll. But from then on there was a sad falling off: from the third day of the contest to the tenth Wray's votes mounted and mounted, Fox's small advantage soon being swallowed up, till on April the 12th Wray had a majority of 318 to his favour.

Nothing seemed effectual in stopping the landslide: Fox's committee put out notices saying that 'the beautiful Duchess of Devonshire is a constant visitor to the sport in Covent Garden: she is generally attended by a party of the finest women in England, round whose carriages the mob crowd and gaze, and gaze and crowd until their senses are lost in admiration, and the pressure of those who push for the same pleasure, drives them into areas, through windows, or rolls them along the kennel to a distant situation, bruised and be-mudded, but not dissatisfied,' or that 'the three seducing Duchesses have been *indefatigable* in their canvass which they have managed in a *different* way. The old Dowager Duchess of Portland has attacked with *chit-chat* and voluble persuasion; the Duchess her daughter [-in-law] with a mildness and sensible moderation; while the *lovely captivator* [Georgiana] has ensnared with a glance and carried her point by the majestic sweetness of her graces.' Or that it 'was observed of the Duchess of Devonshire and Lady Duncannon while they were soliciting votes in favour of Mr Fox on Saturday that they were the most *perfect portraits* that ever appeared upon a *canvas*.' The opposition would delete the word 'portraits' and substitute it with '*pieces*.' From the Shakespeare

Tavern (Fox's committee rooms) would come a notice saying that 'the lovely Dss. of D. is strong in the interest of Mr Fox. Her Grace canvasses every day and has caused a thousand Coalition medals to be struck on the occasion, one of which she gives to every elector who promises a *plumper* for Mr Fox.' This would be retaliated by 'We hear that the D——— of D——— grants *favours* for those who promise votes and interest to Mr Fox.'

Fox might rail against 'back-stairs influence'; Wray retorted that Several ladies of a certain rank in Westminster are exerting very extraordinary *interest* for their friends. Let who will rail against *secret* influence and *back stairs*, there will always be some *influence* and certain stairs which honest men do not scruple to mount on certain occasions.'

Fox would rain blow after blow upon Wray for his desertion; Wray would defend himself by accusing Fox in turn with treachery. Fox would inveigh against Wray's threat to pull down Chelsea Hospital; Wray would retort with Fox's menaces to the 'place holders.' Fox would assert that Wray's Tax on Maidservants would drive 'these lovely virgins' to prostitution; Wray would counter-attack that Fox was going to annul chartered rights.

Fox would put out a mock play-bill 'By Command of their Majesties, the performance to be 'FREE ELECTION: A FARCE!' The cast to be, 'Old Obstinate' acted by Mr King; 'Admiral Broadside' (1st Court Candidate) by Lord Hood; 'Judas' (2nd ditto) by Sir C. Wray. The 'Champions of Liberty and Prerogative' by Mr Fox and Wilkes [who was now in opposition] respectively, whilst there was to be a chorus of 'Female Patriots' consisting of the Duchess of Portland, Lady Duncannon, the Hon. Mrs Bouverie and others, presided over by the 'Genius of Beauty,' the Duchess of Devonshire. The next day Wray would print another play-bill 'For the Benefit of Carlo Khan's Committee' announcing the 'RESTORATION OF OLIVER IInd, Or the TRIUMPM OF FACTION,' in which the 'Coalition Minuet' would be danced by Sir Jeffrey Dunstan and the Duchess of Portland, with a farce called 'THE LAST SHIFT,' in which the Duchess of Devonshire would play 'Doll Common and Canvass,' with Lady Duncannon as her Lady's Maid.

So far Wray's party had given as good as they got, but now their attack became more scurrilous; they flooded the shops with indecent prints and foul notices, Georgiana being the butt of their abuse, though there was no reason why Mrs Bouverie, Mrs Crewe, Lady Duncannon and the Duchess of Portland should not have shared in their vilifications, for they all supported Fox and canvassed openly for him. The Duchess was asked whether she intended to keep up her acquaintance with the *ladies* she had lately visited in Brick Street, Park Lane? Wray's party maintained that 'a *certain lady* has been observed to call at a Bawdy House not far from the corner of St Martins Lane; and the Major Domo, being a man of gallantry has frequently declared that he will not give a plumper unless escorted by the Duchess in her own Carriage.' They said that 'Considering the frequent visits they pay to Covent Garden [then inhabited by prostitutes] it is no wonder that the Ladies catch the *contagion* of party spirit and are so *warm* in support of their favourite *member*.'

It was disgusting and undignified, but Georgiana set her teeth and carried on, driving into every quarter with gentle smiles and winning words. She went as far as St Albans, where her mother was now living, to canvass for Fox's party, and as she stepped out of her carriage to enter a shop, by some accident her shoe was torn, insomuch that it was with difficulty she could keep it on her foot. 'In this embarrassment, the beautiful politician acquitted herself with great vivacity and good humour; she kicked the shoe from her and said, "I gladly serve my friends, even bare-footed!"' This unaffected anecdote could not be allowed to pass, and it was reported by the opposition that 'a certain lady of great beauty and high rank, requests that in future when she condescends to favour any shoemaker or other mechanic, with a salute, that he will kiss fair and not take *improper liberties*.' Most of the squibs are unprintable.

The situation was unbearable alike for Georgiana, her husband, mother and friends, and Fox was revolted by the tactics of his opponents, whose majority grew day by day. But however much her friends consoled her, comforted her with praise, the mud and filth flung at her made her sick at heart and almost disgusted with herself. Why had she and Charles ever thought of this mad idea? It might have brought him a few votes, but was it worth it? Her repulsion was so great that she stayed away at St Albans to breathe its purer air, where she would only hear the echoes of the insults and ribaldries that had been shouted at her for the past ten days.

On the evening of the 13th a letter from the Duchess of Portland was brought to her; at the first glance it consoled her conscience which was pricking her for her desertion, but as she read her heart sank.

My dearest Dutchess, I am happy to tell you of Our Success today for Westminster we beat them by forty five, which has put us in great spirits you may believe. Ev'ry body is so anxious for your return that I do hope you will come to town at latest tomorrow Evening, for if we should lose this (at least they will think) it is owing to your absence. I hope you found Lady Spencer better.

Yours most affect D. P.

I do verily believe Mr Fox will succeed, everybody seems to be of that opinion if people will continue to assert themselves. I am worn out almost and beg of you to Come tomorrow. There are a great many votes that you can command and No One else, and now if You only stop at peoples doors it will be quite sufficient, and really your presence is quite expected—so tomorrow morning pray be here early.

'*No*,' said Georgiana. 'No, I can't.' And she wrote a civil note in reply, saying she was much flattered but that really her mother required her badly and she did not believe she could make so much difference despite her Grace's too complimentary words.

That night her conscience kept her awake; the dancing candlelight fell upon her hat with its 'Coalition Cockades.' ('Coalition Duchess, indeed,' she thought—'they're right, I'm just Doll Common.') But the letters of the word 'Fox' embroidered on a ribbon in gold that bound the cockade in its place seemed to wink at her balefully. She seemed to see Fox himself, her friend, that vigorous black man for whom she had endured so much, and he was tired, tired and discouraged for the first time since she had known him. It had been for him, the first man who had consistently treated her as an intelligent human rather than a beautiful and enchanting doll, that she had striven. If her efforts so far had been as successful as the Duchess of Portland affirmed, they had been dearly paid for and his success was still unassured: the payment demanded of her would not decrease but she could increase her efforts. He should not fail. Her resolution was reborn in her; she would redouble her efforts, dress for the part and fling every ounce of her strength to turn the balance in his favour; she flung, up her head defiantly and opened the doors of her wardrobe.

All the next day she and her maid were very busy; poor Lady Spencer scolding and pleading with her. 'I have fretted myself abominably, I must own,' she said, 'both about you and your sister.'

'I don't see why, Mama,' said the Duchess, 'I am sure we deserve no blame.'

'Naturally,' said Lady Spencer, my first wish is that you may never, either of you, deserve blame; the next that you may never suffer it. If you knew,' she went on, 'what pain the scandalous lies and abuse of you gives me, you would neither of you, I am sure, venture again upon a conduct that subjects you to such insults. There is a degree of dignity and delicacy which a woman should never depart from.'

Georgiana, usually so docile where her mother was concerned, did not seem the least abashed by Lady Spencer's accusations. She knew they were true and that she had resolved to continue in her unbecoming behaviour, so she bowed her head to hide her bitter smile, over her sewing.

'I know it is from the best intention you have both been led to take the part you have done,' continued her mother, 'but let this be a lesson to you, my dearest child, never to go into any matter beyond the strictest rules of propriety.'

Still Georgiana made no reply. Lady Spencer sighed and made a final effort. 'A good humoured moderation in your conduct,' she assured her apparently indifferent daughter, 'especially upon all political points will be a credit to your heart and head and will soon make all the past infamous lies be forgotten.'

At last Georgiana lifted her head. 'Oh, Mama,' she sighed, 'I do indeed hope so.'

On the Thursday morning another letter was brought to her as she was dressing. This time it was from the Duke of Portland:

London, Wednesday Even. 14 April, 1784.

My dear Duchess,

As I believe you to be just as incapable of superstition as of anger I am under no apprehension of incurring the latter by denying my assent to Your account of your own Character and the State of the Poll for these last two days is a better argument than any other I can give for refusing to concur in Your opinion of Yourself. Every one is convinced that your exertions have produced the very material alteration which has happened in Fox's favor, and will continue to preserve and improve it into a decisive Majority, but be assured that if it could be imagined that Your absence was imputable to any other Cause than Your affection to Lady Spencer and Your anxiety (I hope perfectly unnecessary) for the state of Her health, and that a suspicion should arise of Your having withdrawn Yourself from the Election, a general Languor would prevail, Despondancy would succeed, and Triumph of the Court would be the inevitable Consequence. However it may seem, depend upon it, that this Representation is not exaggerated; and if You give the Credit in this respect, which I seriously assure You is due to me, I think We shall have the pleasure of seeing you in the course of tomorrow...

There was a lot more, but she had not time to read it. Her coach was at the door; she ran downstairs, kissed her mother goodbye, and as she went through the hall paused for a second to unhook from the wall an old fox's brush, a trophy of some long-forgotten chase.

Back in London she sent for Fox and received him in that crowded high little room where she used to dress, the room that was the very heart of Devonshire House, whose walls covered with red silk and over-hung with pictures seemed to enclose more intimacy than elsewhere. There was no witness to what passed between them, but knowing what they both thought at the time, if we look closely into the clouded past we may see them staring at each other, their glances meeting in the mirror before the Duchess, both asking the same questions, both denying the answers they knew to be true, Fox before the fire, grinding his knuckles into his eyes as he always did when he was perplexed; Georgiana in front of her tiny dressing table, pushing things about, gazing unseeing into the glass, wondering how she was to convince him of her new plan. Leaning our ears to the thin wall between our times, we can almost hear Fox's passionate outburst. 'It's vile, vile,' he cried. 'That they should touch you, besmirch you like this is unthinkable. You're the only clean woman in London...'

'Oh, Charles,' she broke in, 'how can you say such a thing? Think of Harriet.'

'I don't care,' he said. 'It's you who are their quarry. It's got to stop—you've got to stop.'

There was a silence between them, hot, heavy, unresolved. Fox was muttering, almost to himself. 'I must win, I must. A pocket borough is as good as a defeat. But how—how? I won't have you in it.'

The Duchess stood up, pressing down her immense skirts, and sidled between the furniture till she stood behind his chair. She released her skirts and, billowing out, they almost touched the walls of the little gilded place.

'Fox,' she whispered, and her dress pressed right over the wing of his chair on to his shoulders, 'will you not let me help you?'

'*You?* By God, no! You've done enough already. I've told you—you're out of it.'

'Charles,' she said and sat down near him, 'I've a plan, listen. Nothing can wipe away the filth they've thrown. Let's use it—don't let us be defeated by them.' He did not answer and she went on urgently, fearful lest he should interrupt her. 'You've admitted that my—our—driving about in carriages has done good. Well, I'm going to get out of my carriage. I'm going to *get* the votes. I can, I know it.'

Her new plan made her eyes shine with excitement, or maybe the dancing firelight was the animation in her face.

He gazed at her unwillingly, grudgingly, hating to admit that she was right, that she alone could do it.

'Well,' she whispered, 'I'm right, ain't I?' She laughed with relief at his silence. 'Are you not grateful?' she said.

'Grateful? What do you mean? Politics are a matter of chicanery or integrity. Integrity doesn't seem to exist anymore, but you've given me yours to help me in my charlatanry —so for that I'm grateful.'

Without another word they rose to their feet, he opened the door for her and, smiling at each other, they left the room.

The next day, dressed in a buff gown trimmed with blue ribbons, the party colours, with the fox's brush tied in her hat, Georgiana drove out on her new campaign.

Stopping at a butcher's shop she alighted and asked the proprietor for his vote.

'I will give your Grace a plumper,' said the tradesman, and procure you *five* more, on a certain condition.'

'What is that?'

'That your Grace will give me a kiss.'

'Why then,' says the charming Duchess, 'take one.'

There, now it's out, that fatal kiss that was to set London by the ears and which has survived a century and a half; the kiss by which she is known today, the innocent payment she was said to have made for six votes for her friend and which has grown in magnitude till it might have been paid for with thirty pieces of silver. 'The beautiful Duchess of Devonshire,' they still say, 'the one that kissed the butcher.'

The irony of it is that though she denied it, for in a letter to her mother she wrote that 'My Sister & Ly. —— [the name is illegible] were both kiss'd, so it's very hard I who was not shd. have the reputation for it,' neither then nor now would the world believe her. Today it is regarded as an amusing anecdote, but it was a major scandal then. The opposition pounced on it, whooping.

They printed flaming placards headed 'WESTMINSTER.' 'To be hired for the day,' they read, 'Several PAIR of RUBY POUTING LIPS of the FIRST QUALITY. To be kissed by rum Dukes, queer Dukes, Butchers, Draymen, Dustmen and Chimney sweepers. Please to enquire at Devon & Cos Crimson Pouting Warehouse, Piccadilly.'

Lord Hood's sailors went about the town singing:

> I had rather kiss my Moll than she,
> With all her paint and finery;
> Whats a Duchess more than Woman?
> We've sounder flesh on Portsmouth Common;

Then fill out Nectar in a glass,
As for kissing—kiss my arse.

'A certain Duchess,' leered *The Morning Post*, 'transacts business in a very expeditious manner, and therefore deserves much praise from her favourite member, as in her canvassing for voters she avoids being loquacious but kisses and comes at once to the point.'

There was a general outcry against the indecent slanders, and though they still cropped up from time to time, the opposition changed their tactics, now accusing her of bribery instead of wantonness.

They alleged that she and Lady Duncannon would enter shops, make some small purchase and pay a price out of all proportion to its value, at the same time soliciting a vote for Fox. They were supposed to have given 5 guineas for a bundle of broccoli, 8 for a leg of mutton, and £20 for a French loaf. Finally, 'to convince the public of the shameful effects of undue influence in the present contest,' *The Morning Post* says that 'they hear from a correspondent that a certain Dss. sent an order on Thursday night to two hairdressers of the name of J – –ks–n in Wardour Street, for 50 lbs of hair-powder each at their *own prices* and requesting them to vote for her Grace's cicisbeo. Their alacrity to serve her Grace need not be doubted.' The next day Mr Jackson gave his own rather ambiguous explanation on affidavit. He swore that 'a Mr E., a gentleman in the law in Charlotte Street, asked me if I would take £25 for my vote, to which question I replied that if a bribe had been an object, I might have taken an order for 50 lbs of hair-powder at my own price provided I would vote as I should be directed.' Mr Jackson then affirmed that whenever he voted it would be independent of any pecuniary consideration whatever.

The protests against the many obscene prints of the Duchess were met with a declaration that 'the Duchess is much enamoured with the prints which condescend to notice her Grace in such a variety of canvassing positions. Strict orders are given to buy all that come out and to place them in one particular light apartment, which is to be called the Duchess's *Exhibition*.'

Another paper tried to defend the prints by saying that it must be 'remembered that when people of rank descend below themselves and mingle with the vulgar for mean and dirty purposes, they give up their claim to respect, forfeit their privileges and become fair game for censors.'

She did not forfeit her respect with the simple folk, among whom she moved utterly unconscious of her rank, thinking only of Fox, whilst her rival canvasser, Lady Salisbury, sought to impose her rank upon them, using it as a reason why they should vote for Hood and Wray. The workman who exclaimed that her eyes were so bright that he could light his pipe at them, and the Irish chairman who swore that if he were God he would make her Queen of Heaven, saw the woman rather than the Duchess.

Finally when the opposition saw that nothing would deter her from canvassing and that her unremitting efforts brought in more and more votes for Fox, they maintained that it was essential to her that he should win, as otherwise she and the Duke would be ruined financially. The papers stated that the election cost her £600 a day (which would amount to a total of £24,000), and that apart from money there were three motives for her persistent advocacy. These were, firstly 'to secure the yielding affections of a certain great Personage [the Prince of Wales], which she fears are now *sinking* under the *weight* of her encreasing charms. The second is a love for her husband's family, part of which, it is apprehended, must soon starve unless Mr Fox is again Secretary of State, or rather unless the Duke of Portland is Roy and, as Trinculo says, Mr Fox is *Viceroy over him*. The third, last and weakest motive is her personal regard for Mr Fox himself— *utrum horum mavis aecipe*; and to do justice to her Grace's taste we must pronounce the latter motive to be the least probable.'

Actually, of course, the third motive was the true one—her intransigent loyalty was unshakable and would not allow her to surrender.

What the election cost her, no one knew, though we can catch a glimpse from a letter to her mother written one Sunday at Chiswick:

> I would give the world to be with you, for I am unhappy beyond measure here and abus'd for nothing. Yet as it is begun I must go with it—they will not give it up and they insist upon our all continuing to canvass—in short, they say having begun and not going on would do a great deal of harm. I shall go to church today, but I am really so vex'd (though I don't say so) at the abuse in the newspapers that I have no heart left—it is very hard they single me out when all the women of my side do as much.

Her perseverance brought its reward; despite riots, lampoons and the many false votes that could only be checked by a scrutiny, when the poll was closed on May the 17th at three o'clock in the afternoon, Fox had beaten Wray by a majority of 236. It was all over bar the shouting.

Immediately a vast procession was formed: escorted by a squadron of gentlemen in buff and blue uniforms, accompanied by bands of music, Fox, seated in a triumphal chair decorated with laurels, was borne aloft.

Over the procession flew the buff and blue banners of triumph; it was closed by the State carriages of their Graces, the Duchesses of Portland and Devonshire, drawn by six horses apiece superbly caparisoned with six running footmen attendant on each. The procession wound through Covent Garden to the Strand, down Parliament Street, back through Pall Mall and St James's to Devonshire House, where the Prince of Wales awaited it standing on a platform in the courtyard.

That night there was a great dinner at Willis's Rooms, followed by the famous ball at Mrs Crewe's. Georgiana was toasted and toasted again; the Prince partnered her in the quadrille. Her triumph was complete. She was too tired to care.

The dining room, Devonshire House.

9

Set to Partners

The current of life ebbed slowly back into its accustomed channels, leaving an unsavoury backwash: a trial for the 'murder' of one Nicholas Casson, killed during the Covent Garden riot on May the 10th, and an expensive scrutiny of the poll which proved inconclusive, so that Fox took his double seat (for he also represented the Shetland Isles) in the House. His party had lost 160 constituencies and young Mr Pitt was firmly established.

The scummy flood-mark still besmirched the walls of Devonshire House, and Georgiana, who had looked forward to a year of economy and of peace with her baby, found her debts and her conduct still publicly criticized. It made her cross, miserable and unhappy, and she turned to Lady Spencer who she believed could teach her to regain that which she had lost—her dignity and good opinion in the eyes of the world. Lady Spencer counselled time, piety and a withdrawal from the public stage, and as usual she was right, for gradually the talk died down and Georgiana's interests shrank to their normal size.

For instance she had been a little worried about the future of a negro page she had been given, whom, 'as the Duke don't like my having a black,' she had passed on to her strict and benevolent mother. Now she had time to inquire whether he was making progress as a Christian and turning into a good boy. Above all, she was now free to return to the nursery of her beloved baby daughter who had been lulled to sleep during the election, according to the opposition, by the Duke comfortably singing 'Hey, my kitten! my kitten!' as he rocked the cradle. But even in this innocent haven she found cause for mortification, as the Duchess of Portland remarked, with the candour peculiar to relations, that she feared dear little Georgiana, though a very pretty child, had too Cavendish a face to be a handsome woman. Alas, that aunts should prove so often right.

In Parliament they were settling down to work: for once Pitt and Fox whole-heartedly in co-operation, both detesting and fighting bribery, corruption and place-hunting, were determined to put a stop to this, and a motion was made that 'a Committee be appointed to take into consideration the state of the Representation of the Commons of Great Britain in Parliament.'

The Duchess reports this debate, and mentions the chief instruments of ministerial corruption—Robinson of the Treasury and Rigby, ex-Paymaster of the Forces, in a letter of June the 18th. 'The reform bill,' she says, 'was lost last night by 50—Pitt and Fox for it. Great simptoms of Rigby's changing! He has had it is supposed Mr Robinson to Dinner.'

She goes on to describe a typical day:

This morning I went to Lady Walpole, to my Aunt, to Lady Melbourne—nobody din'd with us and I began dressing for Dadhemar's [Count d'Adhémar, the French Ambassador] ball. I had a white gauze pettycoat, an apron bound with black, my sash with the Queen of Frances pearl buckle under my gown and a Robe turke of white gauze clouded with black and a kind of Spanish gauze hat with feathers hanging down, a gauze puffing handkerchief bound with black and a great nosegay of Corn flowers. My Sister was in a grey gown, plain black hat at the back of her head and look'd vastly well. We went first to Lady George's [the Duke's sister-in-law] where I saw Mrs Digby and Mrs Walpole. We then went to the ball, where there was only married women except Miss Gunnings and Miss Hudson—the room was decorated with sprigs and wreaths and lamps—very pretty but hot. I danc'd with the Prince, with Lord Strathaven and Lord St Asaph—this last is good natur'd and looks sensible, Gentlemanlike and Ghastly. I play'd a little to cool before I came home and won tant soit peu. My S^r danc'd a little and look'd charmingly.

In the manner of their time they were burning up their splendid energies, spending money recklessly—the Prince making alterations at Carlton House on a scale of fabulous splendour, and squandering their forces equally on frivolities or matters of import, men and women discussing political reform with passion and earnestness the same day that Fox, Sheridan and the Prince of Wales are hoaxing Lord Shelburne into thinking they are plotting a treaty under his nose.

Although this set of friends was as closely allied as ever, there took place about this time one of those subtle, almost unnoticeable, regroupings amongst them. Their collective affections were unaltered, but their personal relationships were changing.

Fox, for example, appeared to be settling down: for some time it was known that he had been seeing a great deal of Mrs Armistead, the best-known courtesan in London, the heroine of the episode when her lover, Lord George Cavendish, had found her other lover, the young Prince of Wales, hiding behind her door; who, though never losing her Cockney accent, was a woman of tact and charm, skilled in domesticity, which meant that she was equally companionable in the boudoir and the bed. Fox, whose virile mode of life was taking a toll on him, found her quiet and utter devotion increasingly attractive, and he looked forward, as he told Sheridan after the hurly-burly of the election, to the delights of St Anne's Hill, his small country estate, where, with Mrs Armistead as his companion, he could rest under the trees with a book, preferably Homer.

'Why with a book?' asked 'Sherry,' who was unambiguous if volatile in his desires.

Sheridan himself was veering to all points of the feminine compass: now it was the Prince of Wales's ex-mistress, exquisite 'Perdita' Robinson; next Lady Duncannon; then he hovered around beautiful, political Mrs Crewe. But his wife Elizabeth Linley was the magnetic north of his unstable course.

Yet all these personal interests and loves were eclipsed by the Prince of Wales's latest infatuation. Having dangled in vain after Georgiana, more successfully after Lady Melbourne, having won and discarded 'Perdita,' Mrs Armistead and Mrs Hodges, he was now, at the age of twenty-two, to be struck by the *coup de foudre*.

Maria Fitzherbert was twenty-five years old, twice widowed and the granddaughter of a Catholic baronet, Sir John Smythe. As was customary owing to the anti-Catholic laws, she had been educated in Paris at the convent of the 'Blew Nuns' with other girls similarly placed. She was a good-natured, good-looking, placid and extremely pious young woman. It has been said that the Prince met her at Devonshire House, but whether this were so or not, he immediately poured into his 'Sister' Georgiana's sympathetic ear the troubled details of his love. He was completely unreticent; apart from the Duchess he confided in every Tom, Dick and Harriet.

Georgiana was duped neither by his complaints that Maria was unyielding nor by his demands on her own friendship. The analysis she once made of one aspect of her character perfectly explains her conduct at this juncture. She told her mother:

> It has happened to me, with people who have influence over me, to have perfectly seized the reason of their wishing me to do some one thing or other which I did not like to do, & that tho' they did not disclose their real motive, I have been saying to myself all the time they have been persuading me, 'I know what you are at, & why you wish me to do so and so,' & yet with this full conviction instead of owning it & in spite of disliking the thing, I have done it because I was desired & have pretended to believe every word that was said to me, so that I actually have taken more pains to appear a Dupe than most people do to shew they cannot be outwitted. In things of consequence I hope I should be strong, but in common events I have so great an antipathy to the word no that I expose myself to many inconveniences not to pronounce it. It seems almost as if the activity of my nature spent itself in my mind, and gave me force to feel and reason, but that tir'd with the effort, it yielded to indolence the moment I was to perform.

No one knew herself better than Georgiana and no one was more weak than she in yielding to her fatal good nature, which now led her to help him, partly in the belief that it was only one of his many whims, in making friends with Mrs Fitzherbert.

She invited her—and naturally the Prince—to every party she gave, and Lady Melbourne followed her example, as did the other Whig ladies. But Maria's earlier friends were mostly of the opposition, and when the Prince was observed at Lady Salisbury's or the Duchess of Gordon's, panting anxiously in pursuit of the young widow, tongues began to clack and soon gossip was rife.

The Prince's dilemma was a new one to him, for it was the first time he had either been serious or had met with a persistent refusal. He was in turns puzzled, angry and pitiful; he was completely at a loss and could not understand Maria's attitude. It was not that she was indifferent to him; on the contrary, she was deeply in love, and this made it the more perplexing to the bewildered Prince, for if the many other ladies (who had not cared for him half so well) had said 'yes,' why did she, who had admitted her love, alone say 'no'? He was incapable of understanding that to a young, independent, devout Catholic, her religion was of more importance than her personal inclinations. He lost all sense of proportion; he offered to waive his right to the Crown, to emigrate with her to America, to marry her—anything and everything if she would only say 'yes.' But Maria, as a Catholic, thought that such a 'marriage' would be invalid, and she was not prepared to commit a mortal sin.

While he raved and bellowed, she preserved the discreetest silence, assuring the Duchess that never, never would she even appear to countenance measures she knew to be wrong. Ten years later Georgiana wrote an official 'statement' which is among her papers, blaming and exonerating herself for her share in the subsequent events. Meantime, though Prinny would not rest till he had told her the full extent of his passion for Maria and his design to marry her, vowing to kill himself when Georgiana remonstrated with him, she did not appear to take his threats very seriously, perhaps because they were too frequent to be believed in. At the same time she recognized the need for secrecy, and always referred to him by the codename of '2' when writing to her mother.

By June the 23rd Georgiana was relieved to hear that Maria intended to go abroad, and Prinny talked of following her, which, though undesirable, seemed wise to the Duchess; for Spa was a preferable venue for a decisive battle than London. At last the Prince prevailed on Georgiana to visit Maria in her own house, presumably in the hopes that his 'Sister' would plead his cause. Maria and Georgiana talked over the whole problem, and both agreed that his proposals were out of the question. The Duchess drove home and confessed to the Duke and Lady Spencer that she was much relieved by Mrs Fitzherbert's good sense and inflexible resolve neither to become the Prince's mistress nor to marry him and that she had fixed the date of her departure to Spa for July the 7th.

The demented Prince knew not how to stop her, and on June the 30th he drank three pints of brandy which nearly killed him, confining him to his bed for three days. Even this did not shake Maria's resolve, and she continued with preparations for her journey.

On Tuesday, the eve of Mrs Fitzherbert's departure, Georgiana gave a rather dull card party at which none of her intimates were present. Suddenly she was summoned from the room by a white-faced footman. She found two of the Prince's friends, Bouverie and Onslow, as pale as death.

'Good God, what is the matter?' cried Georgiana.

They told her that the Prince had run himself through the body, missing his heart by a nail's breadth, and that the only way to prevent his tearing off his bandages was for Mrs Fitzherbert to send him some kind of promise to marry him on her return from Spa.

'But surely she will not consent to such a course?' asked the Duchess.

They assured her that any promise made with the idea of saving his life must be void, and that therefore Maria was safe.

They were then joined by Keate, the Prince's surgeon, who swore the news was true.

'But what has this to do with me?' asked the Duchess. 'Let Mrs Fitzherbert send the message if she must, but as to myself ...'

They broke in, telling her that nothing would be of any use but that Maria should go herself to the Prince, that she was waiting without and would not, and indeed could not, go unless the Duchess would accompany her.

Having nobody to consult, impressed by the three men's frightened faces and her pity for Maria, Georgiana gave way and traversed the courtyard, where she found Mrs Fitzherbert in her carriage.

They drove to Carlton House where they found Lord Southampton, whom the gentlemen had sent for with the idea, they told the ladies, of his informing the King, for otherwise, if the Prince should die, they might all be tried for their lives.

It was a nightmare scene—the Prince covered in blood, flinging himself against the walls, back on to his bed, down on to the floor, muttering and sobbing 'Maria, Maria,' 'calming' himself with brandy and water; the terrified gentlemen; the anxious, futile physician, all powerless to control his hysterics, added to the fear that the cries and groans would reach the ear of the King (for the walls of Royalty are thin and scandal travels fast), forced from Maria the jesuitical promise demanded of her.

Lord Southampton, grave and censorious, alarmed Georgiana still more, and on her return to Devonshire House she wrote him a full account of all she knew—the Prince's intended marriage, the events of the night, the part played by her, everything.

His reply saying that he did not intend to inform the King, as he looked upon it as a boyish prank, was an unspeakable relief.

But the next day, this change of front appeared suspect, and to Georgiana and Maria's horror they learned that they had been hoaxed—it was all a sham staged to extort the promise from Maria. The two women, inexpressibly shocked and angry, wrote a joint statement, signed by them both, briefly and succinctly setting forth how they had been duped and that the promise was therefore considered by them entirely null and void.

Whether this statement was shown to the Prince or not, Georgiana wrote a censorious letter to Mr Onslow, intending it, or its purport, to be conveyed to Prinny, in which she demanded, in view that she had reason to believe the suicide to be a fake, that he should submit to examination by her own surgeon.

This called forth a long remonstrance from the Prince, written from Kew on the 9th, and as it must have been delivered by hand, it is quite possibly the cause, and not the result, of the joint declaration. Prinny's letter is far too long: he protests his innocence, his utter devotion to Maria, his noble intentions, the probity of his conduct throughout. He is insulted that he, the most blameless of men, should be asked to submit to the scrutiny of an unknown surgeon. If Georgiana persists in her unheard-of conduct, he can no longer believe in the friendship of his 'Sister,' enjoy her society or consider himself her Brother. Worst of all is that she had conveyed her inexplicable censure and mistrust through one of his gentlemen. He begs her to show his letter to the Duke, whom he knew would see the justice of his cause and approve of his conduct, and he hopes that, despite everything, her repentance would still allow him to regard himself as her ever affectionate Friend and Brother, George P.

She made him wait three days and then consented to see him. After a long scene of mutual reproaches, she allowed him to believe she had forgiven all his follies, but insisted that in future he must lessen his intimacy with her and forbade him to come to Chatsworth until she herself sent for him, which she had no intention of doing. Prinny was contrite, submitted his whole conduct to the Duke, and Georgiana flattered herself that the dreadful business might have good consequences.

Of course it could have no good consequences, for Prinny never kept a promise and Georgiana could never say 'no.'

Lulled by a false sense of security, Mrs Fitzherbert being at Spa whilst she, Bess and Canis were blissfully reunited at Chatsworth, Georgiana thought the danger was past. Actually she was acting most injudiciously; she recommended a courier to the Prince who was for ever writing expresses to Maria, sending many of them, as she afterwards discovered, in her own name. The Prince also persecuted her to write to Maria herself to persuade her to marry him, but the most she ever did, wearied by his importunities, was to write urging Maria to declare her intentions definitely to the Prince. Yet she would not have consented thus far had she not felt secure in Maria's resolution.

Mrs Fitzherbert replied that she was incapable of expressing the cruelty of her situation; that she could not understand the Duchess's letter as she had never swerved from her resolve not to agree to any of the Prince's proposals; that though she condemned the conduct of his friends—Fox and some others—she understood their attitude, which was one of anxiety to placate the Prince as they well knew his proposals were invalid. Finally, she implored Georgiana to exercise her influence over the Prince, as no one had more than she.

After this letter it is no wonder that the Duchess was flabbergasted when she learned in the early autumn that Maria had returned to England. She saw her once, but they tacitly avoided the disagreeable subject and the Duchess stifled her fears.

Before we decide whether these fears were justifiable let us consider what were the attitudes of the other participants in the drama: after Maria's departure for Spa, Prinny rushed to Fox, who in his new-found domestic happiness, listened sympathetically to the heart-broken tale of the deserted lover, but at the same time he pointed out the impossibility of the recognition of any form of marriage: the laws of England, the King's aversion from his eldest son, and his financial situation all made even a morganatic marriage out of the question. Indeed, the Prince's debts were another matter of the gravest concern: Fox urged retrenchment and circumspection.

What had occasioned Maria's return; what had shaken her resolution? If the sight of Prinny, apparently almost fatally wounded, had not broken her resistance, what more powerful argument had prevailed? There can only be one reply—religion. It was on the rock of her religion that the Prince had dashed himself in vain: now she must have taken counsel from the Church and learned that a Catholic marriage is a sacrament between two people; that providing they are both free to marry, nothing in the world can prevent their doing so; that the priest is only the witness of their marriage, not the maker of it—for a marriage consists in the consent of two people joining themselves sacramentally together before the sight of God. A great weight was lifted from her heart; she had fought against her love and her lover valiantly, now she need fight no more, for she was a widow and he was a single man, and if they chose to partake of the sacrament of marriage no Principality nor Power could put them asunder.

Fox, hearing of Maria's return to England, redoubled his entreaties; the Prince listened with suspicious meekness, agreed that his dear Charles was right and categorically renounced any intention of marriage.

At the same moment he invited his dearest 'Sister' to be present at his marriage with Maria.

Her reaction was as dramatic as his request. Seizing a sheet of paper, incoherent and illegible from her horror and distress, she scrawled a letter desperate in its haste, secrecy and fear. She is terrified out of her senses—never would she have consented to see or listen to him had she thought it would come to this. It must not happen—it must not, it is madness to think of it, indeed it is madness. She cannot be present at what is not—can never be—a marriage. She is not frightened for herself, but the terror of the consequences she foresees for them has made her half-wild with fear. On her knees she begs him to see Charles Fox—she will always show Maria every mark of respect, but for God's sake, for God's sake, see Fox—delay, delay—see Fox—delay.... Shaking with fear, she shut her eyes and blocked her ears. She would not know the consequences, she would never hear or suffer the word 'marriage' to be spoken of again by the Prince. She would not know of or recognize what, despite her frenzied appeals, took place at Maria's house in Park Street that night.

What took place was one of those deathly secrets that are bound to leak out. What a sequel to the summer....

For the summer had been an enchanted one. After the events at Carlton House and her 'reconciliation' with the Prince, she had gone to Chatsworth with the Duke and little G., and there they were joined by Bess who had returned to England in June.

Bess brought more than Charlotte William with her to Chatsworth; she brought happiness, and carefree, light-hearted days. Georgiana was more than ever enchanted with her friend and her successes: Lord Jersey, old Sir William Jones, Colonel Crawfurd, witty Mr Hare and the Duke himself all swarmed round the alluring honey-pot, till the Duchess assured her that she was like Susannah tempted by the elders.

The two young women, their arms entwined, walked in the sun by the sparkling fountains, idled in the shade of the great trees; they lured Charles Wyndham under the copper willow, then drenched him with its magic spray; they rode to watch shooting matches between the men; even the Duke unbent and reduced them to fits of laughter by teazing Colonel Crawfurd to run uphill. Then Lady Liz teased the 'Fish' in turn, throwing her whip down the hill for him to retrieve, but the Colonel proved more lazy than gallant.

Their most serious visitor was Georgiana's old friend Dr Johnson, who arrived looking and feeling ill. Young Mr Burke tactlessly asked the great man if he were quite well.

'Sir.' replied the Doctor, 'I am not half well, no, nor a quarter well.' And indeed he was far worse than they knew.

After this awkward opening the Doctor was dry and talked in too high a strain about new friendships and Aristotle. But gradually the talk slipped very commodiously into easier channels, and by the time the Duke had led him under the lime trees, he was wonderfully agreeable indeed. They talked of Topham Beauclerk and asked the Doctor what he thought of him. He said that Mr Beauclerk's mind was unperverted and capable of anything, but that as his wine was strong and high, so was his vinegar sour, which, they agreed, exactly fitted the case. The Doctor added that Beauclerk sometimes succeeded in hurting him, but it was by the design to hurt rather than by the words he used. Furthermore, he was most entertaining about Sir William Jones's learning, and Georgiana and Bess were sorry when they had to leave him to get ready for the Public Day, for it was a Monday, but their regret was lessened when they observed him at dinner with the other less distinguished guests, for he ate much and nastily, though his manners were better than those of a neighbouring clergyman who got so extremely drunk that he almost knocked down Lady Liz and Miss Lloyd.

But, on the whole, they preferred their own company; they were always happiest *à trois*. The Duke, especially, was content, for during Lady Liz's absence abroad he had had a particularly disagreeable time. It is true that his wife had at last borne him a child, but it had proved to be a daughter. Apart from this dubious consolation, life had been very trying indeed. After his unique speech in the House of Lords on which Burke had commented so favourably, he had again retired into his egoistical shell of card-playing, verse-composing and the study of Shakespeare. Accustomed as he was to being considered and deferred to in every way, the disruption of this pleasant existence by the great political upheaval was, to say the least of it, upsetting: the comfortable routine of Brooks's had been disturbed by a tornado of political intrigue, blotting out the peaceful landscape of wagers, magnums of port and literary discussion. Worse still, his wife had become the notorious centre of this upheaval, and to the Duke this was singularly distasteful. He had a horror of any form of unconventionality or departure from the ordinary, and he found himself, linked by loyalty to his wife, his brother-in-law Portland and his friends, in a blaze of unwelcome publicity. Immediately after the distresses of this storm came a lull of absolute peace, perfected by the reappearance of this charming. deferential, amusing woman whom, to his surprise, he found he had missed during her absence. Of course, the business of begetting a son had to be attended to, but meanwhile Chatsworth in the company of Lady Liz was all that was delightful.

Georgiana, always more than a little afraid of her husband—her very respect for him making her uneasy and more impetuous in his presence—sighed with relief as she saw him amused, occupied and happy.

Bess made him jocular too—had he not found a perfect nickname for her—'the Racoon'? Nothing could be more apt, and as he was 'the Dog,' why then it was obvious that Georgiana must be 'the Rat.' So here they were, Canis, Mrs Racky and Mrs Rat, as happy as the day was long.

Besides, no one—even her sister Harriet—understood Georgiana as Liz did. Perhaps there was more than the sycophancy and self-interest, which trustful Georgiana mistook for sympathy and resignation, that attracted her to her friend. Was her passionate love for Bess almost that of a lover? It had the ingredients of humility, gratitude and unbounded admiration, whilst Bess's shrewd pointed pieces of worldly advice gave her a sense of stability and wisdom and her husband's pleasure in the company of her friend created almost a necessity for her continued residence with them. If only the world would leave them alone....

But back in London the world whispered round Carlton and Devonshire House. Mrs Fitzherbert was seen openly visiting the former, but the Prince was so constantly with the Duchess that the rumours contradicted each other. Not only did some of the gossips maintain that she was the Prince's mistress, but they believed they had proof of it, for the Duchess was again with child. But surely that proved nothing? Not at all, for—and here the voices sank to ominous significance—had not the Duke's attentions to Lady Elizabeth Foster been very marked and had it not been rumoured that she was breeding too? The Prince and the Duke were certainly the fathers.

It was not true, for in the long autumn days, declining into winter, the two women, ripening like ears of corn fertilized by the same indifferent sun, were both to become the mothers of the Duke's children. Only the Duchess was blind—'She was always simple, my dear, but now she is positively gullible.'

The fact that the miracle had happened again, that once more the presence of her talisman, Bess, had coincided with her conception, left room for no other feelings in Georgiana's heart but wonder and gratitude. Even Bess's departure for Italy just before Christmas, far earlier than had been intended, did not rouse her suspicions. She had to pay for her joy at being pregnant with the separation from her friend.

But to others Lady Elizabeth's discreet withdrawal aroused speculation; no one knew for certain what had happened, but they had very shrewd suspicions.

Lady Liz spent the first months of the year in Naples and then quietly slipped across to Ischia. Canis wrote to her frequently—he was impatient for her news; he hoped for good news; why had he not received the news from Ischia which he awaited so eagerly? He was alone at Chatsworth, and the sight of the sofa where she used to sit last summer and the blue bed in which she had slept recalled her cruelly to his mind, She must really be careful to write on less transparent paper, and if she had private news, for which he longed, she must send it by a sure hand. In August he was happy to inform her that Mrs Rat had had an easy confinement and another daughter.

Lady Duncannon, too, was great with child; there were no rumours round her name, and in November, to the delight of the family—for she already had three sons—she gave birth to a daughter.

Three little girls had been born whose lives were to be strangely and indissolubly interwoven—Harriet Elizabeth Cavendish, Caroline Ponsonby and Caroline Rosalie Adelaide St Jules.

Georgiana was happy in her nursery, with her child called by the names of the two women she loved best in the world, her sister and her friend, protected by her curious innocence and unworldliness, that never left her through her most worldly existence, from blows that were to fall.

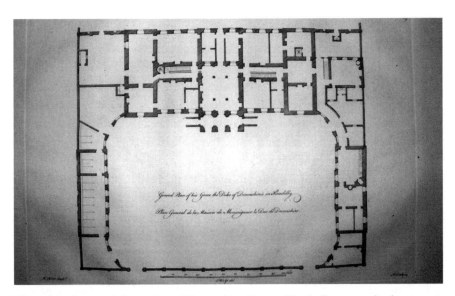

The original ground floor plan of Devonshire House. The ballroom and other 'state' rooms were on the first floor.

10

Chapter for Women

My mind can no comfort or happiness fix
On seventeen hundred and eighty six;
For Sorrow and Folly delighted to mix
With seventeen hundred and eighty six;
Abounding alone in unpromising tricks
Was seventeen hundred and eighty six;
And none was eer worse I can swear by ye Styx,
Than seventeen hundred and eighty six.

G. D.

So Georgiana wrote on New Year's Day, 1787, and by that time she had partly recovered from the shocks and menaces of the past year.

Things had begun to go wrong in January. Her partisanship of Mrs Fitzherbert and the Prince had recoiled upon her, for now she was the unwilling sharer in the secret of their marriage. Lady Spencer, who knew no more but guessed as much as the rest of the world, was worried as to what Georgiana's conduct in this matter would be. She had been deeply distressed at the opprobrium cast upon her daughter's behaviour at the time of the Westminster Election: now she foresaw further scandal if the Prince accompanied Georgiana to Newmarket, as he suggested. She also wished to know what the Duchess would do about going to the opera with Mrs Fitzherbert. She hoped it could be avoided, for it was certainly very plain that both the Prince and Mrs Fitzherbert meant to show they were not upon the same footing as before—and as she could not be his wife, what then was she? Also Lady Spencer wished to know why 'a private Gentlewoman' took a whole box at the opera for herself, when it was the custom among friends to share boxes; why that gentlewoman suffered the Prince to sit and talk to her throughout the performances; why she allowed him to carry her miniature about and show it to people, or permitted his carriage to be constantly seen at her door, especially in a morning to carry him home? All these things put it past a doubt that they were 'married,' but Lady Spencer wished to know in what light Georgiana meant to appear— did she intend to go about with the Prince's mistress, or did she mean to countenance and support such a marriage? The Duke and Duchess of Portland had decided that, should the Prince approach them on the subject, the Duchess would refuse, as she could, under no circumstances, comply with his requests. The Ladies Beauchamp and Broughton had agreed with the Portlands to act likewise, and Lady Spencer hoped that, even if Georgiana would not follow their admirable examples, she would at least remain in the country till the situation was clarified.

Georgiana, unable, as always, to take what appeared to her as an unfriendly attitude, fell back upon compromise. She was sure Prinny would not go to Newmarket, and as to Mrs F.—she would never go to the opera with her, *she* never did and never would, and Mrs F. knew it. What she meant to do was this (and here her certain knowledge of Polichinelle's secret made her incoherent)—as she knew that Mrs F.'s intentions were once perfectly honourable and prudent, seeing another turn had taken place, having strongly dissuaded him from his ideas, she declared:

I do not know that any thing has taken place.... I search into nothing and only wish to keep entirely out of it. I shall leave my name with her and if I have a large assembly, ask her, because Mrs F., an unmarried woman suffering the visits of an unmarried man is no reason for not being civil to her—but this is all I will do and I will avoid the assembly if you like it and indeed from my own choice I shall not have one and only mentioned the possibility of carrying my utmost civility so far.... Surely I am not wrong in having too much pride to let the P. of W. or his concerns alter any of them [her plans], surely I had better quarrel at once with him than be so far a slave to his Caprice that my intentions should be subjected to him?

This was all very well, but how could the Prince of Wales interfere with the Duchess's plans when these were undecided in the extreme? It was this indecision as to her future which was her chief worry.

Once more those debts which she had not had the courage to own had raised their insistent, ugly heads: the Duke knew of them; Mr Heaton knew of them; Lady Spencer, young Lord Spencer and the malicious, mischief-making Duchess of Portland, all knew of them, and they all agreed in one thing—that the debts must be paid and the Duchess prevented from contracting new ones. They all agreed that London seemed fatal to Georgiana's propensity to extravagance, and therefore, with a cruel clarity, they decided she must not be allowed to live in London. The problem then arose where she was to be exiled: to retire to Chatsworth, with its almost regal scale of living, would be no economy; Chiswick was damp and too near London; Newmarket dangerous because of the Prince; to live alone at Washingley, a 'cold, solitary, melancholy house,' would be a sad penance that Georgiana felt she could not face unless she was forced to; Compton Place was but a holiday resort; questions would certainly be asked if she lived alone and for no apparent reason at Buxton or Bolton, while even her potential gaolers seemed to feel the shade of that other prisoner, Mary Stuart, at Hardwick. The Duke, while agreeing with the consensus of opinion that sequestration would be salutary for his extravagant wife, as usual could not make up his mind about it. Meantime the Duchess spent most of her time at St Albans, whether Lady Spencer was there or not; being seen sufficiently often with the Duke to avoid gossip and blessing her baby Hary-o, who while she was being nursed kept her mother in civilized places. But Hary-o was now eight months old, and the miserable moment of weaning and the anxious one of inoculation were fast approaching. The Duchess felt her verdict was approaching too, and prayed it would be delayed. At all events, she assured her mother, at any time, in any scrape or danger, she would fly to her.

Other people were in scrapes and dangers too: Harriet Duncannon's marriage was no longer the happy, peaceful relationship it had promised. 'Harum,' Lord Duncannon, was playing deep and neglecting his wife, and she in turn was reputed to have run away from him with an unnamed lover. False as this report was, it yet occasioned both Georgiana and Lady Spencer much distress, and Harriet's future was as eagerly and anxiously discussed as her sister's. Lady Melbourne wrote offering her help—she had, of course, denied reports of an elopement, but would it not be wise for Lady Duncannon to appear in public with her sister and her friends?

Even from France the Duchess received disquieting news: the Duke of Dorset, then Ambassador in Paris, wrote that her friend, 'Mrs B.,' had been implicated in an unsavoury affair to do with a Diamond Necklace, and that she had father damaged herself in public opinion by her support of the tyrannical, haughty minister, le Baron de Breteuil. However, the Queen sent Georgiana a present of some very fine lace-trimmed chemises, which must not be confused with the 'shifts' of the time, for these were meant to be seen, puffing out above the low-cut gowns, and she felt reassured.

Farther afield, in Naples, Bess (though she wrote gay, affectionate letters to her Dearest Love) was devoured with worry: she was afraid certain rumours had reached the Duchess's ears, and wrote to Canis to ask him if this was true. He assured her that 'the Rat' did not know the chief cause of her uneasiness, and that he, of course, would never mention it to her, unless she so desired him; but that, did he ever do so, he was sure Mrs Rat would acquit Mrs Racky of blame when he had explained how 'the thing' had happened. He did not mention that there was a domestic crisis at home, but hoped that Mrs Bess would soon return to rejoice their hearts.

Though the Duke seemed unmoved by these feminine perplexities, two of which affected him closely, others were not prepared to let the matter drop; the vexed question of where Georgiana was to live was still undecided, and for a time she hoped a solution had been found, for the Duke actually entertained the idea of a visit to Spa. This suited him perfectly, for Bess was preparing to return to England and he hoped that she would join them there. But his lethargy; Heaton's assurances that Georgiana's creditors, especially Martindale the banker, insisted on a settlement of her debts; Lady Spencer's hints that her daughter would be safer in the country, and some other more pointed gossip, retailed to him by his sister, the Duchess of Portland, all combined to keep him in England.

This more pointed gossip was concerned with Georgiana's 'lovers.'

There were several: the 'Eyebrow,' the 'Infernal' (whose identities were hidden by their pseudonyms, the former probably Fox), and the 'Pic,' Monsieur de Fersen, reported to be Marie Antoinette's lover. The fame of Monsieur de Fersen, indeed, had preceded him to such a glamorous extent that Georgiana was actually terrified that she might fall in love with him. It came as a relief to her to discover that, despite his delightful eyes and most gentlemanlike air, she was not attracted, and that in England he was regarded even as ugly. The glamour, raised by his association with Marie Antoinette, was not justified.

There remained, however, one other.

Georgiana was now twenty-nine: it was twelve years since she gazed upon the imaginary landscape of her future when her picture of it had been clear yet remote, at once detailed and fantastic. She had peopled it with herself and the Duke as central figures, surrounded by many children and countless friends, dispensing over them a golden haze of happiness and benevolence. If she had foreseen shadows, they were all transitory, dispersed by the wisdom and courage of her husband. In fact, it was the stock Utopia of a young and ignorant girl. She had imagined leaving her mother's house (that stronghold built upon precept, warmed by charity and shaded by reason), determined to build such a mansion for herself, but she had found a wide territory lay between. Now the landscape had become reality across which wound a tortuous road with many branches, all of which held entrancing promise and each of which she explored only to find them dead ends. There was always a sense of impending storm from which she could not escape; she shrank under heavy clouds of debt which threatened to ruin and obliterate her, and had lost sight of the horizon.

Looking back, we can follow her progress. From the outset life had proved entirely different from what she had imagined.

Neither her husband nor she had understood that a marriage must be more than a ceremony; though her instincts told her this was so, for she had spontaneously approached him, only to be rebuffed.

To him marriage was a matter of convention; his wife was to be his consort, reigning over his demesnes, bearing his children and sharing in his honours. He neither understood nor approved of her attempts to enlarge, and still more to make use of, her education. He did not comprehend why she had desired a laboratory, wished to collect minerals, pored for hours over the pair of Adams' globes that she had bought for five guineas, studied the composition of music or took her versifying seriously. All these were amusing accomplishments, no doubt, but to him they were accomplishments only and not essentials to her development. Even her passionate interest in politics was to him the reflection of her friendship with his friends and not an end in itself. These hobbies, as he saw them, would naturally occupy her leisure—such well-bred interests were sufficient for other women with pretensions to culture, therefore they must be enough for her. He found it a pretty gesture when she endowed her poor school at Edensor on their daughter's birth; he did not realize that she had done so, not only because it was an expression of deep gratitude to providence and a hostage to fortune, but because she passionately believed in education for the illiterate. When she schemed, even in one of her blackest moments of financial distress, to set aside £100 a year with which she would beg from him a few barren unprofitable acres on which to build a small cottage, plant trees round it, furnish it, install some poor people, paying them for their labour, and thereby, by building such a cottage every year, improve his estates and her tenants' lot, he thought it a charming, impracticable fantasy and did not realize that she was serious in her arcadian scheme.

Likewise he found it unnecessary and unseemly to express openly any affection or admiration they might feel for each other: if they lived together

Above left: John Spencer, 1st Earl Spencer (1734-1783), by Thomas Gainsborough *c.* 1763. John Spencer married, 1754, Georgiana, née Poyntz (1737-1814).

Above right: Margaret Georgiana Spencer, Countess Spencer, née Poyntz, by Thomas Gainsborough. The date is unknown, but probably *c.* 1763,

Below left: Georgiana, Countess Spencer, and her daughter, Georgiana (1757-1806), by Joshua Reynolds, *c.* 1760.

Below right: Another depiction of Georgiana, Countess Spencer, *c.* 1765, this portrait by Pompeo Batoni.

Above left: Lady Georgiana Spencer, by Joshua Reynolds, *c.* 1759-60.

Above right: Lady Georgiana, Lady Henrietta Frances and George John Spencer, Viscount Althorp; the first three children Earl and Countess Spencer; by Angelica Kauffman, 1774.

Left: William Cavendish, 5th Duke of Devonshire; portrait painted in Rome by Pompeo Batoni, 1768.

Above left: Dr Samuel Johnson (1709–1784), a portrait by Joshua Reynolds. Dr Johnson was an early admirer of Georgiana—for her spirit and character—not her looks.

Above right: Portrait of a Gentleman, traditionally identified as Horatio Walpole, (1723–1809); by Pompeo Batoni. Walpole wrote of Georgiana in March 1774, 'She is a lovely girl, natural and full of grace'. *Courtesy Norfolk Museums Service*

Below left: Edmund Burke (right) in conversation with Charles James Fox. In Georgiana's family slang, Fox was 'the Eyebrow'.

Below right: George, Prince of Wales by Thomas Gainsborough, *c.* 1783. In Georgiana's family slang the prince was 'Prinny'.

Above left: Georgiana Cavendish, Duchess of Devonshire, by Thomas Gainsborough, 1783.

Above right: William Cavendish, 5th Duke of Devonshire (1748-1811), by Anton von Maron.

Below left: Lady Elizabeth Foster (1759-1824), 'Bess'; by Joshua Reynolds, 1787.

Below right: A miniature of William Cavendish in the form of an unfinished sketch by Richard Cosway, commissioned by Lady Elizabeth Foster in 1782. This was the same year that Elizabeth, known as 'Bess', met William Cavendish, 5th Duke of Devonshire and his wife, Georgiana at Bath.

Above left: Elizabeth Hervey, née Davers, Countess of Bristol (1733-1800), mother of Lady Elizabeth Foster.

Above right: The Earl Bishop, Frederick Augustus Hervey, 4th Earl of Bristol (1730–1803); Church of Ireland bishop of Derry and father of Lady Elizabeth Foster. It is said that Lord Bristol's knowledge of fine things in Europe and love of travelling and staying in luxury inspired the fashion for naming a hotel the 'Hotel Bristol'. The use of this name is meant to be synonymous with the finest accommodation and living throughout the Continent.

Below left: Lady Louisa Theodosia Hervey (1767-1821), as a child, sister of Bess, who married, 1795, Robert Jenkinson, 2nd Earl of Liverpool; a portrait by Johann Friedrich August Tischbein, 1778.

Below right: Robert Jenkinson, 2nd Earl of Liverpool (1770-1828); by Sir Thomas Lawrence *c.* 1795.

Two political cartoons—two out many, published 20 and 26 April respectively, during the Westminster Election campaign of 1784.

FEMALE INFLUENCE; or, the DEVONS—hire—E CANVAS.

Two more cartoons published 3 April and 10 May respectively. Note the allusions to a butcher and to a kiss.

The POLITICAL SHAVER.

Above: Wife & no wife—or—a trip to the Continent, a cartoon by James Gillray, 27 March 1786. Edmund Burke, dressed as a Jesuit, marries the Prince of Wales and Mrs Fitzherbert. The Prince is about to put the ring on her finger. Fox gives her away, holding her left wrist. Beside him (right) stands Louis Weltje, the Prince's cook in back view but looking to the left at the ceremony. A napkin is under his left arm, bottles project from his coat-pockets, and the tags on his shoulder denote the liveried manservant. To the left of Fox appears the profile of George Hanger, a companion of the Prince of Wales. They became great friends, the prince apparently admiring Hanger's sense of humour and his exploits, both military and with women, and appointing him Equerry in 1791. On the left Lord North sits, leaning against the altar wall, sound asleep, his legs outstretched.

Left: The Prince Regent, by William Beechey, 1803. Beechey gave the first version of this portrait to the Royal Academy in 1798 as his 'Diploma Work' (compulsory donation made upon being elected academician). This repetition was painted in 1803 for the sitter's brother and Queen Victoria's father, Edward, Duke of Kent. *The Royal Collection*

L'ASSEMBLEE NATIONALE. __ or __ Grand Cooperative Meeting at St. Ann's Hill. __ Respectfully Dedicated to the admirers of a Broad Bottom'd Administration

Above: L'Assemblée Nationale. A cartoon by James Gillray, 18 June 1804; a reception given by Mr and Mrs Fox to various groups of the Opposition. Three Grenvilles bow to the host and hostess; the Marquis of Buckingham, wearing his ribbon, holding hat and gold-headed cane and showing a gouty leg and foot, bends low. Next is Lord Grenville, clasping his hat to his breast, more ingratiating but less obsequious than his brother. Next is the stout Lord Temple, awkwardly imitating his uncle's gesture. Fox, wearing a sword, returns Buckingham's bow; on his right stands Mrs Fox, curtseying, and ogling Grenville. On the extreme right is the Prince of Wales. Behind Mrs Fox is a family group: the Duchess of Devonshire, with a fan inscribed 'The Devonshire Delight or the new Coalition Reel', Lady Bessborough wearing a miniature of 'Nelson', and, behind them, their brother, Lord Spencer. In the foreground on the extreme left, the Duke of Bedford, sits at a small table holding out an open book. Next to him sits the Duke of Norfolk, fat and gouty, resting on his knee a frothing tankard of 'Whitbread's Entire'. Behind Norfolk, Sheridan, gross and conspiratorial, offers his snuff-box to Windham.

Right: Charles James Fox, a portrait by Joshua Reynolds, 1783.

Above: A coloured aquatint of Vauxhall Gardens, by Francis Jukes, from a drawing by Thomas Rowlandson. This was published 28 June 1785, but as Dr Johnson had died in December 1784, Rowlandson must have drawn it earlier. It depicts Madame Weichsel on a balcony, with an orchestra behind her. Below is a crowd including some notable personalities of the day. Dining in the box on the left are Boswell, Dr Johnson and Oliver Goldsmith. The two fashionable ladies in the centre are the Duchess of Devonshire and her sister, Lady Bessborough. The Prince of Wales is also in the crowd.

Left: Portrait of a Gentleman, traditionally identified as Richard Brinsley Sheridan (1751–1816), by John Hoppner.

Above left: Henrietta Ponsonby, Viscountess Duncannon, later Countess of Bessborough (1761-1821). Henrietta was born Lady Henrietta Frances Spencer (generally called Harriet). She was the younger sister to Georgiana, Duchess of Devonshire. A mezzotint, after a drawing by John Downman, *c.* 1776.

Above right: Harriet, (Henrietta) Ponsonby; by Angelica Kauffman, 1793. Harriet was a leading figure in society and notorious for her affairs with Richard Brinsley Sheridan and Granville Leveson-Gower, 1st Earl Granville, who became her most enduring lover.

Harriet married, 27 November 1780, Frederick Ponsonby, Viscount Duncannon, the Duke's cousin, even though she was unsure of his character. They quickly became part of the Devonshire House set.

Right: Granville Leveson-Gower (1773-1846), at the time of his mission to St Petersburg, c. 1804, by Sir Thomas Lawrence. His affair with Harriet produced two illegitimate children: Harriet Emma Arundel Stewart and George Stewart.

Left: Harriet, Viscountess Duncannon (later Countess of Bessborough) and her two sons, Frederick and John (later the 4th Earl of Bessborough); by John Hoppner, 1787. Harriet became addicted to gambling and amassed thousands of pounds of debt that she could not afford to pay. Duncannon proved to be an abusive husband, desperate to get his hands on Harriet's financial settlement and frequently Harriet turned to her family for help. They had four children, John William (1781), Frederick Cavendish (1783), Caroline (1785) and William (1787).

Right: Lady Caroline Lamb née Ponsonby (1785- 1828), was the only daughter of Frederick Ponsonby, 3rd Earl of Bessborough and Harriet. She was the niece of Georgiana and cousin (by marriage) of Annabella, Lady Byron. She married, 1805, William Lamb, who was later 2nd Viscount Melbourne and Prime Minister. Caroline and William produced a son, George Augustus Frederick, born 1807, and a premature daughter, born in 1809 who died within 24 hours.

From March to August 1812, Lady Caroline embarked on a well-publicized affair with Lord Byron, subsequently giving Byron what became his lasting epitaph when she described him as 'mad, bad, and dangerous to know'. Lady Caroline and Lord Byron publicly decried each other as they privately pledged their love over the following months. Byron referred to Lamb as 'Caro', which she adopted as her public nickname. After Byron broke things off, her husband took the disgraced and desolated Lady Caroline to Ireland. Detail from a portrait by Thomas Phillips.

Right: Henrietta Elizabeth 'Harriet' Leveson-Gower, Countess Granville, née Cavendish, (1785-1862), 'Harryo' or 'Hary-o'. Harriet was born at Devonshire House, second daughter of William Cavendish, 5th Duke of Devonshire and Georgiana, Duchess of Devonshire. Despite her parents' turbulent marriage, Harriet had a happy childhood. Her mother's death in 1806 led to an unpleasant situation in which her father's long-time mistress Lady Elizabeth Foster took control of the Devonshire household; as the unmarried eldest daughter, this should have been Harriet's role. To help her escape this awkward domestic situation, Harriet's maternal aunt Harriet arranged for her niece to marry her lover of seventeen years, Granville Leveson-Gower, 1st Earl Granville. The couple's marriage proved to be happy, and produced five children.

Below left: Portrait of the Spencer Sisters; Georgiana Duchess of Devonshire and her sister Harriet, by Thomas Rowlandson, 1790.

Below right: Elizabeth, 'Bess' Foster, née Hervey (left with basket) and Georgiana Duchess of Devonshire. In 1809, three years after Georgiana's death in 1806, Bess married William Cavendish, to become the new duchess, but it lasted just two years as he died in 1811. She later lived at Rome. A miniature by Jean-Urbain Guérin, 1791. *Wallace Collection*

Above left: Georgiana, with her infant daughter Lady Georgiana (1783-1858), who was born after nine years of childless marriage. In 1801, Georgiana married George Howard, Viscount Morpeth, later becoming Countess of Carlisle upon her husband's accession in 1825.

Above right: Georgiana, Countess of Carlisle, 1853. She and the Earl had twelve children including the 7th and 8th Earls of Carlisle. Another child, the Duchess of Sutherland, was Mistress of the Robes and a close friend to Queen Victoria.

Below left: Portrait of a Gentleman, said to be the young Charles Grey, later 2nd Earl Grey (1764-1845); Prime Minister 1830-34. Grey met Georgiana in the late 1780s while attending a Whig gathering at Devonshire House. Grey and Georgiana became lovers, and she became pregnant. Grey wanted Georgiana to leave the duke and live with him, but the duke told Georgiana if she did, she would never see her children again.

Below right: Eliza Courtney (1792-1859). Georgiana was sent to France, where she gave birth to a daughter, Eliza, on 20 February 1792 at Aix-en-Provence. Eliza was relinquished, shortly after birth, to the care of Grey's parents. She married, 1814, Lt-Col. Robert Charles Ellice; two sons and three daughters.

Above left: George John Spencer, 2nd Earl Spencer (1758- 1834), styled Viscount Althorp from 1765 to 1783, was Georgiana's brother and a Whig politician. He notably served as Home Secretary from 1806 to 1807 in the Ministry of All the Talents.

Above right: Lavinia Spencer, Countess Spencer, née Bingham (1762–1831), was the eldest daughter of the Irish peer Charles Bingham, 1st Earl of Lucan and his wife, the portrait miniature painter Margaret, née Smyth. She married George John Spencer on 6 March 1782, and the couple had nine children. A portrait by Joshua Reynolds, 1781-82.

Below left: Charles James Fox, a portrait by Karl Anton Hickel, 1794. *National Portrait Gallery.*

Below right: Elizabeth Bridget Armistead (1750–1842). In 1784 or 1785, Fox met and fell in love with Elizabeth, a former mistress of the Prince of Wales. He married her in a private ceremony at Wyton in Huntingdonshire in 1795, but did not make the fact public until October 1802, and Elizabeth was never really accepted at court.

Above left: William Cavendish, 'Hart' (later 6th Duke of Devonshire) when Marquess of Hartington; portrait by Sir Martin Archer Shee, 1805.

Above right: William Spencer Cavendish, 6th Duke of Devonshire (1790-1858), who died unmarried. He intended to marry Lady Caroline Ponsonby, his cousin, but she married William Lamb, which he found devastating. Portrait by Sir Thomas Lawrence.

Below: Granville Leveson-Gower, 1st Earl Granville (1773-1846) and his wife, Lady Harriet Elizabeth Cavendish 'Hary-o' (1785–1862), and their four children; and possibly also his illegitimate son; a portrait by Thomas Phillips, *c.* 1815.

within the bounds of good manners, approved by their acquaintance and agreeable to each other's company, their marriage was undoubtedly a success. It was impossible for him to understand her desire to be articulate—the purpose of conversation was the exchange of opinions, not the discussion of personal relationships.

He saw himself as a student of Shakespeare and a writer of verse; a considerate and courtly man with a perfect knowledge of how life should be lived and of a kind and liberal disposition. He recognized that it was suitable that Chatsworth should be filled with a hundred persons at a time, that sixteen sheep and three bullocks should be slaughtered weekly to feed his guests and household, and that the advantages of their being in residence were essentially felt by the neighbourhood. Providing that he continued the boresome custom of the 'Public Days' there was no call upon him to converse with his neighbour unless he happened to be well acquainted and liked him, and then in common intercourse he preferred to listen, weighing over what was said until he gave his opinions, slowly and generally to the point. To his contemporaries he appeared to 'lack *spring* rather than *sense*,' and this verdict would not have displeased him, for he disliked levity, though, naturally, he enjoyed a joke. He acknowledged willingly that it was right for him to allow numerous pensions of £5 a year to poor people in the village, and provided he was left alone he was pleased to receive their respectful salutations. Fox-hunting was rather too strenuous and undignified a pursuit, but he liked shooting, racing and coursing. In fact, considering his great circumstances, he was a very quiet man, giving no trouble to anyone.

In London, equally, he did not interfere with his wife's occupations; in fact her mode of life fitted in perfectly with his own, for he hated early rising and it had been a real act of condescension to get up at midday to record his vote at St George's, Hanover Square, in order to please Mr Trebeck, the vicar of Chiswick. Normally he preferred to rise at three o'clock, and after breakfasting to take a short ride before dinner at the revolutionary hour of eight. He used then to go to Brooks's, where he remained till four or even five in the morning, letting himself into Devonshire House with his own key, not even requiring a servant to sit up for him.

As was only to be expected, he and his wife found they had less and less in common: she had tried to share his interests and, apart from her extravagance caused by their way of life and the prevalent passion for play, had succeeded fairly well in the early years of their marriage, reading the same books as he and identifying herself with his interest in the Militia and in politics. But soon her interest and political skill had outstripped his own, and her eagerness for him to take an active part could not induce him to make more than a solitary speech. He occupied himself more and more in his own ways so that, though their lives passed under the same roof, they became utterly divergent, the only point of contact being Georgiana's concern that he should be happy and their common affection for Bess.

Georgiana had reached a point in her journey when she felt strangely alone; having so many friends, she yet longed for permanent companionship. Now that she had Bess and her two little daughters, she could not understand why she felt her life to be so empty. She loved best when they were at Chiswick and the children were playing with her in the big blue bow-window of her room; but even then she felt there was something missing. She ascribed her sense of dissatisfaction to her own unworthiness and to her follies and extravagances which she could not control.

It was now that she met a boy with high-tossed head who seemed to beckon and promise her shelter. She hesitated, looking back to her mother and then towards the Duke, but he and Liz were absorbed in each other and did not notice her appeal. She went towards the boy with outstretched hands.

Seventeen eighty-six was to be in many ways the climax of her life: having crossed the plain of her youth, for she was long in maturing, she reached the apex of the ridge which divided her immaturity from fulfilment, but the achievement of that climax led to a narrower, more enclosed country rather than to the promised land of her girlhood.

Though it was in 1786 that she came to know Charles Grey and that he fell in love with her and touched her heart, it was not this unique experience of her life that was to set the year apart—there were a whole series of happenings that interlocked and affected her future. But Grey must be considered first, for he supplies the half-heard theme running through this unhappy year.

The whole of Georgiana's love affair is so obscure, so lost to our sight (for there is no documentary evidence of any kind about it), that it is impossible not to feel, despite efforts to throw light upon it, that it is better left a shadowy thing. That it was so is her tragedy, for the clue to her life is that, lovable and longing for love, love passed her by, and she hardly knew she had been brushed by his wings save for the little cold wind they made in passing. That Grey was her only lover is certain; for, many years after, she herself told her son this, and she would not have made the admission had it not been true. He, in turn, told this to his favourite nephew, Frederick Leveson Gower, and there is every reason for believing it.

Why did Grey, among the many who professed themselves in love with her, alone find the key to Georgiana's heart?

Charles Grey, born on March the 13th, 1764, was her junior by seven years. He met her when he had just completed a brilliant scholastic career, which had prepared him for adventure into politics; but his aim was undecided. He had great physical beauty, was still unformed and intolerant, yet supremely malleable. Thus far his meeting with Georgiana

and hers with Fox run parallel. He was attracted by the tenets and the brilliance of the opposition, and Devonshire House immediately welcomed this young man of promise, sponsored by Fox who recognized his undeveloped gifts. There is abundant contemporary evidence that he was formed by Fox and the Duchess, whose influence endured throughout his career; and the Reform, which they originated, was to be achieved by him long after their deaths. He became the justification and crown of their political beliefs.

When they met she rightly believed him to have need of her, for he made inordinate and insistent demands upon her; enchanted, outraged and shocked by his possessiveness (for all the others had been possessed), she would close her door gently upon his arrogance, only to find his foot farther advanced within her defences.

Or did she know with clarity and bitterness what was taking place? I do not think so. For one thing, she did not yet know that the relationship between herself, Canis and Bess was not the ideal one she had imagined and, even had she done so, it was not in her nature to take either an instinctive or a cynical revenge. Another point is that her mother's precepts and influence were still too close to her heart for her to break her marriage vows without deliberation and enduring remorse. Also she had not yet borne that heir upon which so much depended: her rehabilitation with her husband's family and the releasing of moneys (without which she believed the Duke would be ruined) with which to pay her debts.

All things considered, it would appear that she gave her friendship and advice without stint, finding in his wholehearted admiration and need of her a grateful salve for her wounds, until she realized that he had become more to her than a cherished pupil, and that she loved him. But not yet did she yield to her love.

The Duke saw her constant association with Grey in another light. If his wife were to prove frail, which seemed unthinkable, for he had perfect and well-founded trust in her integrity, it was intolerable that a cub of twenty-two should be his cuckolder. Rather to secure himself from the sly hints at Brooks's than from genuine suspicion or mistrust, the Duke joined the throng who demanded, if not his wife's separation, at least her sequestration from him.

The summer brought no solution. The Devonshires went to Chatsworth and the post-bags were swollen with letters discussing the unsolved problem of Georgiana's future. Sheridan joined them, sympathetic and anxious to help—only too well did he know the odium of debt, and he was devoted to Georgiana. His affectionate, friendly face, which he could never keep straight for long, gave her reassurance and a few moments of gaiety, but he could not find a way out of the maze.

Lord Spencer's suggestion that his sister should make her home with him, would have been acceptable to her, if the separation were insisted upon, had it not been for his shrewish wife, Lavinia. Five years of her criticisms and disapproval—no, that would be too much.

Then Lady Spencer suggested that she and the Duchess should live together at Londesborough. Georgiana expressed her gratitude, and said that of the many suggestions this was the only one she could bear, though of course she knew only too well that the choice did not rest with her sinful self; but might she delay before submitting Mama's proposal to the Duke? He was happier than he had been for some time—quieter and more contented. Not that he had dismissed her problem from his mind, of course, but in his present mood he pushed it away from him.

What had occasioned this change?

On August the 17th Lady Elizabeth arrived at Chatsworth from the Continent. During all September and half October she watched the comedy: she sympathized with the Duke's dilemma, with Sheridan's failure to effect a solution, with Georgiana's anxiety. By October the 16th the Duchess was still uneasy about her affairs—nothing was yet settled or likely to be. Lady Spencer awaited an answer to her proposal.

On November the 15th the trio retired alone to Hardwick—the King-Duke, his disgraced consort and their dearest friend. Bess felt it was time she took an active hand: she suggested an interesting and agreeable book which she and Georgiana would read while the Duke was out shooting, make a synopsis and retail it to him in the evening. Then they would play at cards, and dearest Georgiana, who had so much experience, would instruct poor little Bess how to win at whist. She tinkled with laughter and recounted anecdotes about Naples, and then, probably quite casually, she suggested to the Duke that of course she quite saw the reasons for dearest Georgiana living apart from him, but that it would be very sad, would it not, for then she and he could no longer meet?

Canis was horror-stricken; this aspect of his wife's separation had not occurred to him; re-enchanted once more by Bess, the prospect of losing her seemed intolerable.

'And then,' Bess whispered, 'we are not without blame. After all ...'

It would appear that it was about this time that she told Georgiana that she hoped she had made the Duke see reason, and that she confessed to the birth of Caroline St Jules.

The hurt and shock to Georgiana must have been almost mortal. She was neither ignorant nor a prude, but she was innocent and an idealist, and the pain was in finding that the relationship which she had believed so ideal, so unique, was terrestrial and commonplace.

Whatever happened at Hardwick between November the 15th and December the 6th, something took place between the three that caused the vexed question of Georgiana's separation to be abandoned; something that altered the tone of her letters from that time so that they take on a different key; they are quieter and harder, their original bloom of candour has gone and instead there is a melancholy resignation and gentle disillusion. Also from this time it is clear that she knew of the existence of Caroline St Jules, though she does not admit her knowledge of the child's parentage.

At the end of the year she made a resolve to embrace a real spirit of exertion and reform, but she doubted any chance of becoming pregnant until her nerves were much stronger.

Early in the New Year, which she hoped would be so different from its forerunner, the Devonshires journeyed to London, posting over a hundred miles in one day.

Life began once more, but on a different plane.

The Prince, who was plunged in the deepest financial crisis of his life, again incurred the Duchess's displeasure. She and all her set were shocked by the events in the House of Commons, when Fox, asking that the Prince's debts should be paid, gave a categorical denial that any marriage had taken place. Grey and Sheridan were both involved in the undignified and hypocritical proceedings instigated by the Prince; this caused a breach between Fox and Mrs Fitzherbert (who was assured by the Prince that Fox 'had exceeded his instructions') and a wider and more serious chasm opened in the Whig party: the women supporting Mrs Fitzherbert and the men Fox, while Sheridan remained the only link between them.

Not only did the Prince shock Georgiana by his public behaviour and disloyalties, but he played another of his small scurvy tricks upon her: he had a certain living in his gift which Lady Spencer was anxious should be bestowed on a worthy clergyman with a large family in whom she was interested. She asked Georgiana to approach the Prince, who immediately promised the living to Lady Spencer's protégé. Lady Spencer was delighted and the impoverished cleric overwhelmed with gratitude; but the official notification of the benefice did not materialize. Instead the Prince sent the Duchess a present of a diamond key, and at the same time she learned that he had given the living to another. It was really too bad ... she ought to have known that he never kept a promise ... she was a fool to have believed in him. She sent Lady Spencer money for the poor parson, sold the diamond key for his profit (for it was rightly his), and promised to find him another living. Really her erstwhile 'Brother' was beyond the pale.

However, on the whole, the first half of the year passed pleasantly enough between Bath, London, Cheltenham and Newmarket. In March, thanks to Mr Heaton's spirit of order and regularity in business, Martindale the banker was paid. There were still large sums owing, for, needless to say, Georgiana had not made a full confession of her debts; but her chief anxiety was allayed, though false reports ran through London that she had lost £4,000 at Newmarket and a like sum to Lady Essex.

There was one disagreeable incident caused by Georgiana's good nature and sense of justice. Lady Spencer's sister-in-law, Mrs Isabella Poyntz, had a daughter, another 'Georgiana' known as 'Jockey,' who was married to Frederick Fawkener. Jockey and John Townshend fell in love and there was a divorce. The Duchess was accused of complicity, and the Duke for once emerges from obscurity. He wrote to Mr Fawkener with great dignity and sense, defending his wife from the accusations levelled against her, and identifying himself with her. Although the guilty pair were now married, the Spencer family were shocked and horrified; it was agreed that Jockey could not yet be received in Society, and Lord Spencer exacted a promise from the Duchess that she would not call upon her. Mr Fawkener was constantly with Mrs Poyntz, who was as ardent in her defence of him as she was adamant in her refusal to regard Jockey any longer as her daughter. Then Georgiana learned that poor Jockey was miserable at her ostracism and her mother's attitude and went to see her. She comforted Jockey, dissuaded her from writing to her mother, which the Duchess insisted would be useless until Mr Fawkener left England, and having played the Good Samaritan was stricken with remorse. She had broken her word to her brother, her aunt was 'outrageous' with her and the Duke blamed her, not for her visit but for breaking her promise. She wrote imploring Lady Spencer's advice and forgiveness, 'but what you have often told me is very true—I come too late when the mischief is done.'

Lady Spencer acted with justice and kindness; Georgiana was to write to her brother confessing her action and, in future, she must try to consider consequences before it was too late, but it was evident from the tone of Lady Spencer's letter that, she thought her daughter a better Christian than her sister-in-law.

The last act ended happily, as is proper to comedies: Jockey and her John had a baby girl; the Duke and Duchess stood as godparents, thereby reconciling the Dowager Lady Townshend to her disgraceful daughter-in-law; but stipulating that Jockey must still remain in retirement. The unrelenting mother poured out expostulations to her niece for condoning immorality and inflicting injustice on 'nice and good people,' and the Duchess, secure in the knowledge that she was acting with the support and approval of her mother and her husband, turned, rent and banished her from the scene.

All was well that ended well. The Devonshires and Lady Spencer went to Chatsworth. Curiously enough, Lady Spencer left on October the 20th and Lady Elizabeth Foster arrived on the 23rd.

The ballroom, Devonshire House. The furniture was removed when balls were due to be held.

11

Rachel and Leah

The arrival of Liz was a triumphal entry. The Duke's spirits soared; he played cards, read and rode with her, and Georgiana's headaches, to which she had always been subject, became acute.

She had always ascribed these headaches to nerves, and indeed they were more frequent when she was worried or distressed. She could not understand why she was so afflicted now that she had so much cause for happiness and content—the worst of her debts were paid, she was with her children, her husband and her friend. But Chatsworth was somehow different from last year, though then she had been so miserable she had wished she could die. Now it was as though she gazed at those lovely woods, those splashing fountains, through clouded glasses. Everything seemed lower in tone, and she had little zest for life.

Her mind went back to the party she had given in May for Madame de Polignac and Comte Fersen: of the faro table in her room, the dancing, the supper in the hall, and she remembered her fête at Chiswick stirring enthusiasm in her visitors from France and how they had admired England and freedom. She thought of her thirtieth birthday and how she had then resolved to bid adieu to many, many follies as a great period of her life was over, and believing that reflection would help her to surmount too great a love of dissipation, admiration and dress. She believed that she was sick of these—or was she sick of life itself?—but she hoped to renounce those follies that arose from the impulse of the moment, from a careless and unthinking head.

Above all, she thought of Bess, Canis and herself. She was not jealous, she could not be jealous, for had not her greatest happiness been the companionship and affection her husband and her friend found in each other? But something had changed now—she tried to explain it to herself and failed. She felt torn in two parts: on one side was her instinctive revulsion from an association that with her upbringing, her belief in her mother, she knew to be immoral; on the other was Bess's fascination for her, the fact that Bess had brought her, not only closer to her husband, but was actually the magnet who had drawn her children into being. But Bess and Canis had brought another child into being. Could it be that she was jealous of that child? No, she thought, no—never could I be so wicked as to be jealous of a child.

How best to resolve this conflict was her problem. What was she to do? If she denied Bess, she denied her closest friend and destroyed her husband's greatest happiness. She would be separated from him and her beloved children today had it not been for Bess's influence. She herself had still to bear that son. She wondered how much longer she could endure the polite and recurrent inquiries of the Portlands, the George Cavendishes, of Lavinia Spencer and the county.

If she were great enough to realize that Canis and Bess were necessary to each other, that therefore their love could not be regarded as sinful, would she not, perhaps—perhaps be rewarded by a son?

Utterly perplexed, blinded by the pain in her head and the ache in her heart, she finally came to an important decision; she must go against her mother's fundamental teaching.

It has rightly been said that people can only be judged according to the customs of their own times. Today, she would have left her husband, thrown in her lot with Grey and started life afresh. Had she done so then, or had she even gone to live with her mother, she would have been cut off from all her friendships, and she was gregarious by nature; she would have had to live in an atmosphere of seclusion and austerity and, worst of all, she would have been for ever separated from her beloved children. In her state of nerves and unhappiness it was impossible even to contemplate such a future.

Early in January she wrote to Lady Spencer that Bess was to go abroad and that she and the Duke were to accompany her on part of her journey. Lady Spencer replied, expressing her strongest disapproval of this plan.

'But it would occasion my being out of town—I am extremely anxious to accompany Bess on her road, it would be the greatest comfort to me. The sea voyage might occasion my breeding—the expense would be trifling. Please, Mama, *please.*'

Lady Spencer, however, was adamant; she, and the necessity for the Duke to attend Warren Hastings's trial, won the day. All the same, the

Devonshires accompanied Bess as far as Dover, staying with her two days until the wind was favourable, before returning, as amateurs of oratory rather than interested witnesses of history, to be present at the Hastings trial.

In May Bess bore a son—Leah and not Rachel had triumphed once again. The boy, unlike his sister, was given a name which indicated his parentage; he was called Augustus Clifford, for the Duke's mother had been Baroness Clifford. Less than two months after his birth, Bess returned to England and Devonshire House.

That summer there were two new visitors to Chatsworth—Monsieur and Madame de Calonne. The ex-advocate-and procurator-general, now in exile, was to replay in Georgiana's life, though on another scale, the part he had played in the finances of France. His brilliant but unsubstantial qualities had not been of the kind to bring order into the chaos of French finance. Eventually, when he found that his policy of growing expenditure and extended credits had hopelessly increased the problems of the Treasury, he had proposed to the Assembly of Notables suppression of all privileges and that taxes should be levied on all property without distinction. The howls of fury that greeted his proposals caused him to expose the national bankruptcy. Alienated from the Court, he was exiled to Lorraine, and thence made his way to England, being soon invited to Chatsworth.

Georgiana, charmed by his sympathy and with implicit trust in his natural financial genius, confided to him her money troubles and asked for loans and advice. Though she had practically given up gambling, the interest on her earlier and still unadmitted debts was crippling. She was in urgent need of money. Like Marie Antoinette who, when she had asked him for a large sum, had added, 'Ce que je vous demande est peut-être bien difficile,' Georgiana apologized for her request, and Calonne made her much the same reply as he had given to the Queen. 'Madame,' he said, 'si cela n'est que difficile, c'est fait; si cela est impossible, nous verrons.' It seemed to Calonne the most natural thing in the world that the Duchess should want money and that she should ask him for it, for he believed that 'a man who wishes to borrow money must appear to be rich, and in order to appear rich, it is necessary to make a display of expenditure. Economy is doubly fatal; it warns the capitalist not to lend to a treasury involved in debt; it causes the arts to languish, while prodigality enriches them.' He could not have given the spendthrift Duchess worse, or more acceptable, advice.

So relieved was she to be saved once more from exposure, that she took to writing her 'little' verses again; brushed up her grammar in order to teach little G., and sent an example of her parsing for Lady Spencer to correct.

Her headaches, however, grew worse and more frequent. She was terrified lest she would have one during the approaching centenary celebrations of the Glorious Revolution. Once more M. de Calonne gave her advice. 'Eat roast chicken only,' he said. 'I once cured an obstinate and painful stomach complaint by eating three hundred and sixty-five roast chickens in a year.'

Georgiana, therefore, ate roast chickens and saved her eyesight by employing Charlotte William, now promoted to Chatsworth, as secretary.

The preparations were tremendous: every inch of orange ribbon in Derbyshire was snatched up, and poor, sallow Mrs Heaton was forced to make-do with scarlet substitutes. The whole great house was in turmoil; there was to be a great ball and then a procession and jubilations at Chesterfield. Chatsworth flamed with orange: the maids' caps and aprons, the footmen's shoulder-knots, all sported orange favours, while Georgiana, encouraged by M. de Calonne's philosophy, and justified by her position and politics, devised an extravagantly magnificent costume. Dressed in this, she was drawn to Chesterfield in the state coach, the horses and postilions all decked in orange and accompanied by great Whigs and small: Cavendishes, Osbornes and Molyneuxs heading the cavalcade of eight 'Revolution Clubs' with their flags and emblems.

In London, the Duke of Portland took the chair at a banquet of the Whig Club at the 'Crown and Anchor' in the Strand. Sheridan made an eloquent speech, suggesting and carrying a proposal that the statue of the hero of the Revolution should be erected on Romney Mead. The triumphant Whigs challenged Pitt to combat.

England rang to the chorus of 'Fall, tyrants, fall, fall, fall ...,' and it seemed that heaven heard the invocation with commendable promptitude, for two days after the Devonshires' Ball, the Duke of Portland sent an urgent summons to his brother-in-law at Chatsworth to come to London as the King was reported to be very ill.

Canis, who hated any hurried decision and had planned to go to Buxton, refused to go, though Whig hopes ran high at the long-deferred prospect of power under a patron-King.

Portland sent more insistent messages, and on November the 19th the news was so critical that Georgiana and the Duke hurried to London, driving all night and arriving exhausted at six in the morning.

They were told that the King had had a less restless night than the preceding one, but was still in a feverish state. To this official bulletin was added the report that His Majesty was 'very mad indeed.' Parliament was adjourned for a fortnight and then there was to be a full attendance.

The same night Devonshire House was thronged with people. Now that the crisis had come, pity and distress for the King were general, though many of the stories about his frenzy were so ludicrous that it was impossible not to smile. Every sort of anecdote and rumour was afoot and the London fog was full of whispers.

These whispers had first been heard the previous May. Then various causes of the King's derangement had been suggested. The favourite of these were that he was suffering from hereditary gout which had settled in his head; that he had sucked in madness from a lunatic wet-nurse, and that indulgence in quack medicines had brought it on.

During the summer the King had been taken to Cheltenham; but as he was observed embroidering with the young Court ladies, and running a race against a horse, his amelioration was doubtful. Certainly the King's madness brought a lightness and fantasy into his staid and ordered life, though, naturally, his entourage did not see it in this light. He would pretend to play the fiddle; he showed West how to mix his colours and demonstrated with his foot; he was star-ridden—'Hush, hush,' he would say, 'don't talk about stars.... You know I am Mopsimus and don't like French mottoes.' He pulled off Sir George Baker's wig and forced him to star-gaze on his knees. With unwonted imagination he declared Lady Pembroke to be Esther, and the Queen, Vashti. When Dr Warren was called in, he addressed him as 'Sir Richard Rascal.'

Back at Windsor, he dictated Cervantes and the Bible simultaneously and at incredible speed. He was equally given to creating his pages Baronets and Knights of the Holy Roman Empire, and to attacking them with physical fury.

These, and many other stories, were recounted at Devonshire House, and the assembly were unanimous in their opinion that, if not a new King, a Regent was at hand. Georgiana decided to keep a diary.

This diary, published by Mr Sichel as an appendix to his life of Sheridan, has a double interest: firstly from its day-to-day account of the Regency intrigues, written in the very centre of the storm; and secondly because its preface, written thirteen years later, shows Georgiana's political and personal views of both the principles and protagonists of the drama.

The Whiggish creed of putting Parliament and the Constitution first and individual interests second was theoretically sound but impracticable. The party members, having been so long in opposition, save for their deplorable administration in 1783, naturally thirsted for power. The weakness of the Regency intrigues lay in the Whigs' inability to sink their individual ambitions. Sheridan's unshakable character of personal honesty and the integrity of his own opinions threw his colleagues into confusion and common mistrust. The strength of his character was also his weakness, for it betrayed the flaws in his party. This was recognized by Georgiana, who, in her preface to her diary, acquits him of duplicity and is convinced of the honour of his sentiments. As this preface was written after the breach between Fox and Sheridan, it is largely coloured and biased by Fox, for she went on to say that Sheridan could not resist playing a sly game alone, though, actually, he was continually used as a cat's-paw.

History was to repeat itself: Sheridan's defence of the Prince at the time of his marriage to Mrs Fitzherbert, and now his secret negotiations, commissioned by his leaders, both drew upon him the blame of having committed his friends.

From thirteen years' distance, Georgiana remembered four points of interest. She was chiefly impressed by her husband's and her brother's conduct; she lamented the entire destruction of the Rockinghams, and of the Duke of Portland's 'dereliction from those highly valued original principles' of the Whigs. She also blamed him for abandoning his friends. Above all were sown those 'seeds of disunion among the Whigs which operated so fatally' for the party and the country. She remembered as outstanding characters the young Duke of Bedford, who 'was very eager on the subject,' and Grey, 'who gave proof of his talents, integrity and attachment to Fox and also of the imprudent warmth and eagerness that afterwards was the means of his being so shamefully misrepresented and misunderstood.'

Actually, at the time, the stage was so crowded that it was impossible to distinguish the merits of the players.

The course of events from November to January fell into 'two Epochas,' the first being that period when there seemed to be no doubt of the Prince becoming Regent. Therefore the formation of a new administration occupied all minds, and produced the rivalry and anxiety which ever attend a new Ministry. The Duke of Portland, on whom the mantle of leader would naturally fall, was advised by his wife 'not to be Minister, unless the proposal came absolutely from ye Prince himself,' as it was supposed the Prince was still angry with him for having opposed the payment of his debts. Though the Whigs intended to form the new administration on 'the true Rockingham principles,' they were constantly diverted by such questions as whether Lord John Cavendish, Sheridan or Grey was to be Chancellor. M. de Calonne reported that the City was in favour of Lord

John; Sheridan said he preferred to attain such a post 'by degrees and when he had proved his capabilities to the public'; Grey arrogantly said he would be content to be either Chancellor or Secretary for War, but nobly added that he would stand aside for Lord John, Fox or Sheridan, but not for 'those Norfolks, Wyndhams and Pelhams.'

Fox was absent in Italy from these preliminary skirmishes. He reached England after a journey of eight days from Bologna, so thin and tired that he liked people to talk to him in order 'to avoid thinking, which puzzled him.'

The Prince, who apart from some evidence of thoughtlessness was acting reasonably and with some degree of dignity, sent a message to Portland 'cancelling all former discontents,' and summoned the Cabinet that they might verify the King's disorder and take charge of him.

His Majesty's condition did not improve: he nearly set the Queen on fire; he took the Duke of York's regiment away from him as a punishment for removing the fireirons; he ordered a tye-wig and danced with Dr Reynolds. Also in attendance were Dr Addington, Pitt's family physician, Dr Warren and Dr Willis the alienist. On December the 1st, Dr Warren told the Duchess that the King might improve but that he thought it improbable.

Night after night Sheridan, Fitzpatrick, Grey, Calonne, 'Fish' Crawfurd and Fox met at Devonshire House, where they would pool their news and weave the tangled threads of prospective office into an inextricable maze.

The real issue lay between Fox and Pitt, the former insisting on the natural and undeniable right of the Prince to act as Regent; Pitt denying this.

Standing aloof and inscrutable was Lord Chancellor Thurlow. When he had first seen the poor King in his madness, he was so deeply affected that he allowed himself to have an attack of hysterics and 'iron tears rained down Pluto's cheeks.' He realized clearly that were the Queen and the Prince, or the Prince alone, appointed Regents, he would in truth 'cease to make that impression' he had long enjoyed; it was unthinkable to him to be bereft of power, and soon he sent Sheridan a message saying he was 'not a party man.' Sheridan, taking the hint, visited him in secret to find out how the land lay. Fox, discovering this on his return, was furious with Sherry for treating with the enemy, but Sheridan convinced him that only by bringing Thurlow over to their side could they hope to defeat Pitt. Though Sheridan was depressed and hurt by Fox's attitude of censure, he was sure he had acted rightly, and soon Lord Thurlow and the Prince were closeted together. The Prince was no match for the wily, brilliant

Chancellor, who easily convinced the young man that he might expect the same support as he had previously given his royal father. Fox, therefore, on December the 13th, reluctantly sent Sheridan with a written proposal to Thurlow, Sherry protesting it was too late as Hurlo-Thrumbo had openly pledged himself to support the Statute of Limitations. They were together from three till ten o'clock at night. Thurlow assured Sheridan that he was bound to uphold the limitations to the Prince's Regency, but suggested that Sheridan could undermine Fox's opposition. Though Sheridan was furious, he concealed his anger. Thurlow went on to divulge Pitt's plans, the chief of which was that the Queen should control the royal household for six months. After all, there should be no difficulty about this, as the King's madness had largely healed the antagonism between mother and son.

'And what will become of your head when he is King?' asked Sheridan.

'You may hang the Chancellor, but you cannot alter the law,' replied Thurlow.

Although Sheridan came away convinced that the Chancellor was 'a great rogue,' the result of the interview was that he had accepted the view that the best thing for the Prince was for him to accept the limitation of peerages. This would mean that, though Regent, he would be unable to create a majority favourable to him in the Upper House. Fox was bitterly opposed to this concession, and the Whigs were thrown into worse confusion than ever.

Thurlow surveyed the scene and smiled sardonically when Sheridan told him that his faction proposed employing Georgiana to convert Fox. 'Ah,' said Pluto, 'she would have been a powerful, indeed almost an irresistible advocate.' He was completely satisfied with his work: he had both his opponents and his allies in a state of confusion from which only he could extricate them.

The reports varied from day to day: the King was better; he was much worse; he was recovering; he was tied down to his bed.

At Devonshire House persons and offices were shuffled like cards, but no one dealt a playable hand.

On December the 31st Pitt sent the Prince a letter 'insolently couch'd,' stipulating peerages, Patent places and the Household under control of the Queen. The Whigs considered a way to arrange that the Prince's reply, which was to be 'a noble one,' be made public.

Burke first drafted this reply—it was 'all fire and tow.' Loughborough attempted another—it was 'all ice and snow.' Sheridan was deputed to make both into one, and it was due to be ready by January the 2nd. He worked on the famous answer all New Year's Night at Devonshire House, his fire and style animating and dominating the whole. By his side sat his wife, copying the pages as they fell still wet from his quill. His promise to have the reply ready by the 2nd was pinned up on Fox's mantelpiece, but it was a composition that needed much time and thought. Also he was sent on various missions by the party. Finally it was finished, and in so masterly a fashion that it has always been attributed to Burke, until the publication of Georgiana's diary made it certain that Sheridan was the author.

Burke was furious that his original reply had not been considered good enough, and quarrelled with Sheridan. Everybody's nerves were on edge. Fox quarrelled with Sherry and made it up again: the Prince quarrelled with him and then was reconciled. They were all wrangling in an undignified squabble and scramble for places which made them appear, not as statesmen, but naughty, selfish children. Only Sheridan's good humour and Georgiana's tact kept the party together. For, impetuous and unthinking as she was in private life, there is not a single instance of her acting either indiscreetly or tactlessly when politics were concerned.

On January the 6th the House decided on a report of the King's condition by a committee of physicians; a new issue had been invented, for while the Whigs believed him incurable, the Tories were sanguine that he would recover.

Overstrung nerves and frayed tempers caused accusations, denials and counter-accusations to follow one another with blinding rapidity. It was a disgraceful mêlée. Georgiana's diary is a breathless confusion.

When the King's partial recovery revived the hopes of Pitt's friends, the opposition seemed only to differ on the part the Prince and themselves were to take.

Thurlow, the only man who had preserved his balance on the dubious fence, lifted his eyes to heaven in full view of the House, vowing, 'When I forget my King, may my King forget me.'

'He'll see you damned first,' growled Wilkes audibly. The Whigs were reunited, but the essential unity of the party was gone for ever.

From Georgiana's summing-up of the events of 1788–9 we may trace:

... the facility with which the Prince yields to the pleasure of making himself agreeable to those with whom he happens to associate—his aptitude to yield over his better opinions to foolish and even ridiculous counsellors if they happen to convince him. ... the same facility that made him promise places in the Regency, has since driven him into Society and Manners unworthy of him, for his talents are good, and his manner and deportment superior in grace to any thing I ever saw. And however he may have appear'd to deviate from strict honor, or to be capricious & unsteady, I cannot believe his heart to be bad—but he has obeyed the Star of the moment which has unfortunately been in a general Malignant.

Rereading her diary she finds that:

We can trace in these fragments, the Virtues & foibles of Mr Fox, the comprehensive mind, undaunted genius, & unabating kindness which added to the most unaffected simplicity, constitute his Character, but we may also trace ... a contempt for even neccessary expedients, a great imprudence in conversation and above all, a fear of seeming to yield what he thinks right to the bias of public opinion. ... [I had] long lamented, and often been provok'd with his negligence, sometimes even to decent attention ... [but] I must say that this kind of carriage in a Man whose Idol was popularity, is perhaps the greatest proof of the real greatness of his mind—& must give security to the sentiments he possesses.

Finally she says that she:

must ever regret the loss of the Rockingham phalanx, who were ever ready to secure the Constitution on the basis established at the Revolution. For it appears to me that the overthrow from French principles, so far from giving rise to more power in the Crown, ought to make us more jealous to keep our own within the limits which alone have seem'd capable of binding & uniting the genius & sentiments of Englishmen.

The tumult having died down, Canis, who had steadily refused to be drawn into any of these imbroglios, decided to go abroad.

12

The Hollow Crown

The visit to Spa was planned in the hope that it would cure the Duke's ever-increasing gout, and that the waters and the change of air would result in the Duchess becoming pregnant. M. de Calonne was an advocate of the move.

On the last day of his visit to Chatsworth the previous October, Georgiana had written him a letter. In it she expressed her gratitude for his help and understanding and told him how her superficial gaiety screened her terrors and fears. She assured him that her greatest wish was to live quietly with her husband, her children and her friend, and he was probably the only person who could bring this about; for without his financial assistance, her debts must have been disclosed, which disclosure would result in her ruin and separation from her family. She proposed that he should meet another of her true friends and believed that between them they could secure her peace.

This friend was Mr Thomas Coutts, the banker, and he was indeed the best friend she ever had. Early in 1787 she had confided in Mr Coutts, who had not only advanced her money, but had given her both wise, fatherly advice and his loyal and undying friendship. He had spoken and written to her frankly, setting forth the horrible dangers to which she was exposing herself by gambling, predicting her future ruthlessly, foretelling the ruin of her health and character, if she did not forswear play and curb her natural generosity which, though he deplored, he could not help admiring. He reminded her that she, above all other women, enjoyed titles, character, friends, fortune, power and beauty. To these—we fear as an after-thought—he added conjugal happiness. He assured her that she risked all these advantages, save the first, if she persisted in her destructive passion for play. He implored her to set her house and heart in order. He himself would teach her the value and management of money. He placed all his knowledge and experience at her disposal if she would only listen to him.

Appreciating his candour and desire to help her and touched by his goodness, she replied with gratitude, assuring him that her gambling was a thing of the past. In future she always wrote to him as a fond but errant child, and often signed her letters as his 'ever affectionate eldest daughter.' Nevertheless, like many affectionate children, she listened to parental advice but did not act upon it.

Recognizing the qualities of these two men, she hoped that by bringing together the two financial geniuses, so different in their character and outlook, they would resolve her difficulties. Unhappily her debts by now had acquired a malignant life of their own. These evil weeds, sprung from the few early seeds she had thoughtlessly sown, had spread and multiplied, sending out suckers in all directions, the new shoots nourishing their begetters, until they had formed an impenetrable jungle. She was never certain of, nor could she bear to explore, the extent of this jungle. She would venture in a little distance, assuring whichever helper accompanied her that the clearing ahead was the limit of the forest: and would then retreat, hoping that the growth had been cleared away, only to find she was hemmed in on another side. She would confess to Mr Heaton and the Duke a certain amount; another sum to M. de Calonne; a third to Mr Coutts; she would borrow from her brother, her oculist, her doctor; but she was unable to admit the full extent of her liabilities. By forgetting them, she hoped they would lose heart and die. Had she brought herself to a full recognition and confession of her liabilities, marshalling her helpers together, they could have razed the haunted forest to the ground. But she lacked the strength of mind to disclose her weakness.

All through the time of the Regency intrigues, she had been in constant communication with M. de Calonne and Mr Coutts. In March, when the visit to Spa had been determined upon, she asked the former whether he could procure a further sum which would settle her most pressing debts and thus enable her to go abroad. She recognized that he must have some security beyond her gratitude and sense of indebtedness, and that her husband must be told of the pecuniary aid she had received from him. She went on to say that the doctors hoped that the treatment at Spa would result in her bearing a son. Should she become pregnant, she would immediately inform the Duke of *all*, since the birth of a son would bring their troubles to an end, as a direct heir to the Dukedom would release entailed moneys. In case this happy solution did not take place, she promised to tell the Duke in precisely a year's time. She would even leave a letter behind her, confessing the extent of her indebtedness to M. de Calonne and copies of the receipts of moneys which he had lent her. Lady Elizabeth knew of all these negotiations.

There remained one other matter which had to be attended to before the Devonshires could leave England.

For some time Lady Spencer had been more definite in the expression of her disapproval of Bess's association with her daughter and son-in-law. She refused to meet her under their roof. As Lady Elizabeth was always with them, Lady Spencer's absence became extremely obvious, as formerly she had been a constant visitor, and when in London she had nearly always stayed at Devonshire House. Now she preferred to be in Bolton Street, and refused even to dine with the Devonshires if Bess were present. Georgiana felt that, apart from the gossip caused by Lady Spencer's attitude, she could not bear to be wholly separated from her mother; in her extremely nervous and agitated condition she felt more need of her than ever before. She therefore implored her mother to visit her and the babies of a morning; she assured her that she would order her day to her mother's convenience. She would give small, quiet dinners and whist parties for Lady Spencer and her friends, and only sometimes, for otherwise it would be too obvious, would Bess be present.

Georgiana pleaded with such good effect that Lady Spencer agreed, with extreme reluctance, to enter Devonshire House.

Her occasional calls, and the fact of her living in Bolton Street, did not allay the gossip. Nothing could do this but that Lady Spencer should receive Lady Liz *chez elle*.

Finally, moved by her daughter's pleadings, she agreed that Georgiana might bring Bess and Canis to spend one night at St Albans. Georgiana's gratitude was painful to witness. She knew her mother so well, and therefore recognized how much this concession had cost her. Never had their relationship been so clearly defined.

It was a curious evening: the Duke, heavy and silent; Bess, servile and effusive (her servility and effusion doing her little good with her hostess); and Georgiana, humble and grateful. Lady Spencer, who never varied in her manner, was as always well-bred and self-contained. Perhaps, but only perhaps, she was a shade more astringent than usual.

Magnanimity and good manners had prevailed; convention had triumphed and the Devonshires were free to go abroad. On Friday, June the 24th, they set out.

The party consisted of the Duke, the Duchess and Bess. With them was also Charlotte William, the development of whose character was not entirely satisfactory. She had been for some time with the Duchess at Chatsworth and in London, and it was now decided to settle her in some suitable establishment in Paris. Paris, therefore, was to be their first port of call.

Though for the past five or six years constant rumours of changes and disturbances in France had reached the Devonshires, they had been reassured by the amusing and malicious anecdotes of the Court given them by M. de Calonne. He had etched for them biting little descriptions of the King: how Louis, bored to death at the Council meetings, had either fallen asleep or occupied himself by cutting his nails and picking the pomatum out of his hair. He had recounted how His Majesty loved to sing, and how the Queen refused to allow him to do so, as his voice was hoarse and out of tune. M. de Calonne added that in Chapel, where the Queen could not interfere, a strange harsh voice would ring out, dominating all others. Even the national bankruptcy and M. de Calonne's disgrace were explained away by the blindness and selfishness of the nobles and clergy who would not agree to be taxed. However, the accounts given by M. de Fersen and Mme de Polignac the previous summer had done much to allay apprehensions in Devonshire House that there was something rotten in the state of France.

They were therefore somewhat unprepared for the news they received from Lord Tichfield on their meeting at Clermont three days after they had left Dover. He gave them some very strange accounts of, Paris, and told them that the King had prevented the Tiers État from meeting and intended to dissolve the assembly. At Chantilly the next day they heard more: that Necker had been dismissed and that their arrival would coincide with a moment of great change. It was all rather vague and ominous. At Paris, the same evening, they learned that the King had addressed the Tiers, admonishing them as to their proceedings and ordering them to desist. After he had left, the Tiers annulled by vote everything he had done or said. There were reported to be 25,000 men at Versailles and that all was very quiet. They did not recognize the unholy quiet that comes just before a storm.

However, the next day it was hard to believe in the gravity of these reports: it was June, and June in Paris with the sun shining on the chestnuts and the high mansard roofs is holiday-time. The Duchess's ante-room was crowded with stay-makers, milliners, bonnet, dress- and mantua-makers. Mlle Bertin herself waited upon her old client, hoping for new orders and the settlement of old accounts. The deeper tones of the jewellers and coiffeurs blended with the shrill voices of the modistes. Her Grace protested that she was in mourning and had neither the means nor the occasion for extravagance. They denied her, laughingly: they knew her Grace of old, her exquisite taste and her generous patronage. She bought but little—a cloak and a snuff-box for mama; some fine, coloured sand for the babies to sprinkle over their childish letters and a sheaf of miniature note-paper, as tiny and multi-coloured as the petals of field flowers, on which to write to them. She added three fans; one for her sister and two for G. and Hary-o. (Where are they now, those fans that spread their painted vanes like butterflies on the sunny morning of June the 24th, 1789?) She wrote to Lady Duncannon of the new coiffures and said that she believed the bustle was doing her good.

Later she set out to pay calls on many old friends. Mesdames de Talleyrand, de Coigny, de Boufflers and de Chabannes welcomed her delightedly. They admired her beauty and charm, and they were deeply devoted to Lady Spencer, agreeing with Miss Burney that her sensible and sagacious character, intelligent, polite and agreeable, made her one of the most exemplary women of rank, while her quick; logical mind and preference for conversation rather than play had always appealed to them. Of all Englishwomen, Lady Spencer was the one who was the most at home in the incisive, cultured society of Paris. So Georgiana was doubly welcome, and when she produced the miniature of her two little girls, their smiling faces and baby charms called forth cries of admiration. It seemed so short a time since Georgiana and Harriet had been equally admired by these same women in the same elegant rooms; now it was the turn of their namesakes.

She expressed a wish to see her dear friend, Mme de Polignac, at Versailles, but they shook their heads and advised her to defer her visit: the tumults had increased so much that it was difficult to get there—indeed, a coach belonging to the Archbishop of Paris, they believed, had been held up by the mob who thought it was the King's. Still, in a day or two ...

Evidently the alarms were exaggerated, for the very next day she and Bess went to Versailles, as well as the two days following. At night they went to the theatre, making use of either the Comte d'Artois's or the Duc d'Orléans's box. The theatres were crowded and gay: after the play they would dress and pay visits. Large dinners and assemblies were given for the two lovely Englishwomen; they met their old, friends of the Noblesse and the latest recruits to the ranks of Elégants and Elégantes. Georgiana argued furiously with Messieurs de Lafayette and de Noailles, defending the Court policy on account of her friendship with Mme de Polignac and the Queen, while the men found it amusing and smart to side with the Tiers État. They went on delicious expeditions in the Bois; an immense aristocratic company driving in coaches and calèches and riding on horseback; they visited Bagatelle; with the Duke as escort they strolled in the Champs Elysées, the Tuileries and the Palais Royal. They received visits at home: took Mr Coutts's three charming daughters to the play and gave a great dinner to their compatriots. And to her 'Dearest G.,' on a little piece of shiny yellow paper, edged with pink and black spots, the Duchess wrote that she had seen:

> ... some very curious beasts in the King of France's Menagerie—a Rhinoceros—very ugly, large and cover'd with scales—a lyoness, very fond of a little dog that lives with her. A Porcupine cover'd with sharp quills and a pelican, a pretty white bird who is suppos'd to bleed itself to feed its little ones.... God bless you my
> Dear little girl
>
>   G. D.

Versailles itself appeared exactly as Georgiana remembered it, apart from a new, delicious mock hamlet by the lake in the Petit Trianon; but its inhabitants had altered. Not little Mme de Polignac who was as gay and bird-like as ever, but the King and Queen had changed. Georgiana was shocked in the alteration in Marie Antoinette, who had grown stout and lost all her hair, though her *éclat* was as great as ever. The Queen was gracious and friendly, inquiring affectionately after Lady Spencer, and she, too, admired the children's portrait. Naturally, she was depressed by the events of the times. Only the day before she received Georgiana (who had then been walking in the Trianon), the populace had broken into the Palace, but had been appeased by the sight of the Royal Family. The King, unlike his wife, had improved in appearance; he was less fat, better looking and better dressed than formerly. Bess and Georgiana had watched him from the Chapel Gallery during the 'King's Mass,' and he had stopped and spoken to them at length on his way out. It had been he, the Duchess was told, who had ordered his nobles to side with the Tiers, and they had obeyed with reluctant loyalty, tears in their eyes and with heavy hearts.

So many old friends to see, and so many strange happenings....

To Georgiana the strangest wonder of all was that Canis delighted in Versailles; in fact, he actually 'doated' on it—there was no other word for his enthusiasm. He would rise at nine in the morning without complaint, and, arrayed in full dress, feathered hat and powder, set out for Versailles, where he was presented at 'all the Courts' by the Duke of Dorset, and expressed himself perfectly at home. Actually, apart from the physical effort these visits entailed, it was natural he should enjoy the French Court, for he had always liked and approved of splendour, etiquette and formality.

When Georgiana set out to call upon the Duchesse d'Orléans at the Palais Royal, she was terrified to find the palace surrounded by a seething rabble, screaming and huzzaing. She thought the crowd was hostile, but was told that they were rejoicing because the Guards had been released. 'What guards? Why?' 'The Guards at the États Généraux who were imprisoned for laying down their bayonets,' she was told. Safely inside the Palace, the Duchesse received her very kindly, and promised to drink tea with her at the Cirque if the times would permit. 'Indeed,' thought Georgiana, as she dressed for a great dinner that night, 'its all licence and confusion.'

However, if her French friends could treat these manifestations so lightly, there could be no reason why she should not enjoy herself, and indeed Paris was vastly amusing. Even the aristocrats could see a joke against themselves, and when yesterday's hero, M. d'Espremont, asked Mme de Coigny, 'Pourquoi l'année passée me couronnait on de Laurier, et à présent me brule t'on?' she had replied, 'C'est que rien ne brule comme le Laurier desséché.'

As an amateur of oratory, Georgiana was charmed to attend a session at the Salle d'États at Versailles, though the motion of the Bishop of Autun (Talleyrand) to abolish the 'Mandats Impératifs' was less interesting than the style of the various orators. She considered she was most fortunate in hearing such accomplished speakers as Lally Tollendal, l'Abbé Sieg and M. de Clermont Tonnerre.

The main object of her visit was not yet accomplished, as she had still to find a suitable home for Charlotte William. However, she was lucky in discovering a charming couple called Nagel, to whom she and Canis decided they could safely entrust the troublesome girl. M. Nagel, though well instructed, was a great bore, but Mme Nagel was delightful; musical, reliable and, though perfectly kind, yet with a nice understanding of discipline. The Duchess wrote to her mother that she had been fortunate to find them, especially as they had only one other *pensionnaire*, a Mlle St Jules, 'a very young lady from the provinces,' of so tender an age that Mme Nagel could devote herself wholly to Charlotte.

Miss William being comfortably installed, the Devonshires made ready for departure. While their trunks were being packed, she, Canis, Bess and Lady Sutherland went for a last walk in the Tuileries. It was July the 11th; a lovely evening, and the setting sun shining through the high trees was delicious.

The next day all Paris was in confusion: Necker had been dismissed; a dreadful riot was expected; bank bills were being refused as payment; it was reported that Versailles was already attacked. If the twenty-two thousand foreign troops surrounding Paris could not control the populace ...

But such a thing, they were assured, was impossible. They took leave of Charlotte in perfect confidence that she was in safe hands. The future of little Mlle St Jules did not, of course, concern them.

It was a strange journey to Spa: they were forced to travel all night, as the better inns were full—it was almost as though they were in flight themselves. But from what? All would be well, they were told, in a few days.

Then they began to hear rumours: Necker's coach had been seen; he was in full dress, without luggage or passports of any kind; his wife dying, yet unable to stop. Messieurs de Fersen and d'Esterhazy at Valenciennes were struck with dismay that he had slipped through their hands, though he carried a letter, desiring his safe passage, from the King. If his conscience was as clear as he asserted, he must *know something* to fly with such precipitancy. At Brussels the rumours increased: of dreadful riots in Paris; the Bastille fallen; revolt among the mercenaries. That the streets were full of a pitch-forked rabble shouting '*aux armes*'; that nothing was sacred. To think they had left poor Charlotte in this danger. The Duke really cried from anxiety.

In dull, quiet Spa, the three people who had left two helpless children in danger were powerless to save them. They did what they could; sent a courier post-haste back to Paris to rescue the children but, before he could return, they received letters from M. Nagel and Mr Hare saying the worst was over and the children safe. Canis dried his eyes, Bess recovered from her hysterics and Georgiana decided that Spa was too dull to describe.

Almost immediately, however, other visitors began to arrive—creatures fleeing from the storm. First came two lovely little boys, dressed in men's finery which made them appear like dwarfs. These were the sons of the Comte d'Artois, who had escaped in another direction. Then came reports that Mme de Polignac had fled, barely saving her own and her children's lives; that M. de Calonne intended to return to France; that the fashionables were no longer driving in the Bois but posting towards the frontiers. It did not seem possible that less than a fortnight ago they had all been laughing together at Bagatelle and the play.

Yet once again the Devonshires believed the rumours to have been exaggerated, for they shortly received letters from Mme de Polignac saying that she and her friends had reached safety and intended forming themselves into a little republic. The word sounded idyllic rather than ominous.

Canis even contemplated returning to Paris, which was 'quite safe but very stupid,' as he planned to install the whole of the Nagel establishment in England, including the mysterious little girl who was referred to as 'the little Pensioner,' and once as the 'little Comtesse.' He was easily dissuaded from this project, however, as it meant another move, and gradually, as Spa filled with agreeable, if slightly battered, friends from Paris, and as he was benefiting from the waters, he decided to remain. A house in Chelsea was taken for the Nagels, whose arrival in England was planned to coincide with the Devonshires' at the end of September.

Georgiana, who was always miserable when parted from her children for any length of time, welcomed this return, and deplored the alternative, which was to take a house in Brussels for six months. Separated from her little daughters, she found life as monotonous and colourless as the white muslin gowns in which she dressed. If only she could get back to Mama, G. and Hary-o. Still, the Duke's wishes must come first.

By the end of September she announced calmly and fatalistically that she believed she was pregnant. The rapture, anxiety and exaltation accompanying her earlier pregnancies were all absent. The fevered letters, hopes and fears were all past. Her chief preoccupation was not relief and delight that she was at last to bear a son (for she had no doubts as to the baby's sex), but that her condition might prevent her rejoining her daughters.

For once it was Canis who was in a fever. He made innumerable plans: to pay a rapid visit to England to see to his affairs; to transport Lady Spencer and the little girls to Brussels, where he would take a house; to bring the Nagels, Charlotte and 'the little Pensioner' to Brussels instead of to Chelsea.

All these plans were made and remade a dozen times, but on one point he was adamant—the Duchess was not to risk a miscarriage. Whatever else happened, his future heir must be protected.

Georgiana literally made herself ill with homesickness and longing for her children. Scheme after scheme was made to bring them to her, but each plan fell through. First, it was a complicated business to arrange the journey for Lady Spencer and the two little girls, with their cortège of nurses and governess, innumerable maids, footmen, couriers and postilions. Then, as soon as all was settled, there were fresh revolutionary outbursts which made it hazardous to travel.

Surely, asked Lady Spencer, it would be easier, simpler and less dangerous for Georgiana to return home,

The Duke, however, would not hear of it, and the Duchess fretted silently, but with the knowledge that in sacrificing her desires she was pleasing her husband. She was astonished by his anxiety, and attributed it to the fact that he had previously given up all hopes of an heir, and now thought only of the safe delivery of his son. She, herself, felt almost indifferent, and was puzzled by this. Had she not worn her nerves threadbare for years, longing for the very thing now happening to her? Yet, with Bess by her side, and the third and essential miracle taking place, she had only 'duty feels'; there was no wonder, no gratitude, only a grim certainty that she must make the future secure. She was only a vehicle: if love had begotten the child—if Grey ... She put such thoughts from her and renewed her efforts to bring mama and the children to Brussels. Apart from her joy when reunited with them, it would be more satisfactory for the children's education. It was time that they should become proficient in French, but it was impossible to find a suitable French girl in London, and the 'little St Jules,' though a sweet child, was too young to send over. This was a pity, as the Duchess was certain mama would be interested in *Mme de Polignac's* protégée. Meanwhile the Duke was sure the best thing, if possible, was for them to come to Brussels, since he was determined Georgiana should not risk the passage to England.

However, the revolutionary infection spread to the Low Countries, though in a less virulent form, whilst the local disturbances caused yet another postponement of the family reunion and entailed the Devonshires moving from Brussels to Lille, where their 'habitation was stinking and uncomfortable.'

As soon as things were quiet again, they returned to Brussels, planning that Lady Spencer should arrive in time for the Duchess's confinement. Indeed, if this could be arranged, and possibly a visit from Harriet Duncannon as well, Brussels would prove a paradise. Lady Duncannon contrived a short visit, but Lady Spencer, left in charge of Caroline Ponsonby, as well as the Cavendish children, could not leave England.

These constantly thwarted plans were not Georgiana's only worry. There was the ever-recurrent question of money. She had early informed M. de Calonne, as she had promised, that she hoped to bear a son, so she had no fear that he would press for repayment before her lying-in, but in England strange stories were gaining credence. The almost royal pomp with which her pregnancy was announced did not prevent the acid comments that it was singular that the Duchess should at last be breeding, and odd that she should remain abroad at such a time. Next it was openly asserted that she was not with child, and that the whole story was an opportune canard. 'If only they could see me,' she wailed, 'they would have an evident answer to their infamous lies.'

Furthermore, she learned that old Mr Henry Cavendish, the Duke's wealthy relation, had stood as godfather in person to a new George Cavendish baby. Because of their absence abroad, and Canis's previous neglect of Mr Cavendish, she foresaw that he would probably leave his money to 'the Georges,' and that her children would be impoverished.

Worst of all was a secret 'transaction' of hers that made her almost wild with torment. The whole business is complicated and involved, but the details are irrelevant. Briefly, the gist was that she had borrowed moneys belonging to the Duke, in advance from his bankers, intending to repay them before they fell due to his account. To do this, she had had to borrow sums elsewhere. Now before she had left England, Canis had made her bind herself by an oath in which she pledged her 'wishes for the Salvation of her Children, of the Duke and Lady Eliz., not to sign any paper to raise money *upon interest.*'

In the course of these intricate negotiations, she was suddenly terror-stricken lest she had broken her vow. She was not sure whether interest was expected on the second loan or not, though she had stipulated that it should be free. Unable to bear the thought that she had been false to her word, she attempted to raise a third sum to pay off the second.

The point of the whole sorry business is that it is typical of her usual lack of logic and judgment where her own affairs were concerned. The woman who never lost sight of the major issue in politics could not see that she had forgotten the essential spirit of her personal resolutions, but was tortured by the idea that she had sinned against the letter of the law. To rectify this sin, which she was not even sure she had committed, she involved herself in a web of deceit and anxiety.

On one point only was she clear: she would not confess to the Duke, who, because of her condition, would be compelled to act with magnanimous forgiveness. She was weak, untruthful to herself and tortured by misery. To salve her conscience she wrote an incredibly complicated secret memorandum of the affair, dated at Lille on November the 25th, 1789. At the same time she wrote to M. de Calonne, asking him not to press his claims until he heard from her again.

The year ended in a welter of unhappiness; uncertain plans and an uncertain future under a dark cloud of debt and deceit. She tried to calm her fears and awaited her confinement and the children's arrival in Brussels as quietly as she could. At last, it seemed, they were to set out from England in the charge of the inestimable Miss Selina Trimmer.

This young lady, 'the eldest daughter of the exceeding worthy Mrs Trimmer,' authoress of moral tales for children, was a protégée of Lady Spencer's, and regarded by her with affection and trust. She had the care, as Miss Burney describes it, 'of the young Lady Cavendishes, but was in every respect treated as if one of themselves.' She was a 'pleasing, but not pretty young woman and seemed born with her excellent mother's amiableness and serenity of mind.' Though of a serious nature, she was fond of pretty clothes, and there was a constant small, friendly battle between Lady Spencer and the Duchess on this account; the Duchess giving Selina caps and gowns, and Lady Spencer deploring this unsuitable encouragement of frivolity. On the journey to Brussels. Miss Trimmer was to be assisted in her responsibilities by a small army of servants and couriers.

At last, on March the 4th, the Duchess was able to write to her eldest daughter:

My Deareast Georgiana,

I send Louis to meet you at Calais, and I wish I was strong enough to go there myself; I should enjoy so much your surprise at all the changes you will see.

I hope you have not been very sick at Sea; how happy I shall be my dear dear child to see you; I count evr'y minute.

I send you a little cup to drink your breakfast out of on the road.

I hope french goes on a little; I have got you a charming little companion in Melle de St Jules; she is like Caro Ponsonby but as she don't speak English she will soon teach you and Dr Harryo french in play.

I will now tell you some thing of the chief towns you come thro', and Miss Trimmer will shew you them on the Map I send her. Calais is in the province of Picardy; it was conquer'd to England by Edward the 3d, in 1347. It was retaken by the french in Bloody Marys reign.... Lisle is capital of French Flanders: it is a fine town, and was taken in Queen Annes reign by your great great great grandfather, the Duke of Marlborough....

God of Heaven bless you.

Alas, when the children arrived, despite Lady Spencer's and Miss Trimmer's loving care, G.'s white cheeks and delicate look were in sad contrast to Hary-o's rosy round cheeks. She was very far from well.

Back in England the talk continued. The known fact of the Duke's and Bess's liaison, the Duchess's debts and Devonshire's desire for a son, all made the subject of the coming baby of absorbing interest. In April it was learnt that Dr Crofts, the accoucheur, had been summoned by the Duchess: it was indeed strange that the long-awaited heir was to be born on foreign soil. On May the 4th the scandal blazed out, as the London papers announced:

> ... that a courier from Brussels had been stopped by order of the Government and that the Duke and Duchess of Devonshire's letters to England had been taken out on suspicion of containing a correspondence inimical to the views of the Autocratic Faction which now presides over the Netherlands.

Hot on this news came an announcement stating that the Duke was:

> ... said to have made a formal complaint of the disrespect shewn towards his amiable consort by the Executive Powers at Brussels in stopping Her Grace's letters.

The complaint lodged by Canis was unheeded, and it was reported in England that it was feared the Duchess was obliged to leave Brussels.

The control of events had passed from the Duke's hands; the very thing he had striven to avoid was forced upon him. It was just a fortnight before the birth of the child on whom all his hopes were fixed.

Throughout her pregnancy, the slightest physical exertion had caused the Duchess agonizing pain. Now, when her hour was at hand, how would she support a long journey, over the rutted roads, across the cobbled streets, shaken and sickened by the jolting, swaying coach?

They left Brussels on May the 7th, driven out by the inexorable Secretary of State, praying that they would reach Paris safely and in time, and that Lady Spencer, who had set out on the 4th, would be there to meet them.

Having arrived in Paris, Georgiana was installed at the Hôtel de l'Université, while Bess and Canis hurried to inspect a house in Passy. This house had two recommendations—it belonged to a nobleman and it was very large. The latter qualification was essential, as it had to house not only the Duke and Duchess, but Lady Spencer, Bess, G. and Hary-o,

Miss Trimmer, Dr Crofts, Mrs Bartho, the midwife and a host of personal servants and menials.

Early the next morning, May the 20th, the midwife came to Bess and informed her that the Duchess had not been well throughout the night.

Bess got up immediately and sent off two housemaids to prepare the house at Passy. As soon as the Duchess had had a little breakfast, and the horses had been harnessed, she and Bess got into the carriage.

It was an anxious drive, but thanks to the coachman, who drove slowly and with great care, they got there safely.

They had run it very fine.

Throughout the long day, relays of servants, children and baggage continued to arrive.

It was decided that Bess should attend the opera, and she shared a box with Lord St Helens.

Presumably on account of the persistent gossip in England, the Duke, Lady Spencer and Georgiana agreed it would be wise to have disinterested witnesses in the house at the time of the birth. Lady Spencer, therefore, wrote to the Dowager Duchesse Deremberg and to Lord Robert Fitzgerald, Secretary to the English Embassy, requesting their immediate attendance. By the time the note to Lord Robert was delivered, he was in bed. His servant, thinking it of little consequence, decided to hold it over till the morning.

Bess found the labour far advanced on her return from the opera and hastened to Georgiana's room. Here were assembled Lady Spencer, the midwife, Dr Crofts, Bess's maid, Ann Scafe and the Duchess's two women, her faithful Dennis and Hannah Bunting. Canis waited in the next room. At a little after one, he was joined by the Duchesse Deremberg and at the same moment the baby was born.

'There never was a more welcome child,' wrote Ann Scafe, and she echoed the delight of all present, for the baby was a boy. The Marquess of Hartington had arrived after sixteen years of hope and disappointments.

The child was put into Ann's arms, and as soon as the Duke heard a thin, new cry, he came into the room and looked at his son. Ann carried the baby into the next room, where there was a little fire, and held him on her lap till the nurse took him to be dressed.

It was all over. Georgiana had done her duty; she had redeemed the reproach that had shadowed her life. She had saved herself and given Canis his heir. With a little sigh of exhaustion, she fell asleep.

She made a good recovery and the baby thrived. Preparations were made for a splendid christening at the end of June, but by this time little G.

was definitely ill and the ceremony was postponed, a simple baptism being performed by the Ambassador's Chaplain.

One ceremony, however, could not be put off. Marie Antoinette, who too had waited many years for her son, sent for Georgiana. She was fond of the Duchess and wished to congratulate her in person. As Georgiana was nursing the baby, she took him with her to Versailles. The two women, whose lives bore so strange a resemblance, looked at each other, as Georgiana held her son towards the Queen. Marie Antoinette stooped, took the tiny hands in hers and kissed them twice. It was the last time that she and Georgiana met.

Despite the precious baby, the house at Passy was filled with sorrow, for G, was now critically ill. Her life was despaired of and the whole family was distraught. Fortunately the care that was lavished upon her was not in vain, and by August the 10th she was well enough to travel, though still extremely weak. The large company set out for England, travelling by easy stages, and reached Devonshire House towards the end of the month.

On his first birthday, May the 21st, 1791, the Marquess of Hartington was formally christened at St George's, Hanover Square, being given the names of William Spencer Cavendish.

Devonshire House from Piccadilly, 1906.

13

Prelude to Exile

Georgiana was sitting in the Captains' room in the 'Ship' Inn at Southampton. It was both cold and stuffy; panelled in mahogany and upholstered in dark red repp, it reeked of rum, smoke and fog.

The packet was to sail that November evening and they were waiting for the tide. Lady Spencer was in another room, where Harriet Duncannon was lying on an uncomfortable sofa. Georgiana had felt that she must be alone, that she could not even bear the company of her adored mother and sister.

'What has brought me here?' she asked herself. 'Why should I be here, waiting to sail into exile, when with every fibre of my being I long to remain in England?'

The door opened for a moment and the icy fog surged into the room, making the fire belch smoke, so that Georgiana's eyes filled with smarting tears. Or so she pretended to herself, trying to keep her misery under control.

As the fog swirled about her, she seemed to see Charles Grey. He stood before her with a faint smile on his beautiful mouth, his head tossed high and his eyes looking past and beyond her.

She wondered for the thousandth time whether he knew, as she knew at last, how much she loved him or how much her surrender had cost her. Did he long for and dread the coming of their child, as she was longing, yet dreading? Would the child of love be different from those other three children, whom she loved for themselves, not for their begetting? What would be its future?

She pressed her hand over her eyes, as though she could not bear the vision of that future.

And the other three children? What would become of them? Would she ever see them again? She must, she must. Suppose she died? What would become of them? Mama would look after them, and Bess, and Selina Trimmer.

Here another train of thought started. Was it Mama's dislike of Bess which had communicated itself, unconsciously she was sure, to G. and Hary-o? Why did her darling little girls remain so obstinate in their childish hatred of poor Bess who was always so good to them?

No one could have been more tender or devoted than Bess had been to G. during the little girl's terrible illness in Paris last year.

The remembrance of that agonizing spring and summer at Passy blotted out all other thoughts. She remembered how they had watched, week by week, day by day, hour by hour, the little life fading in front of their eyes. Neither Dr Crofts nor his French colleagues, Mama nor Selina nor Bess, had been able to strengthen the loosening hold of G.'s little hands on the slender thread of her existence. The child had been so patient and good and had borne her suffering with gentle, uncomplaining courage; while Georgiana, longing to comfort and tend her, had been forbidden to do so, for her first duty had been to baby Hart. She was his nurse, and others must look after her darling, her eldest. She could remember nothing of that summer in Paris, neither politics nor friends, nor even her little son, only G.'s white face and frail tossing body.

And then, when the tide had turned, and life had slowly flowed back into the wasted child, and they had returned to England, then what had happened?

The homecoming had been almost worse than the vigil in Paris. She had been right to dread it, for no sooner had she set foot in England, than Canis had forced her to confess her debts to him. She had put off the day of reckoning so long, that now it had come it seemed as though it were her death sentence. She recollected how she had had to write the hated truth, for she could not bring herself to speak of it. She had had to admit her transactions with Calonne; how she had raised money to pay back the sums she had borrowed from her husband's agents; how she had feared she had broken her oath to him not to borrow money upon interest; that she owed more than £61,000.

That confession had deprived her of all her strength, and when she had turned to her mother for comfort and forgiveness, she found these denied to her.

She remembered, with horror, how Mama had told her that unless she severed her friendship and all connexion with Bess, she would have nothing more to do with her—with her, *Georgiana*.

She supposed it had all arisen from the mistake she had made in allowing Mama to see little Caroline St Jules at Passy. But whilst G. had been so ill, and Hart had needed her loving attention, she had not given a thought to other things. She had been sure that, after all the hints she had given Mama about Mme de Polignac's interest in the little girl, and how careful she had been to stress Caroline's French parentage, she would not have alighted on the truth. She supposed she ought to have known that nothing could have been hidden from Mama's clear grey eyes. But after Mama's capitulation when they had fought their first battle about Bess in 1789, she had not expected this new ultimatum.

She recollected her miserable distress in her dilemma: it had obviously been out of the question for her to withdraw her friendship and support from Bess. Apart from her own love for her, there had been Canis. She remembered how she had been threatened with separation from him and the children, and how it was Bess who had saved her, had made him see reason. How could she be expected to repay her with ingratitude; worse, with treacherous denial?

Those long months at Passy when she, Canis, Bess and Mama had lived under the same roof had evidently left no doubt in Lady Spencer's mind of the nature of their triangular relationship. She could neither do without her mother nor her friend. There had been no alternative than to defy, whilst appealing to, Mama; bluffing it out, knowing full well that she would see through the bluff, praying she would relent and pretend to believe in it. So she had written the one false letter of her life, because on one subject she must remain unalterable—Bess must stay.

She remembered that letter as well as though she were writing it now, in the cold, smoky room at the 'Ship.'

You are wrong, grossly wrong, Dst. M., I often wish you would talk to the Duke on this subject; he would prove to you that you are wrong and shew you likewise how resolved he was that no lies of the world could make him authorize them by abandoning a person he has every reason to esteem and think well of—after all the Lies made abroad, a Separation when we came home, would have this effect.... I have just been speaking to the Duke about your objection to Ly. Eliz. He has often told me that (if we continue to live together, which my unfortunate conduct about money renders very doubtful), that If I had a moment's uneasiness about her, He would be far from wishing her to live with us—nor would she, I am sure, one moment. But, good god, how far is this from being the case. I have, as well as him, the highest regard & respect & esteem for her as well as Love. In this case, Dst. M., you must feel how impossible, how cruel, it would be to expose her to the malignant illnature of the world & to expose ourselves to all the misery of parting with her, for what we know to be unjust and false....

I can only add, Dst. M., that I am born to a most complicated misery—I had ran into errors that would have made any other man discard me; my friend who had likewise stood between him and my ruin, was likewise his friend, her society was delightful to us and her gentleness and affection sooth'd the bitterness [of the] many misfortunes I had brought upon us. And the Mother whom I adore, whom

look up to, whom I love better than my Life, sets herself up in the opposite scale; forgets all the affection her Son in Law has shewn her & only says I will deprive them of their friend and of my countenance....

She remembered how, just as she had written those words, Dr Crofts had come into the room and had been terrified by her wild look, her shaking hand.

She remembered the twenty-four hours of torture she had endured while waiting for Mama's reply. When Lady Spencer's letter was brought to her the next day, she had hardly been able to break the seal.

Her heart had overflowed with relief as she read the clear, dignified words. She had not expected Mama to agree with her, but she had hardly hoped for such magnanimity.

'Dearest M., dearest M.,' she had replied, overwhelming her mother with gratitude, and expressing a hope that the subject would never again be mentioned between them, and that Mama would join with her trying to make it of as little consequence to their peace and living together as possible. Otherwise, Georgiana remembered telling her, she would either deprive the Duke 'of the Society so soothing to him,' or run the risk of depriving her daughter of what was her dearest happiness on earth, 'seeing you in Ease and comfort.'

Deep down in her heart she knew, however, that Mama, 'convinced against her will, was of the same opinion still' and would ever regard poor Bess as 'the Obstacle.'

The door opened again, and with the fog there entered the sound of her sister's voice.

'Oh, poor Harriet,' she thought, 'pray God she may recover.'

As the door swung-to again, she reflected that it was a miracle that her sister was well enough to undertake this hateful journey.

First there had been the summer in Paris by G.'s sick-bed; then the next summer in Bath by Harriet's. Georgiana could not believe that it was possible to be so near death as her child and her sister had been, and yet live. She thought of Harriet's paralysis, her useless arm and leg; of the numbness; the racking, blood-stained cough; of her weakness and exhaustion; yet of her feverish will to live. Even when the doctors had ordered her to Bath, and she had resigned herself with fortitude to death, the small vital flicker had persisted.

Bath … a fresh gust of smoke blew another picture into the room. Not the town where she and Canis and Bess had been together, but a larger, finer, cleaner town whose improvements had decreased its charms. Instead of her sister's sickbed, she had thought of the grey, steely pond where they had skated; in place of Mama's Sunday schools (one of which she had taken under her immediate patronage) Georgiana remembered the little, firelit rooms where she had taken guineas from the Bishop's lady at whist; instead of the odour of death she remembered the kindling of life.

Had she known it, her comparisons had shown on her face; for Miss Burney, that neat, precise, observant little woman, had remarked that when she met the Duchess previously, she had seemed 'far more easy and lively in her spirits and consequently, far more lovely in her person.' Furthermore Miss Burney noted that in Georgiana she had not found so much beauty as she expected:

> … notwithstanding the variation of accounts; but I found far more of manner, politeness, and gentle quiet. She seems to me to possess the highest animal spirits, but she appeared to me not happy, I thought she looked oppressed within … Though there is a native cheerfulness about her which, I fancy, scarce ever deserts her … vivacity is so much her characteristic that her style of beauty requires it indispensably; the beauty, indeed, dies away without it.

Had Georgiana read those words, she would have agreed with them, for her heart had been heavy and oppressed. Instead she only remembered how Miss Burney had been present at Hary-o's sixth birthday party, when half a dozen charity children had been clothed by Mama to celebrate the event. She would have remembered her children's pretty behaviour on that occasion, and how she, Queen of the Regency faction, had listened with civil attention and sympathy to Miss Burney's account of the poor King's 'illness.'

She did remember how once, as she was being carried in her chair to the Rooms, she had seen the neat little lady on the side-walk and how, though she had waved and kissed her hands towards her, Miss Burney had been too shortsighted to recognize her, until she cried, 'How d'ye do? How d'ye do?' at the top of her voice.

She also remembered how Miss Burney had inquired very kindly after Hartington, then fourteen months old, and how surprised she had been to learn that he had a separate establishment and carriage of his own.

She would have been pleased to know that Miss Burney thought that:

… the fame of her personal charms was obtained from the expression of her smile, which was very sweet, and that her countenance had an ingenuousness and openness so singular that, taken in those moments, not the most rigid critic could deny the justice of her personal celebrity.

Instead her thoughts returned to the early days in England after those unhappy months in Paris: how she had given dinners at Devonshire House, inviting the guests to come upstairs to see the new Lord Hartington while she nursed him at her breast. Among these visitors she remembered Mr Selwyn, who had remarked pointedly upon the baby's resemblance to his Grace. Poor George, did he know her so little as to have thought she would have given Canis a bastard heir? She supposed he had been fool enough to listen to that absurd story of her and Bess substituting children in Paris. What an old woman he must be!

But if he and his kind could believe a story like that, what would they not do to her if they learned the real cause of her withdrawal to France? She shuddered, and then reflected bitterly, that perhaps Harriet's illness was a blessing in disguise. At least it was a blessing to her, affording her a chance to conceal her frailty. If they ever learnt the truth they would tear her to pieces, mercilessly and with enjoyment. 'They'd be justified, at last, I suppose,' she thought.

Once more the door opened and a messenger pushed his head round the corner: 'Winds favourable and the tide on the turn,' he yelled.

Georgiana shook herself and called for Hannah, her maid. 'Bring me my writing desk,' she commanded.

While she was waiting she thought:

I *must* never let them forget me. G. won't forget me; she's old enough to remember. But Hary-o is only six, and Hart—he's too little to remember long. I must make them remember. I'll write every day—keep journals—send pictures—everything possible so that they shan't forget.

When Hannah brought the little red leather travelling desk she opened it, and taking a piece of paper, her eyes dim with tears, she wrote:

Southampton, the 3rd Nov. 1791. We embark in half an hour....

The green room, Devonshire House.

14

The Exile

Hope of my life! dear Children of my heart!
That anxious heart to each fond feeling true,
To you still pants each pleasure to impart,
And more—oh transport! reach its Home and You!

Georgiana's Passage of St Gothard

We will follow Georgiana in exile through extracts from her letters to
the nine-year-old G. in England, and from the journals that she kept for
her. There are three of these copy-books of rough blue-grey paper, on the
covers of which Georgiana had painted labels—wreaths of flowers and
the initials 'G.C.' in a flowery rope. They are profusely illustrated and
closely written. Most of the illustrations are by her, drawings in sepia and
colour, full of grace and charm. In the journal she kept while at Rome
the illustrations are small, brightly coloured little prints, and into it she
crammed every scrap of information she could lay hands on, about Roman
history, monuments, pictures and churches.

The first journal opens with the words: 'Left Bath very miserable at
leaving my Dear children.' As an after-thought she inserted 'the Duke &'
before the 'dear children.'

The serious business of the journal, which was to educate G., then opens
with a description of France, its former situation and history and goes on to
recount the state of affairs at the time of writing. The Duchess enumerates
the thirty-two old Provinces, the principal rivers and towns, and continues:

Since the Revolution they have attempted to divide France into 83
departments—the names chiefly taken from the Rivers etc. I do not give

them to you as they are very puzzling & probably will not last, or at least will not make the old names forgotten.

There are four kinds of Government in Europe:

Despotick, where the Sovereign alone follows his own will & may dispose of the Lives of his Subjects; fortunately the only example of this barbarous government in Europe is in Turkey.

Monarchial, where the King has the chief command, but is subject to the Laws established by his Predecessors, such as was in France and is in Spain.

Aristocratical, where the principal Noblemen govern, as at Venice.

Democratical, where the people govern, either in Publick Assembly, or in assemblys of men whom they have chosen to explain their sentiments, such as in Switzerland. The English government is reckoned the wisest and certainly is the happyest of all, being composed of the 3 last.

The Duchess then writes a short history of France, enumerating the Kings and the principal events of each reign. Opposite the French Kings, she puts a similar synopsis of English history, the whole being very clear and comprehensive. This work took her all her spare time while she was at Paris, where Lady Spencer, she and Lady Duncannon were to meet Bess, Charlotte William and Caroline St Jules. It made it doubly hard for Georgiana, pining for her children in England, to see her sister with little Caro Ponsonby and Bess with Caro St Jules; and several times each day she was forced to shut herself in her room in order to hide her misery. She determined, however, to devote herself to the unattractive Charlotte. On November the 22nd she writes, 'Charlotte is much grown & improv'd; but she still stoops—this must shew you how much consequence it is not to let any trick get into a habit.'

After many adventures, the four ladies, each with her maid and footman, and with a corresponding number of coachmen and couriers, reached Lyons on December the 14th. Here they were detained by bad weather, and Georgiana writes a long description of the town and its history, though they were unable to go out much because of the rain. She says:

It is a very good Hotel we are in, but as a Nasty Man will not give up his room, Bess & I are oblig'd to go along an open Balcony evr'y night, & sometimes in the Rain.

Our great amusement is drawing & I have made myself very happy here in getting a piano forte & playing your Dear Sonatina which makes me think you are very near me.

La nouvelle ville est bien belle, la Place de Bellecour et la Place de la Charité (où nous demeurent) ressemblent Bruxelles—et les quays le long du Rhône sont superbes.

Lyon est fameuse pour ses manufactures—on y fait les plus belles soyeries du monde; on y brode comme de la peinture et on fait du fil d'or que l'on met autour du fil de Soye, ce qui devient ce que nous appelons *gold thread*.

They have a new way this year of embroidering which is beautiful & which yr. Dr Grandmama admires very much—it is Muslin for Pierrots; at the Bottom a fine black net, laid smooth & embroider'd with Roses— it is beautiful.

The fashionable couleur is a brown call'd cuir de bottes—Boot leather.

Give my love to Dear Selina & my own Harryo & Willy & the inclos'd to Mrs Brown [Hart's nurse].

God bless you dear darling love.

20th of Dec. '91. Pont St Esprit.

Dearest Georgiana,

We set out from Lyons on Sunday the 18th—in a flat bottom boat something like the scratch underneath. [Here the Duchess draws a picture of a boat with an awning like a 'covered wagon.'] The cover'd part divid'd into two rooms with a stove; but only boards, straw & a poor kind of tapestry & very cold. The maids & men set in the back one; & your Uncle, Aunt, Grandmama, Bess & I, Dr Nott & the 2 little girls in the big one. We were very cold & the motion sometimes made us think of the Sea; but the river is beautifully broad & the sides delightful—I longed for you except for the cold. We were call'd at 6 & in the boat by 8—you [would] have laugh'd to have seen all our cold & odd figures in night caps & great coats.

They had many adventures, running ashore and in danger from rocks. At Coudrieux, where they slept the first night, the country girls came into the inn, 'dancing & threading the needle.' They continued in the boat from 'lovely Avignon, no longer gay & happy but deserted' to Tarascon, as the roads were so bad that river travel was more comfortable.

Georgiana illustrated her journal and letters with charming little watercolours and drawings in gouache, sketching the arch at Orange, the

Papal Palace at Avignon, Vienne and all the lovely places through which they passed.

On New Year's Day she drew a little picture of Bess and 'the 2 Caros,' and the two dogs, Lill and Lubin. Bess is dressed in a redingote, puffed kerchief and top hat tied on with a scarf—she makes a very chic and Revolutionary figure. The two little girls are dressed alike in long blue frocks and long red redingotes, with white kerchiefs and black hats. They hold each other by the hand, while the dogs run about the rocky landscape under the olive trees.

The same day the party reached Marseilles and the Duchess described some of the outlandish figures she saw: Greek women, Armenian men with high caps and baggy trousers and the Arlesiennes in their long 'Folettes.' There was a feud in progress between Aix and Marseilles and to avoid the battle of the mob-army of 1,500 people in Marseilles, they pressed on, passing the deserted towns, the inhabitants having fled to the hills, till they reached Toulon. Toulon was in confusion with refugees from Aix, but the harbour was 'neat, and the arsenal well-manag'd.'

On January the 11th the party separated; Lady Spencer and Harriet Duncannon, with her doctor, settling at Hyères, and Bess, Georgiana, Charlotte and Caro St Jules going to Aix.

On the 15th Georgiana writes to G. sending her

… our first view of the mediterrain Sea & Marseille; … I was in the carriage with your dear Aunt and never saw anything equal to her transport at seeing it. She said she was sure she should recover by it—God grant she may! … Pray remember whilst you are labouring at French I shall probably have begun Italian at Nice—addio gioja mia.

She clung to every scrap of news from England: that the little girls had been to see Sir Ashton Lever's collection, where they had admired the corals and Derbyshire spars. She hoped that G. would share her love of geology, as she wished to make a fine collection whilst she was abroad. She planned the tea-parties she would give for them on her return and promised to learn the local dances so she could teach them to the children. She prayed heaven that would be soon.

On January the 29th she says:

I send you the two parcels sewed up—you will find a little figure I have made for you with three changes of dresses—the Dress she is in, is the dress of Provence about Arles & Tarrascon, the Romans formerly had settlements in that part of Gaul and it is suppos'd the long Robe came from there. The other of the Cauchoise is in Normandy, their caps are gold & Silver; & the woman spinning is near Moulins, bourbonnaises.

I cannot persuade myself that Hartington can run quite alone; how I would wish to see his dear little face.... Caroline St Jules is a dear little girl; living so much with her in this journey I have learnt to know her better than ever; she has great good sence; attention like yours; and sweetness of disposition & manner like you—and has wonderful piety for such a little creature. I wish your cousin Caroline was as good; however I believe she is mended with your dear Grandmama—yr. grandmama is the only person she minds at all. God bless you, my darling Love; the longer your letters are the more precious.... ... Je vous aime de tout mon coeur de tout mon âme; embrassez votre chère sœur et cher frère. G. D.

Bess and Georgiana left Aix on February the 3rd, and on the 11th the Duchess writes from Montpellier:

We arriv'd at the Comtesse de St Jules near Aiguesmortes ... We found him so extremely ill that we came here last night ... We had some people of Business to see [at Montpellier] about Caro.... I send these three violets for my three darlings and a kiss for each which I would travel on foot to give you.

Three days later she continues: 'The accnts. of yr. Aunt continue to be very good; she walks on her crutches with much less fatigue and pain....'

History was repeating itself, for little G. now had the famous violinist, Giardini, who had taught her mother and whom the Duchess had re-met in Paris, to teach her music.

From Aigues Mortes, Bess and Georgiana, with Caroline and Charlotte, made their way along the coast and joined Lady Spencer and Harriet Duncannon at Nice on March the 11th.

Nice the 8th April, 1792.... I will give you an account of the manner in which I have spent this day, Easter Sunday. I got up at 9 and after having read one of Blairs Sermons, I went to the Cathedral with the two Carolines—the Bishop performed High Mass & his countenance & manner is so good, it gives grace to any ceremony. We then came home & yr. Dr Grandmama read prayers—I then went to pay visits with your Grandmama and to see the children of the English Consul. I read a little Italian with your Aunt before dinner & we din'd at half past 2. After dinner we rode; I have a little poney—very quiet & pleasant and your Aunt rode upon it and gallop'd a little (with two people holding her on). We met a Country woman with a Snake, very long & venomous that she had just caught near the Var. We are now all come in and are thus Employ'd in the drawing room—your Dear Grand-mama arranging her beautiful Hortus Siccus—her plants are beautiful. Your Aunt, Bess & Ld. Duncannon drawing. I have been idle about drawing lately, but then I study Italian tho' I make but little progress. I am begining too to study mineralogy that I may be able to go to Lever's with you—there is a very clever man here, Dr Dreux [Drew] but he will not come to one as he is busy with his sick people—the day we saw him at a cabinet of natural history we were delighted with him.

We set out on the 18th & tho at first we go a little further I trust it is a begining of our return to England. Oh my Dear Love, with what Joy shall I embrace 'oo all three—en attendant give 2 kisses to yr. Br. & Sister for me—& to Selina too—who tho' she is not my child is very dear to me from her kindness & care of my own Dear brats.

They sailed from Nice, where Georgiana had been horrified by the sight of chained galley-slaves working in the harbour, to Genoa in a felucca, but the weather was so bad that they put in at Monaco, where Georgiana went for long walks on which she collected mineral specimens. Wherever they went in France, she had been struck by the extreme poverty and misery of the people, and on April the 24th she wrote:

Une pauvre femme, à qui to Grandmama à donnée 12 sols, lui à offert tous les fruits de son giardin; et lui a demandée si elle vouloit qu'elle lui baise les pieds.

Finally, on May the 1st, they arrived at Genoa

… where I found yr. Dear letter. Oh my dear child, I can only assure you that your Love and the hopes that you will not forget me is the comfort of my life now that I am absent from you—when I am now to return is very uncertain—I hope it will be soon as I do not feel that I have strength to bear so long an absence. Kiss dearest Harry and yr. Brother. God bless you my darlings.

Apart from her unhappiness that her return had been postponed, Georgiana enjoyed herself at Genoa, where she found much to admire.

She wrote a long history of its government, its nobles and merchants, and enlarged upon its beauty.

The Doge, never must leave the Palace during the 2 years and is ev'n imprison'd in the Palace Spinola for to days after he ends being doge when if any one is discontented they may accuse him. He has great attendance; his pages are drest in green velvet & gold and his palace magnificent. Each Doge new furnishes it ev'ry two years for the sake of commerce; but what spoils his Palace is that the understory & the attics are Prisons; so in the midst of his grandeur he is inclos'd by wretchedness.

The English ladies were much impressed by the Genoese custom of calling men and women by their names, instead of by their titles, such as Angellina Pallavicinna, Clelia Doria and: 'I should be call'd Georgiana Devonshire. We thought this custom very pretty.'

From Turin she sent Hart a doll dressed like a page of the Doge of Genoa, and a kiss to Hary-o. Ten days afterwards she wrote to G.:

This is Dear Hartington's birthday, my own Georgiana—I write him a letter but give him a kiss from me—when shall I see you all? it will not be long now I trust & I beg of you Dst. Love to make 'oo Papa come & fetch me soon.

This is the letter she wrote to her son on his second birthday:

My Dear Little Boy—As soon as you are old enough to understand this letter it will be given to you; it contains the only present I can make you—my blessing written in my blood. The book that will be also given to you is a memorandum of me you must ever keep. Alas! I am gone before you could know me, but I loved you. I nursed you nine months at my breast; I love you dearly.

Now my son observe my best wishes. Be obedient to your dear Papa and Grandmother. Consult them and obey them in all things. Be very kind to your sisters. Join with your dear Papa when you can in increasing their fortunes.... Love always dear Lady Elizabeth and Caroline. Be kind to all your cousins especially the Ponsonbys. Make piety your chief study; never despise religion: never break your word; never betray a secret: never tell a lie.

God bless you my dear child. O how dearly would I wish once again to see your beloved face and to press you to my wretched bosom. God bless you my dear little boy. Your poor mother, G. Devonshire.

On a separate piece of paper is her brownish-red life-blessing: 'May God Almighty bless and preserve you my dear Hartington and make you good and happy. God bless you my child. Your poor mother, G. Devonshire.'

Now the party turned northwards, crossing the Mont Cenis on May the 24th. They were carried in chairs and dined, at the top of the pass in the Curé's house, off delicious trout. Lady Duncannon and Lady Elizabeth suffered very much from the cold, but Lady Spencer was in her element, briskly gathering Alpine flowers among the snow. Georgiana felt that as they crossed the pass, she was a step nearer home.

I cannot tell you how happy I shall be to get to Geneva ... I shall feel myself much nearer you and getting nearer home at Geneva, and I hope your Papa will come for me very soon: I am sure he will as soon as he can for he knows how much I long to see you.

At all events I think I shall now be coming very very soon. How happy I shall be to see you & never to leave you again I trust....

But there was delay in returning after all and they remained at Geneva until October. On June the 5th she writes to G. that she

... cannot resist telling you how much we have been pleased here with M. de Sanssure [?] a great Philosopher. He is a most interesting & amiable man—much attach'd to his wife and has two sons & a beautiful daughter.

There is a very high mountain call'd Montblanc cover'd with Ice always, and so high that nobody for many centuries had reach'd its top—a person got to the top and Mr de Sanssure was desirous to go (tho' very dangerous) to try experiments on the Air.

His Wife, tho' she dreaded his going on acct. of the danger, had courage and Love enough to tell him, as it had been done, he, as a great Philosopher, ought to try it. He went up—he was two days & so frozen with cold tho' in July, that his victuals froze and he was so weak he could not buckle his shoe. Often he was oblig'd to crawl over a ladder plac'd across the cracks in the Ice hundreds of Feet deep.

When he got to this height, he saw underneath him all the snowy points of Mountain and rivers of Ice shining like diamonds—the whole country of Switzerland—Savoie and part of Piedmont—the Lake of Geneva—and the sky appear'd to him a deep prussian blue—but what he delighted most in, was to distinguish, which he had the happyness of doing, his Wife and Son at Chamouny where he had left them, and to see them wave a flag which was the sign he agreed they should make if they saw him and knew he was safe.

I think this story quite affecting. He has given me two bits of Granite he pick'd up from the rock at the summit of Mont Blance, which I shall preserve as great treasures & he has given yr. Dr Grandmama beautiful flowers for her Hortus Siccus.... Yr. Dear Grandmama Aunt & Bess study Botany very much; I do a little but my favourites of all favourites is mineralogy and I have already a pretty Collection of my own collecting.

Yverdun the 10 of June '92.

What can I say to you my Dearest Love—but that I am convinc'd it will not be many months before I see you —I think not above two. I feel that it is much better that I should stay but I cannot accustom myself to it, and I shall count the moments till this sad absence is past....

Yverdun 13 July '92.

I am going to describe to you, my Dearest Georgiana, the manner in which we kept your Dear Birthday yesterday. We had made a little purse, your Dr Grandmama Aunt Bess and me to cloathe 9 poor children in honour of you and Frederick—the boys were drest in jackets and trowsers of blue & white, the girls in pink & white. We gave them a dinner ... in the middle of the table was a basket very prettily adorn'd in flowers, & each of the Children had a nosegay and red beau. Your Grandmama helped to work the ribbons for their caps.

The two Carolines distributed the nosegays and pence a piece to each child.

We had a number of people to see them.... This was the morning part of our little fête and I liked it the better from thinking we were occupied in the same manner, as I believe you cloathed 9 children for the same day.

In the Ev^g your Dear Aunt came to a Thé in my room: my room is very small but looks at the Lake and I had taken my bed out of the room where I sleep. I had ornamented my room with drawings of your Aunts and Dr. Besses. I had a quantity of flowers, especially in the ribbons of my Bookcases—and besides tea we had Ices and fruit & Swiss cakes.

We had about 20 people—a young gentleman who sings very well, sung; and Miss Fellows (who is with the Dss. of Ancaster) Princesse Joseph & Mr Trevor sung. Caroline St Jules play'd and she and Caroline danc'd their little courante which is very pretty & which I shall teach you.

The little girls were very happy, but Caroline St Jules with her usual goodness said that she liked the morning part much the best....

Georgiana meant to write a Swiss story for Hary-o, but there seemed to be

... a spell against it, instead I send you a little Italian song which I have wrote out myself for you—it is very pretty. The begining and ending which are nearly alike, should be play'd slow & very piano. The words are foolish like most songs—they are:

> *I am wounded*
> *in the midst of my heart*
> *and Love wounds me.*
> *Why cruel Love*
> *dost thou wound me thus*
> *Alas unhappy and poor me*
> *Alas what pain, what sorrow.*
> *I am wounded in the midst of my heart.*

The words sound pretty in Italian tho' as you see extremely foolish. I don't know any thing that has given me such pleasure.... Your Dear Aunt comes on in walking and can play with both hands perfectly well.

Tuesday, Aug. 7th, '92.
    ... We have been very gay and dissipated these last two days, by this I mean that Your Dear Aunt has been for Bess and I never go out without her.
    Last night she was at Mr Gibbon's and went all over his beautiful garden—she has been very often as he lives a great deal with us, but we have never had so fine an Evening. He has a beautiful little Pavillion on his Terrace where after tea we had musick and our little Russian Princess and her friend danc'd Russian dances—afterwards they sung a great deal.
    Mr Gibbon is very fond of the two Carolines—and Caroline Ponsonby does what she will with him—and would teach him to do the Kings; that is, to put her map of the Kings of France together.
    Mr Gibbon is very clever but remarkably ugly and wears a green jockey cap to keep the light from his Eyes when he walks in his garden. Caroline was quite entertained with it & made him take it off & twist it about.
    He is a very famous man as he wrote a celebrated history of the fall of the Roman Empire—which makes it very comical to see him play with the two Carolines.

He comes to us almost evr'y day & sometimes whilst we are dressing they undertake to amuse him; they dance to him & they sing to him. One day Caroline Ponsonby out of kindness wanted one of the footmen who had been jumping her, to jump Mr Gibbon, which was rather difficult as he is one of the biggest men you ever saw....

We take lessons in mineralogy & chemistry and Mr Gibbon attends them with us & in the Evenings we have a great deal of musick which you would like I am sure. Your Dr Grandmama has almost learnt German, but she learns what she will—she rides on her Bourrique & I think likes Lausanne better than any place since we have been away. The country is so uncommonly beautiful & and the people so good that I sd. like it too if my longing for England did not encrease dayly. But evr'y hour that I spend away from you seems an age to me....

Sept. 30, '92.

... Caro [Ponsonby] really talks french very well & the little faults she makes are very entertaining. She talks to any body & t'other day she took it into her head that Psse. Joseph de Monaco was a Widow & she would call her Veuve Joseph. She is very naughty and says anything that comes into her head which is very distressing—she told poor Mr Gibbon, who has the misfortune of being very ugly, that his big face frighten'd the little puppy with whom he was playing....

Lausanne Oct. 6, '92.

... Oh my Georgiana, do not let your dear little heart sink—I trust I shall return to you soon; but it would not be proper for me to return till yr. dear Papa fetches me for we ought not to travel alone thro Germany which is full of Troups.

My Sweet Love when I do see you, oh may we never be parted again; I shall never leave you if I can help it for a day—& this sad absence has if possible made me love you all more than ever. I have no thought & wish but you. I am grown a very different creature I believe; for instead of loving to move about I only wish for quiet with my Dst. children....

However, the Duke did not come and the party set out for Italy in October. Georgiana, in her journal to G., described each stage of the journey, collecting little pictures and facts both past and present. The cold and dreary journey over the St Bernard Pass made her really quite ill, but she maintained it was nothing significant. 'We slept for 4 nights in beds without curtains and our matrasses like bags of stones.' She was struck by the beauty of the Vale of Aosta:

> ... but on ye other hand human nature is very ugly there for all ye men & women almost have hideous faces & swellings on their throats & are call'd cretins.

She sent the children a phosphorescent stone from Bologna; she described the old Masters, among whom she had an unfortunate admiration for Guido Reni, and she wished G. to write and tell her which pictures at Devonshire House and which painters were her favourites.

> I try my dearest G. to cheat away the time of absence by employing myself for you.

Nov. 24, '92, Florence.
   ... I shall content myself today with giving you an account of one room out of about 20 which there are at the grand Dukes Gallery.
   It is an octagone room call'd the *tribune*—it is pav'd with the rarest marbles—its Ceiling is inlaid in Mother of pearl—and the hangings are of crimson silk. The pictures are few but are all by the great masters— and there is a little St John in the Desert by Raphael that seems starting out of the Canvas. But the beauty of the room consists in four statues— the Venus of Medicis, which is so soft and graceful she seems really alive—a man listening and sharpening a (knife) who is suppos'd to be a Spy discovering a conspiracy or a Sacrificator, waiting to hear the high priest order the Death of the victims—the other two statues are two gladiators fighting and a young Apollo.
   But what I am sure will shock you as much as it did me, there is in ye Gallery (tho not in any of the best rooms) a venus combing cupid's air [*sic*] and really hunting for a little animal too nasty to mention.

No. 1, 2nd year, Florence, Nov. 30th 1792.
   Your letter dated the 1st of Nov. was delightful to me tho' it made me very melancholy my Dearest Child. This year has been the most painful of my life. But if I have been of use to your Dear Aunt & an assisstance to your Grandmama, I shall be rewarded, and when I do return to you, never leave you I hope again—it will be too great a happyness for me Dear Dear Georg'ana, & it will have been purchas'd by many days of regret—indeed evr'y hour I pass away from you, I regret you; if I amuse

myself or see any thing I admire I long to share the happyness with you—
if on the contrary I am out of spirits I wish for your presence which alone
would do me good....

They then went from Florence to Pisa where 'our house is pretty but
very cold—it belongs to the English consul & therefore is very clean &
with neat furniture but it is very cold indeed.'
It was here that she met:

... poor Mme de Calonne. I am sure your compassionate heart will
suffer at the situation that she & other french people whom we have
seen in prosperity are in now. Their distress for money is in general very
great and now they are not permitted to stay in any town of Italy least
the french shd. be offended....

The news from England that Hart had been successfully inoculated for
the small-pox put her into a flurry of spirits and thankfulness.

Jan. 7, 1793.
    ... I send you four visiting cards from a Lady of your acquaintance,
the Dss. of Devonshire. They are according to the custom of Italy with
views of Pisa—at Rome they are made with views of Rome & cc....

Florence, 18th of Jan. 1793.
    ... The prophecy [in Goldsmith's 'Traveller'] has been verify'd today,
for it is quite summer. It is the Carnival & the Streets are full of masks—
the fine Sunny Street call'd Lung Arno was Crouded with Shepherdesses,
Turcs, old Women & cc.cc.c. Miss Hervey has been a beautiful Sultana
and all the Servants mask of an Evening. When we are well of our colds
I am to dress as a gypsey with Caro Ponsonby at my Back; and we are to
go about the house telling fortunes with Miss Hervey & Caroline little
Gypseys.

She then spent a long morning writing out a music lesson for G., chords,
variations, scales and cadences.

This is enough of musick dear Love, I only wish you to accustom yourself
with Mrs Parkes to go up and down the chords and Cadences, in all
the keys—this will give you great facility when you learn to accompany
yourself in singing & cc.

... The Carolines have been very gay lately having a great deal of masking—especially with 4 Italian girls, who came to play with them—tonight one of the Italian girls was a Sultan & Miss Hervey a Sultana and the two Carolines & ye 3 other girls were slaves. Their names are Assunta, Fortunata and Giji, which is short for Louisa.

How I do wish to receive the hug you promise me my Dearest Dearest Child in one of your letters—I think it cannot be very long before I see & kiss your face....

What books are you reading, Dst. Love? Still Rollin, I suppose. I am still reading the Roman History—Tasso—and some Italian books occasionally....

Do you ride? I have a little ugly poney [that] has prov'd a treasure to me, as I ride it about everywhere. It is a famous little horse for it came over the St Bernard with me.

I have just recollected how amazingly stupid it is in me to send you chords when you have so much better of Giardini's—but as they are wrote they shall go—and I wish you by yourself often to practise over the chords up & down the octaves in evr'y key and use yourself to find out the 5th & 6th of ev'ry note....

1st of Feb. 1793. Pisa.

... I am delighted at your attending upon the Poor children at Chiswick—oh my Love what would I have given to have seen you—I often flatter myself that you have many things in your character like yr. Dr Grandmama, and one is, not only your charity and wish to do good, but your activity and willingness to be of use for there are many things one cannot do by money sometimes which one can do by zeal.

I assure you I allow myself the least expense possible for the terrible storys one hears of the poor french makes one wish for money more than ever. Your Aunt, Bess and I have begun a purse for the poor french we know of & we have already 23£. When it is 50£ we hope to send it to a family in great distress & without our names.

I am glad you reading the Illiad. If I can get it in Italian I will read it too. I have almost finish'd the Gerusalemme Liberata—it is very beautiful indeed....

We were at the Opera last night and much entertained by the number of Masks who came into our box chiefly however in peasants dresses. The Carolines are very fond of tying a Mask with the Eyes to the back of their head and walking backwards which gives a very odd appearance....

4 Feb. 1793. Pisa.

… Nous sommes dans le plus grand chagrin, étonnement et indignation, ayant reçues l'affreuse nouvelle de la mort du Roi de France—c'est pour la Reine et sa pauvre famille que nous souffrons car pour lui il est à present tranquil, libre et heureux. Il étoit un homme bien vertueux, et par son extrème Réligion, parfaitement préparé à la mort. Il a été massacré par des sujets qu'il avoit tendrement aimé et comblé de bienfaits—et sa mort est édifiante au possible.

Adieu chère amie, chère enfant—embrasse to Sœur et dis lui que je serai bien fière de porter sa cravate.

Viterbo, 10th of March, '93.

Tomorrow I shall be at Rome, tomorrow I shall see the City so long call'd the capital of the world…. I assure you the idea of seeing Rome gives me great Emotion. Its origin from two abandon'd children & a race of Robbers—its courage in early times—the bold Character of the people —its becoming Mistress of the World—& when its vice & Luxury brought its decay, yet the famous authors & poets it produc'd— and in later times its painters & Sculptors, make it the most interesting of places. Think of seeing the remains of the temples arches & Theatres of the ancient Romans—but you shall learn from me the effect they occasion upon my mind. As it is I can hardly believe I shall be in Rome tomorrow.

March 14th.

I cannot express to you my delight & rapture at this wonderful place; but I keep a very exact journal for you & will make you as well acquainted with Rome as I am….

Rome the 16 March, '93.

… I must give you an acct. of ye life we lead here. Mr. Morrison the antiquarian, comes early & reads us a lesson upon some part of Rome famous for its being the habitation of some Hero or Statesman, or famous for some great event. We then go with him for 4 or 5 hours amongst beautiful temples & Ruins; we trace the remains of ancient magnificence & see what famous actions were performed; we also trace the manners & way of life of the ancients—all this I am keeping a journal of for you & hope to transport you as I am myself, into ancient Rome and amongst ancient Romans….

I can only now tell you how much I love you—you will know by this time how shocked I was at ye poor Kings death, I am very glad you have a mourning ring.

God bless you & yr. Dr Sister.

Rome, 17/18 March.

... There is nothing in England gives a better idea of the buildings and Villas of Italy than Dear Chiswick as there is nothing here in better taste. God bless you my Dst. Love—oh how delightful a desert wd. appear to me if I cd. people it with my Dearest Children—& how insipid is Rome itself separated from you.

Terracina, 15 April.

... The Inn from which I write is under a Rock & close to the Sea; at the top of [the] Rock are remains of the Palace of Theodoric King of Italy & the Rock is like Bristol full of Marble & Spar. I have a comfortable little room that wd. stand upon your table. I am writing by an open window & Balcony with a view of the Rock & my Room is full of great pieces of Spar which I have pick'd up & my little Canary bird singing at my Window.

The Duchess then wrote apologizing for the poverty of her letters from Rome, but there had been so much to do and see. She would forward the journal soon, however, and possibly an account of Naples by Sir Godfrey Webster.

Naples, the 16th.

I arriv'd last night at this beautiful place, my Dst. G. with so bad a head ach that I have been in bed till this moment & am now in delight at having been at my Window actually to see Vesuvius throwing out fire—I never saw anything so fine.... I am just going to see yr. old friend Ly. Hamilton, who is ador'd here not only for her beauty & her talents but for her Charity—they say she assists the poor to ye greatest degree....

Naples enchanted Georgiana; she was enraptured by the bay, the mountain and the town. The museum at Pompeii, the discovery of Herculaneum and above all, Virgil's tomb, moved her deeply, and the presents she sent her children were cinders from Portici and a sprig of laurel from the tomb. Her chief delight though was that:

I have made great additions here to my collection of minerals—I shall have a most complete collection to study. I don't allow myself to buy—as I am not rich enough, but people have been very good to me & have given me many specimens—indeed ever so small a piece satisfies me—& when I say I don't allow myself to buy I mean I don't allow myself to lay out above 3 or 4£ in a place. I bought a collection of Marble at Florence for half a guinea & here the productions of Vesuvius for 2½; but as I don't mind scrambling I pick up a great deal myself. You wd. laugh to see me climbing up hills with a hammer in my hand—& seeing me with 3 or 4 Natural Philosophers ev'ry Morning.

I have some great curiositys, but when I return you shall help me to arrange my Cabinet.

In Earths I have ye following curiositys—some fine specimens of Rock Christal—one piece with a substance in it that looks like gold thread— call'd les cheveux de Venus. I have some marble with a shell that looks like fire. I have some spar that looks like Mother of pearl—and I have one little christal that looks like a cluster of beautiful pearls—these I carry with me, but my larger boxes are to go to England by Sea & I fear will never arrive safe.

I was at a Gentleman's today who has a very fine collection. But amongst other things he has 2 live Serpents which he keeps quite tame & allows to crawl into his bosom. I own I started from them—but yr. Dear Grandmama longs to go to see them.

I send you a little specimen of the works of this place—Tortoiseshell inlaid with gold....

Naples, 30 April, 1793.

I must give you an acct., my Dst. G. of a very interesting ceremony I saw yesterday—it was a Young Ladys taking the veil. I confess it would have entirely got the better of me had I not known that she was still to have a year to repent of leaving the world if she chose it. She was but 18 & rather pretty and daughter to a Duke who invited all the English to the Ceremony.

The Chappel or rather little Church belonging to the convent was richly decorated in Gold Tissue in Festoons with flowers & the altars in massy Silver and Wax tapers.

The bottom of the Church was filled by Ladys in diamonds & full dresses & two orchestras with beautiful musick & the best singers from the Orchestra. Her poor Mother did the honours & receiv'd the company.

The young girl came in between two Duchesses—in a very fine dress but all white like a bride—she knelt at the Altar & then before the Cardinal who sat in a Gold chair & consecrated her with holy oil. She then withdrew with a torch in her hand & enter'd these gates from which she is no more to come out. We all went to a small grate where she soon appear'd, in a close black dress & her beautiful hair cut off—here she knelt whilst the Cardinal preach'd her an affecting sermon upon her happyness at having chosen a quiet & peaceable retreat from the tumult of the world—afterwards whilst she held a lighted candle in her hand an old Nun put on the veil & Mantle & pin'd upon her head a crown of Roses.

We went afterwards to the Door of the Convent to see her; the nuns had thrown open a large folding door & ev'ry body went so far but no further to wish her joy.

The inside was decorated with garlands of Flowers grapes & oranges— and the Nuns were all around her.

It is said it was perfectly her own doing but we thought we saw traces of tears—& her poor Mother left the Church when her daughter retir'd to the Grate.

Oh my Love what a blessed religion is ours, when a religious turn is not accompany'd by this sullen retreat from the world—& when above all no one can be forc'd to take the veil.

This is enough of a very melancholy subject for it made me melancholy all day. Tell yr. Dr Brother I will write him a pretty letter next post.

8th of May, Naples.

This is your Grand-mama's birthday my Dst. Child. Why are we not all together to enjoy it? the Carolines gave her nosegays & made me wish for you my Dst. Children to have perform'd this agreeable ceremony— you should have given her

> *From your fresh gardens budding side*
> *Roses, that with your cheeks had vied*
> *And lillys of the Vale, whose hue*
> *Bespoke your minds, sincere and true—*
> *However sweet the flowers you brought*
> *Yet hearts like yours, with feeling wrought*
> *Would to your parents Eyes have prov'd*
> *Flowers, fresher, sweeter, more belov'd.*

Excuse these bad verses my Love, but I am tir'd to death with a bustling day—I could not help telling you how I miss'd you on this Dear day. I gave yr. Gdmama a Cup of the Naples China with Herculaneum figures which she was so good as to say she lik'd.

Thursday the 9th.

We have been to a country seat of the Kings which was render'd very gay by a number of Country people & by some horse races. This day was however more pleasing to me from receiving a dear letter from you. your acct. of the Shawl manufactory pleas'd me so much that I read it to Ly. Hamilton who makes, you know, so good a use of shawls. I think it must be beautiful for beds.... We have been riding along the Stygian lake & I send you & your dear Sister a flower each for you from the Elysian Fields....

... We din'd or rather breakfasted with the King at Cardeletta where he has his dairy farm & horses. we din'd at a table which was very comfortable—as no servants wait'd & the different things that were wanted came up from a room below at pleasure—the middle circle of the table contain'd the dinner & by ev'ry place was a moveable trap door which according to your pulling a bell brought up wine, water, bread & c.c.—the Carolines who din'd with us were delighted.

... We have had the musick of a regiment quarter'd here, we have been dancing & I like an old fool join'd in the English country dances & danc'd with both the Caros....

11th of May Naples.

My Dearest G.,

I dispatch'd one packet & begin another with pleasure.

I went today to see some Chinese—they are masks & were stole from China by some papish Embassys. They are yellow & with small eyes. I have preserv'd for your Journal my name written by them—they write with a hair pencil, very slow & holding it upright.

12th of May.

O my G. how can I express my happyness to you. We were dining today at the Arca felice—or rather under it—in the most pitturesque situation in the world—when the post arriv'd and your Dear Dear Dst. Papas letter telling me to return to you in the middle of the summer. God of heaven bless him for his kindness to me—in 3 months at latest I shall be with you my Dearest Children and this cruel absence will be amply made up by the delight of seeing you—oh my Dearest Love what joy it will be & how very very good yr. Dear Papa is to me.

13th.

Dearest Love my hurry of spirits has been too great to be able to write much but the good news contain'd in this letter will make up for its shortness.

In less than 3 months I shall embrace you—I shall see my dear, my Dearest Children—oh how good yr. Dr Papa is.

Another view of the green room, Devonshire House.

15

The Return

Along the dusty autumn roads, the corn still standing in stooks beside them, through the golden-moted air, through the blue-hazed twilight, through the gusty autumn night, posted the messenger to Devonshire House.

When he reached Piccadilly it was long after midnight, but the Duke, his foot wrapped in flannel and supported by a gout-stool, was still playing cards with his cronies, Messieurs Hare, James, Grenville and Fish Crawfurd. The news spread from the porter in his lodge to the footman on duty, who was bidden by the Duke to have Miss Trimmer wakened and informed. The news spread from the footman to the nursery-maid, roused to act as his feminine counterpart, who knocked at Selina's door, the candle flickering over her startled face.

Selina was awake in an instant; drawing on her dressing-gown she hurried through the dark passages, up the dark stairs and knocked on Mrs Brown's door. She opened it, crossed the room, drew the bed-curtains and shook the astonished Mrs Brown by the shoulder.

'She's at Dover,' she whispered, so as not to wake little Hartington, 'she's on her way—she's coming back!'

Soon all the house was awake: little lights of candles, greater lights of candelabras, steadier lights of lamps, broke the gloom. In the attics and the basement alcoves there were lights, and through the great house went Mrs Brown, clutching her shawl around her, dabbing at her eyes with a wet handkerchief, followed by a footman bearing a great jug of wine. She woke them all; the scullions and the still-room maids, the major-domo, the maître d'hôtel and the chef; she woke the housemaids, the lackeys and even the two boys who cleaned the boots. To all of them, a strange bulky angel, she made her annunciation: 'She's coming back,' she said. 'Her Grace is on her way!' And to each she gave a glass of wine.

There was no more sleep that night; the house hummed like a hive of happy bees, and the morning sun shone no more brightly than the polished brass and silver or the gleaming floors over which the striped petticoats of the maids made a sound like the rustling, falling leaves outside.

The children were dressed earlier than usual, the little girls in scarlet coats and beaver bonnets, and soon they and Miss Trimmer were bundled into one carriage, while Mrs Brown with the nursery-maids and the solemn precious heir to all the splendour, the three-and-a-half-year-old Marquess of Hartington, followed in another. But the cortège, bound for Dartford, was not complete, for swinging on its silver springs, like a great pumpkin painted pale blue, drove the new coach that was to bear the Duchess to London.

Little G. was silent with excitement, for, being the eldest, she remembered her mother the best, and when she had written those many letters she had felt she was writing to a real person; that her own beloved mother would read the very words she traced so carefully. But she wished she had not got such a cold; it made her feel so heavy and stupid. And indeed she was a deplorable sight, her large, pale blue eyes watery and suffused, her rather long nose pink against her white face, and her full Cavendish lower lip swollen to twice its size.

Selina was much distressed that the Duchess should see G. thus, but she was not to blame and had dosed the child with manna and bark.

At any rate, she thought, no one can say that Hary-o does not look well. Hary-o was bouncing about on the seat with excitement, though she was not quite sure about what; her fat little body wriggling like a puppy's, her round face and rosy cheeks making poor G. look more anaemic than ever. 'My darling G.'s a rabbit,' she told Miss Trimmer, who asked whatever she meant by speaking so of her sister. 'Well, she is like my rabbit at Chiswick,' persisted Hary-o, 'her eyes are pink and her face is white and her teeth stick out.' Miss Trimmer sternly bade her be silent and beg her sister's pardon, though to be sure, those new teeth of G.'s had rather a rabbity appearance.

But to the Duchess only one thing mattered—they were her children and she could touch them at last. She hugged and kissed the two little girls till G. was breathless and Hary-o wild with spirits, but baby Hart behaved in a lamentable way.

He would not look or speak to this strange lady, but clung to Mrs Brown, burying his face in her comfortable shoulder. But later a memory came to him, and he asked 'for himself.' At first his mother could not understand what he wanted, but she soon realized that it was his miniature that had hung, together with his sisters', in her coach throughout her travels. She sent for it and showed it to him; he nodded solemnly, looking absurdly like his father, kissed his portrait as though bidding it good-bye now that he was really there and then turned it over. 'There is my little hair,' he said to the Duchess, pointing with a fat finger to the silver-white lock. After that he put up his arms and kissed her a little, so that her heart was filled with hope. They were all tired out; the drive to Dartford, the emotion of meeting their half-forgotten mother, the return to London, the sight of all the servants drawn up in the courtyard to greet her, had made the day seem as unreal as a fairy-tale.

The Duchess was exhausted too; half dead from fatigue and the intensity of her feelings. But she could not rest; she ran from room to room, touching the remembered and loved pieces of furniture, stopping in front of strange ones, especially a very pretty new bed in the Duke's room. At last she bid him good-night, hoping that his gout would not prevent him from rest and telling him, a little shyly, how glad she was to be home. He put his hand in his pocket and brought out a miniature of Lady Spencer. 'I thought you might like it,' he said, and before she could thank him for this crowning kindness,' he added, 'I had it in my drawer.'

At last she was ready to go to bed; she had written to Mama ('I have seen them, I have seen them ...'), she had greeted the servants, Canis was kind; with the children beneath the same roof and her mother's portrait in her hand, she felt surrounded by everything she knew was dear. 'I shall sleep tonight,' she decided, 'in the room with my dear Father's picture.'

Still holding Mama's picture, she blew out the lights. She was so happy to have this new possession. It was now hers and she had not many things she could call her very own. She remembered how she had made her will a year and a half ago at Aix, and how difficult it had been to find enough things to leave as remembrances, for all her jewels belonged to Canis. There had been her Petrarch for Hart; the blue Turkey stone earrings for G.; an amethyst for Hary-o and her wedding-ring and the children's portraits for Mama. There had not been much else; a garnet necklace and her Dante for Harriet Duncannon, and Canis's miniature, that she used to carry in her pocket, for Bess. She had hoped that Canis would comply with her wish by maintaining her poor school at Edensor and by paying her two former maids small annuities. As for money, there had only been £350, and of this she had left £100 to Caroline St Jules and £50 to Canis. But why think of all this now? She was alive and at home and the children were with her at last.

The flurry of her spirits died gently down and her dreams were all of the morrow.

The next few days were among the happiest in her life; she was too agitated to look about her, too happy and, perhaps after a long journey, too idle to do anything. She got up early to see the children sooner, sat by the fire, and the litter of her room would have made Lady Spencer cluck with horror. There was so much to learn and decide about these three little beings, who she thought she knew so well and who were so strange to her.

It was evident that G. had outgrown her strength and needed tonics. She had an unfortunate stoop and poked her head forward, and her teeth needed straightening, but a 'silver' would soon put that right. Otherwise she was perfect—loving, docile and obedient. She would follow her mother round the house like a shadow and was quietly and rapturously in heaven. Her mother thought her the most interesting child she had ever seen and very pretty.

Hary-o was quite different; determined, witty and gay. She had one great passion in life—her sister—and when it was decreed that G. needed longer nights, Hary-o suggested herself that she should go to bed half an hour earlier so that G. should still be able to sit up later than her younger sister. But she showed more spirit than the gentle G., and had to be reproved for insolence to the maids which, though shocking, made the Duchess laugh, for Hary-o walked out of the room in silence with a grand and desperate air. There was no doubt that she was very odd: what was one to make of a child who told her father that she was melancholy because her eyes were too big? Or to her reply to the startled Duke, when he asked her why, 'Because I see too much of the world'? She was a great mimic and musically precocious.

As to Hart, Georgiana could hardly recognize in the little boy the eighteen-month-old baby she had left two years ago. He had just been breeched, and his mother adored his beautiful little body dressed in a pepper-and-salt suit with white buttons. He was full of contradictions: his naturally sweet temper alternating with violent fits of passion, when he would kick and fight like a little colt. He was both sensitive and brave, refusing to be seen when he was ill or to be held on to his rocking-horse the first time he rode on it. And how proud and happy she was when, only a few days after her return, he had gravely asked her not to go away again!

How could anyone expect her to pay calls or waste time away from these three children? Indeed, it was out of the question, and though she rose at nine to be with them and though they dined with her at seven, the days were never long enough. Great Devonshire House had shrunk to the size of the nurseries.

The Duke, too, demanded her attention, and though he showed her every courtesy and kindness, he liked her to sit with him in the evenings, after they had supped at eleven, while he played cards with his friends. The poor Duchess, used to the early hours of the Continent, could hardly keep awake, and by three o'clock was almost ill from want of sleep. 'Cette chienne de vie me tue,' she cried to Lady Spencer, 'but Hardwick will set me up again.'

Sometimes, and with reluctance, she was obliged to visit the outside world, where even her old friends bore a different appearance. She had become accustomed to the new modes of the Continent: 'Greek' or 'Turkish' dresses with 'a simple Turban and feather, very neat, noble and pretty,' but in England these fashions had been caricatured, so that the women, wearing their girdles under their armpits, all looked with child, while they tortured their hair into Medusa-like locks.

Her heaven was at home, and no smart assembly could rival the joys of the servants' ball which Canis, dear Canis, suggested in honour of her return. The children were present: G. danced with Mr Cugge and looked really very beautiful; Hary-o, shy for once, soon joined in; Hart made his bow to the company, and Georgiana's heart swelled with pride at her three children. They were all there: Mrs Howden, Mrs Cole, the whole family of Townshend, Mrs Marsden, Mrs Bourchier, Mrs Brown, Hannah Bunting, the devoted Dennis who presided over the card table, and Mrs Venables from Chiswick, 'as fine as hands could make her.' It was the happiest and most successful party ever given in Devonshire House.

Plans for the future were hard to decide. The Duke's gout was obstinate and Bath was clearly indicated, but Hardwick, Chatsworth and Chiswick had all to be inspected.

Finally it was decided to go to Bath, but first Georgiana visited Chiswick to decide on the necessary redecorations and repairs. The mournful gardens, where the cedars and yews stood blackly against the grey-brown autumn grass, seemed infinitely more beautiful to her than had the dazzling, frosty acacias and golden mimosas shining against the southern skies. 'Mrs Venables,' she said, 'we shall soon all be here together again.' 'Oh, your Grace,' said stout Mrs Venables as she dropped her curtsy, 'I have no doubt that now your Grace has come, the dry-rot will soon cease.'

By December they were all at Bath, all, that is to say, except the little girl, Eliza Courtnay, who had been born during the exile, and who could never enter the circle of children round the Duchess, though Caroline St Jules and a little refugee, Corisande de Gramont, daughter of the Duc de Grammont, had found their way in.

Though Georgiana often thought of and longed for her, the other three kept her fully occupied. Hartington was her special problem: his uncontrollable fits of rage were alarming, but Georgiana ascribed them to the indulgence of the doting Mrs Brown. Once, when his temper was so violent that no one could approach him, the Duchess called to the Duke and, as soon as he came into the room, Hartington stopped screaming. Afterwards, when he was alone with his mother, she noticed that he was thoughtful. Suddenly he said, 'Papa made me good directly—*why for*? Do you know, I believe I was frightened?' Georgiana snatched him up and held him tightly to her. Even when he had kicked and pinched her till she was black and blue, she cherished her bruises, for they had been given by her darling little son, who was only spoilt, not bad. She decided that she must find some punishment he could understand and, as he was very proud of his Sunday suit, a miniature Derbyshire uniform, he was not allowed to wear this when he had been naughty. One day, when he was asked why he was not dressed in his red coat, he said that it had gone to the tailor's as a pattern, and won the battle. Soon her patience had its reward, and when she asked him why he had been so naughty, he said that the Bath air had not agreed with him. Georgiana thought his intelligence miraculous and repeated all his sayings to Lady Spencer, especially how he had chosen as New Year's gifts a pair of breeches for Selina Trimmer and a humming-top for the portly Mrs Brown.

The Duke and Duchess decided not to return to London, and instead of going North, they accepted the loan of the Duke of Bedford's house, Oakley, where they remained till June. Though the state of Canis's health alarmed Georgiana, she was supremely happy in this small house with the children. Gradually the regular country life corrected his condition, caused by indulgence in harmful habits and impossibly late hours; the spitting of blood and exhaustion lessened as he settled down to normal.

So in April Georgiana could enjoy to the full the sight of tiny Hart reviewing the Derbyshire Militia at Bedford. He was a pretty sight in his regimentals, standing in the centre of the parade ground. As the men saluted him, he took off his hat so that his silver hair blew in the wind. And when, of his own accord, he desired that the soldiers should be given bread, cheese and ale, Georgiana's delight knew no bounds.

The family's return to Chatsworth was as of long-exiled and much-loved royalty. The villagers, remembering Georgiana's consideration and care; how she had given them a school, medical attention and, best of all, her interest, welcomed her deliriously. They chose G.'s eleventh birthday on which to give full expression to their feelings. The Duchess wrote a description of the occasion to her mother who was still abroad:

It was the prettiest fête I ever saw. Besides my school we had 11 little girls cloathed—they formed a little procession carrying flags, garlands and Nosegays. They had pretty good musick and were clos'd by an excellent train of Morrice dancers, very good looking and finely drest. They march'd through the park along the garden to the Green House which was decorated with flowers and G.'s cypher in Flowers and there they din'd. We had a very good Ball in the Evening and a transparent with G.'s cypher: the girls presented her nosegays with verses (very touching and written by George) and a basket with 11 little trifling presents and cover'd with flowers. The Children sat up till 1 and G. certainly the happyest creature there.

In September Lady Spencer made her way back to England. Her daughter went to Harwich to meet her, but Lady Spencer was delayed, so that her travelling carriage arrived before her. When Georgiana saw Mama's poor dear brown chaise, containing her books, phosphoric candles and paraphernalia, she was flooded with memories of those long years abroad.

Lady Spencer's homecoming was marred by the news that Georgiana's headaches were increasingly frequent and painful. Her eyes were hurting her and she could neither read, write nor work for any length of time without bringing on the pain.

Lady Spencer also learnt that the Prince of Wales and Mrs Fitzherbert were parted, it was said in obedience to a wish of their Majesties, and that there was talk of a 'real' marriage at last. Georgiana confessed to her mother that she was thankful that she had been so much out of town and that, therefore, she had not been involved in the Prince's affairs. Apart from his domestic concerns he was being more than usually tiresome, promising positions and then going back on his word.

Once more the patterns of all their lives were shifting: Prinny was to marry a royal and suitable German cousin; Sheridan was a shadow of his gay self, for his heart-rending letters written to Georgiana and Harriet Duncannon whilst they were abroad had ended with the death of his adored wife, Elizabeth; the shocking news of the execution of the King of France had been followed by the even more harrowing end of Marie Antoinette. Old friends were vanishing and new ones filled their places, though not their memories.

Harriet Duncannon returned to England in the autumn, very nearly cured, and full of anecdotes of Lady Webster, Lord Granville Leveson Gower and Lord Holland whom the sisters had known in Naples. Of these three, Lord Granville was the most frequently mentioned, and when she, the Duchess and their children went to Teignmouth in December, he stayed nearby at Saltram, paying them daily calls.

Though Georgiana's few parties at Devonshire House had delighted her friends, Lady Melbourne and Lady Webster, she preferred to remain in the country, the children proving compensation for more sophisticated society. She had found Charles Grey fractious and exigeant, and now that he was to be married, perhaps it were better that she should stay away. Even Bess and Canis were in temporary disagreement; also any form of exertion brought on those blinding headaches which were becoming the dread of her existence.

With her children, by the sea, however, she could relax. Life was becoming a strange mixture of simple pleasures and crippling pain. Her delights were a New Year's play acted by the whole band of children; a rage for 'devises' play acted by Mme de Staël—she chose a sun for Lady Spencer's devise and the motto 'Bénie par ses bienfaits'; for G. a rosebud and 'Je serais Rose,' and for Dr Drew a flint with the words, 'It shines when struck.' To arrange mock concerts performed by 'La Signora Gina,' 'Signor Guglielmo' (Hart) and the 'Signorinas Henrighetta and Carolina,' which nonsense amused the 'artistes' and encouraged them to practise; to deny herself all luxury so that she could assist her émigré friends, many of whom were practically destitute; to obtain small posts for deserving young men; and to laugh at Hary-o's query, 'Why do the waves spit at me?' seemed to her the height of bliss.

Unhappily her headaches and eye-trouble were becoming so bad that she decided, reluctantly, to return to London, and she communicated this to the Duke. He, however, with his usual negligence, did not reply, and when he did write was inexplicit and unhelpful. By April she was forced to town in order to undergo treatment. This consisted in applying leeches to the eyeball into which the blood was forced by a tourniquet round her neck. She bore this agonizing remedy with the greatest courage and derived some temporary relief.

She longed to resume her country life of the previous year. Her former interests no longer held the same charms; she was neither well enough nor inclined to go into Society, whilst the days when Fox, Sherry and she had been happy and active in political work had gone.

The country was engaged in the first stages of that single-handed resistance to Continental tyranny which was to liberate Europe and justify the faith in freedom which was the very lifeblood of England.

Fox and his adherents, to whom the year 1788 was ever a bright beacon, had seen in the germination of the French Revolution a glorious manifestation of all their ideals, and were therefore bound, by loyalty to their creed, to oppose the war. The more long-sighted of their supporters, headed by the Duke of Portland, while realizing that the ideal of Liberty was threatened by the very liberators who now menaced the liberty of the entire world, could only stand aside, while their political enemies, under the leadership of Pitt, prosecuted the war. These two points of view are most clearly set forth by Georgiana, the idealist and faithful friend of Fox and all he stood for, and by his other disciple, Lady Sarah Napier. Georgiana wrote that:

> Thinking so ill of the war as I do, and being disgusted with politics, and lamenting the ruin and downfall of that glorious phalanx of name, probity and property, which so long had stood between the people and the crown, *the Rockinghams*; my only comfort is my Brother [then at the Admiralty], for I see him amidst the wreck, sacrificing every thing to the prosperity of our only stay and hope—the Navy.

Whilst Lady Sarah believed Fox 'more glorious than ever, with a *few* friends upholding his well-founded opinions in the midst of the confusion of prejudices, frights and abuse and resisting all temptation to fall from his noble height of principle into mean power and adulation.' Later she added that though she abhorred:

> 300 and odd of the French murderers, I pity the rest who are slaves to tyrants; I pity the deluded multitude, 'and I wish them success at home but ruin if they go one step out of France. I think our war, the King's war, very wrong and very foolish, but still I wish it success.'

Georgiana was happy to escape from London again and spent a quiet summer with the children at Bognor. Here she found a few old friends: Pembrokes, Rutlands and Speaker Addington. Sheridan paid flying visits to his second wife, Hecca, who was staying there with her blind mother, Mrs Ogle. He was so wrapped up in his bride, whom Georgiana thought a good-hearted, odd little thing, that he had little time for the Duchess.

Yet she was content as long as she was with the children, and marked the occasion of G.'s twelfth birthday with the present of an emerald cross which she had long hoarded against the day. She knew G. for the child she still was and yet, such is mother-love, every young man appeared as a potential husband, and she eyed each one anxiously, wondering whether he would prove worthy of her paragon.

The winter was productive of little save rumours about the Prince of Wales, his wife and Lady Jersey. It was agreed by all that the open favour with which Prinny honoured her Ladyship was scandalous and unbecoming, especially as his wife was about to be confined. At two o'clock in the morning of January the 7th, 1796, the Prince sent to Canis, desiring his presence at Carlton House where the Princess was in labour. The Duke struggled into a dress coat and spent a long, dull night waiting with the Duke of Leeds and the Prince's Household, till the birth of Princess Charlotte, at ten in the morning, secured his release, when he promptly went home to bed.

In February the Prince summoned the Duchess and Harriet Bessborough (as she had now become) to dinner, in order that they should meet his consort. He greeted them in an ante-room and said he had decided against a formal presentation. He and Georgiana supported Lady Bessborough between them, for she still walked with difficulty, and the Princess advanced to the middle of the room to meet them. Her manner to the sisters was affectionate and almost coaxing: she admired their dresses very much and inquired after Lady Spencer. The dinner was simple and agreeable, the company consisting of the Harcourts, Cholmondeleys and Jerseys, Mr George Pitt and Lord Harcourt's daughter-in-law, Mrs Vernon. Before they left, the Princess kissed Georgiana, calling her 'Ma chère Duchesse,' and expressed a wish to see her again. It was all very friendly and well-mannered, and the Duchess was as much puzzled as the rest of the world when in June the Princess retired to her own house in Pall Mall and Lady Jersey announced she was going to publish an 'Eclaircissment,' which would alter public opinion in her favour. Lady Jersey maintained she was maligned; whilst the men in Georgiana's set assured the Duchess that Lord Jersey was not complacent but only deceived. One thing was clear—the royal couple were definitely parted and all talk of a reconciliation proved false.

Such were the small events in Georgiana's life. In August she was again ill: the former drastic treatments to her eye were repeated, but less successfully. Canis wrote phlegmatically to Lady Spencer announcing the certain loss of one eye, though he was assured the other would not be affected and the outward appearance unaltered.

Georgiana's recovery was slower than she had been promised, and it was not till November that her health was partly restored. She was quite blind in one eye and still suffered from her terrible headaches. She was obliged to use an 'invention' when writing, so as not to use nor strain the remaining eye. This made her handwriting large and sprawling as though she were a girl again. There was but little left of the girl she had been.

16

Towards the End

In 1786 when Selina Trimmer first brought her corded boxes to Devonshire House, she arrived with some trepidation and Lady Spencer's blessing. It had required the latter and much persuasion to overcome her mother's natural reluctance to allow her daughter to take up a post in a house famed for its splendour, brilliance and profligacy. Mrs Trimmer was torn between admiration of Lady Spencer and fear lest her daughter should be contaminated by the notorious and worldly Duchess. After the publicity accorded to the Westminster Election, there was hardly an English home where Georgiana's name was not synonymous with beauty, indiscretion and extravagance. It was not surprising that a minor civil war was waged in the neat house at Brentford, as to whether Selina should accept the post of governess to the Ladies Cavendish or not. Lady Spencer and Mrs Trimmer's good sense won the day.

Still, Selina had been cautious. She was on the defensive against the Duchess's charm, and particularly wary of Lady Elizabeth Foster. Before Lady Liz's return from Italy, Selina's fears had been somewhat allayed, but with Bess's advent her hackles rose again. She disliked and disapproved of her from the first, and she sensed that her feelings were shared by Lady Spencer. Naturally the children's grandmother never spoke to her on the subject, but there were indications.... G. would sometimes beg grandmama to come again soon, and Lady Spencer would reply, 'Perhaps; we'll see—but there are Obstacles....' And a current of understanding would run between the governess and the Dowager. Selina had determined that she would not acknowledge Lady Elizabeth's self-appointed right to treat the nurseries as her own territory, and went so far as to remain seated when her Ladyship entered the room. Afterwards, when Lady Spencer sent for her and gently but sternly rebuked her for treating his Grace's house as her own, she felt ashamed of her breach of manners, but her dislike and disapproval were unaltered.

Before the Duchess went abroad in 1789, she confided the care of her two little girls to Selina. 'My mother will always help you,' she had said, 'but it is to you I must entrust them.' Selina felt honoured and touched by this confidence, for by now she knew how much the Duchess loved her children, and fulfilled her trust with unswerving loyalty and devotion.

She was touched, too, that whenever the Duchess wrote to the children, there was always a message for her, and when they received little presents from Paris and Spa, there was also a fairing for her.

Yet it was in Paris, after Hart's birth and during G.'s illness, that she had come to feel that she was really a part of the family. They had all been united in their anxiety and unhappiness, and even Selina had had to admit that Lady Elizabeth had nursed the sick child with unexpected tenderness. Selina had become fond, too, of little Mlle Caroline St Jules: she was a sweet child and exactly the same age as Hary-o, who therefore found a companion who kept her from fretting while her adored G. was ill.

Now they were all settled in England and the children were growing fast like sturdy plants, and like young plants needed much attention. Both the girls' teeth needed regulating, and this was accomplished by two methods: either by the gradual pressure of a silver wire, or by loosening the teeth in their sockets and then setting them straight. Hary-o had to undergo this torture when she was twelve years old and the operation lasted three hours. The Duchess could not bring herself to witness it, as she felt her horror and pity would communicate itself to the suffering child and break down her courage; but Selina stayed by the whole time, encouraging and consoling, though she owned it was almost too much for her.

Then again both girls were inclined to be bilious; Hary-o was very greedy and G. had inherited her father's sedentary nature, and constant doses and regimens had to be administered by the implacable Selina.

Education was not wholly a matter of book learning, for the graces and accomplishments were of importance to girls whose birth decreed a public, rather than a private, life. So the Duchess had constant small tussles with Selina, who was inclined to put needlework before music, and who regarded the necessary proficiency to be attained in dancing, painting and conversation as time stolen from the globes, history or mathematics. These, of course, were as essential as languages and literature, but Miss Trimmer must remember that a noble, graceful carriage, ease of manner and ability is be agreeable were as important to the Cavendish girls as the more serious branches of her teaching.

Though it was as impossible to teach G. to hold herself upright and keep her head from drooping as to curb Hary-o's over-exuberant spirits, it was not difficult to foster charity and good sense in either of the children. Something of Lady Spencer's unceasing and active benevolence had been transmitted to her granddaughters, and with Miss Trimmer to encourage their inclinations and with their mother's example before them, both the little girls took a lively and real pleasure in doing good from their earliest days. When Hary-o was only eleven she wrote to her sister of a new plan for the biggest of her drawers: 'I mean to keep in it,' she decided, 'all manner of clothes of different sorts for the poor people and when I hear of any in distress, I shall always have my drawer ready.' There was not much money to give away: the Duchess had a 'play purse' limited to fifty guineas, and on the little girls' birthdays she could only afford largess in half-crowns instead of guineas as formerly. But what there was, was given freely and with pleasure.

Both girls had inherited their mother's love of music, though their talents were executive instead of creative. It was now that the Duchess composed the music for Sheridan's song, 'I have a silent sorrow here,' in his production of *The Stranger*, which became the rage; but its popularity did not give her as much pleasure as the sound of the girls playing on the harp and piano. She had engaged the world-famous harpist, Mme Krumpholtz, and her former music-master, Giardini, to teach them these instruments and was delighted by their progress. She took them to hear Mrs Billington and Arioli, but though Hary-o had a passion for the theatre, she had to fight a battle with G., who disapproved of the opera.

G. was going through an acute stage of adolescent piety which threatened to turn to religious mania. The Duchess, who was naturally religious and *pratiquante*, approved of G.'s devotions, but felt she must prevent the girl's inclination to forswear the world. So she wrote her the following letter:

I speak so ill on any subject I am anxious about my darling G., that I have just thrown down my ideas on paper.

Selina is always right & certainly could the world be new form'd & no impropriety suffer'd, how far happier it would be. Also it would perhaps be happier to lead a retir'd life. But your lot is cast in another line; & to do your duty in the world & be an example to it, is my ardent wish.

Public entertainments have at least this good, that they support a number of poor & give cause to employ & exercise industry.

I would not wish any young person to arrogate themselves as a judge, or to blame those amusements that the wisest & best allow themselves temperately. And also be assur'd that neither now, or when you are presented, shall I ever introduce you to a place which I think improper. Of the Opera I think otherways—the moral is never bad as in too many English plays. The company is the best & you are not expos'd to improper intensions as at the play house & you have the advantage of the excellence of the musick. As for encouraging the performers, whilst it is establish'd under the protection of government, I cannot see how any one person keeping away can have any effect. Perhaps Selina does not know that this establishment in the Theatrical line [comes] particularly under the Lord Chamberlayne—& I own I think it as rational as any other public entertainment. You may be certain when the ballets are improper, I should not let you go.

No, my Dr Dst. Child, We have no right to arrogate ourselves against custom, when there is nothing criminal. But my anxious wish is to warn you from taking too much interest, giving too much thought about amusement. Let them never get into a habit, let them never interfere with Sunday, with your prayers & daily religious duty, and being (God grant it may be a happyness to you) plac'd in an exalted situation. Let your modest & reserv'd manner, your chearfulness, but yet temperance in amusement, & your religion, piety & modest deportment distinguish you & exalt you beyond the power of the world to do.

G. bowed to her mother's opinions, but evidently took them too literally, for shortly after the Duchess had to write to her again.

My Dearest G.,

I was half asleep when I spoke to you. I have wrote to Selina & explain'd to her that nobody can have a greater veneration for Sunday & a more serious idea of it than I have; but it was always instill'd into me by my Dr Mother, that it was also a very chearful day, & this was my Mother's opinion so much that tho' she avoided cards, she had musick on Sunday Evening both in the country & town. I know many people think otherways, but this is my opinion; that after the Dutys perform'd, nothing is more innocent.

However as I always like to comply with Selina & with you, we will put it off tomorrow & I will stay with you, Dst. & drink tea with you.

God bless you, I am better & I hope I shall be quite well tomorrow.

Apart from such small differences, they were in perfect accord with their mother and adored her. Whether they were reading in the bow-window of her room at Chiswick while she wrote her letters; reading sermons or Voltaire with her or, best of all, playing chess with her; as long as they were with her the days were happy, and without her, lifeless. She was so gay when she was with them and Cornelia-like in her love. 'I go to Court,' she wrote to them, 'in a beautiful purple & white body & train with gold cord & a pettycoat with gold fringe—no Jewels but your picture; & if I had Hart's finish'd, I should think I carry'd my best Jewels about me.' The girls and Georgiana were close companions: they called her 'dearest Emy' or 'Emma'; studied her every wish and even Hary-o would stay quiet as a mouse, instead of scampering about like a 'march hair' or dancing hornpipes all over the house, when she had one of her headaches.

The two girls and their cousin, Caro Ponsonby, were unrelenting mimics and used to copy Lady Liz's baby-talk, linking their arms together as they strolled in the garden and telling each other that 'Oo know, dearest 'ove, that I 'ave so 'ittle time for 'ose things 'at it is impossible for me to 'ite.' They teased poor Selina, vowing she was secretly married to Bob Adair, and drove her nearly wild with their noise and racket.

Selina sometimes wondered how she managed them at all; it was like driving a flock of wild birds all flying in different directions. G. was the easiest, gentle, pliable and serious. Hary-o was very clever but never stuck to anything long: she would read her eyes out of her head or refuse to read at all; lie in bed till ten o'clock or be up by six: was loving, tempestuous, wild with spirits or melancholy about nothing. Caro St Jules was almost too good; pious, gentle, self-effacing and sensitive to a fault. Caro Ponsonby, wild as a hawk and impertinent as a squirrel. Selina found a verse on the schoolroom table one day: she read:

> *The orange and the lemon pale*
> *With Selly's cheeks do vie.*
> *But, ah! no maid that is not frail*
> *Has such a roving eye!*

'Caroline's writing, of course!' she thought and did not know whether to laugh or be annoyed, when little giggles came from behind the screen and whispers of 'Oh! fie, Mrs Trimmer-Adair!' and there were G., Hary-o, Caro and Hart all convulsed with laughter.

Hart was proud and passionate and would argue with her for hours on a point of authority, but in the end he always gave way and even after he went to Harrow would write her loving letters. He was a constant anxiety: sometimes he would be missing for hours and Selina would search the house fruitlessly from cellar to attic. But she did not climb high enough, till one day she discovered his hiding-place was at the feet of the statue of Minerva, the highest, topmost pinnacle of Chatsworth, where he sat with a book, perched astride the dizzy slope of the pediment a hundred feet above the ground.

Then there was serious little Augustus Clifford who, though he was two years older than Hart, always followed the younger boy's lead.

In 1796 there were two additions to this little world. Lady Elizabeth's husband had died, and her two sons, Augustus and Frederick Foster, came to join her from Ireland. On December the 17th G. received three letters: the first two from her mother, the third from Lady Elizabeth. They read as follows:

Dearest G., They came at six—I never saw a more touching sight. They clung about poor Bess, who cried terribly. Frederick, tho' plain, has an interesting countenance & a manly person and manner. Augustus is a pretty, lively fair boy. It was quite a picture to see them support their poor mother, all drest in black & her picture hanging at Frederick's bosom.

Later the Duchess wrote:

Dearest G., they are all gone to bed—Bess calmer than I could have expected. They are interesting creatures & their love for her quite touching.... I like the interesting affectionate looks of Fred—they have very little brogue & seem to adore her....

Lady Liz's letter was in the same tone: she is sure G. will conceive of her happiness at having her sons with her; she finds their affection for her delightful and the manners of both very engaging.

The Cavendish girls, especially Hary-o who was clear-sighted and unsentimental to a degree, did not find the Fosters such 'interesting creatures,' as they soon tired to death of Fred's laboured jokes and Augustus's pedantry, and found the brothers lacking in good taste and good feelings.

The Fosters, however, made themselves quite at home and teased the girls, Fred vowing 'how happy I could be by myself, if both the dear charmers ...'

Selina quite liked the two boys who, though 14 and 16, had to submit to her jurisdiction, but her dislike of their mother was undiminished by time. This dislike was reciprocal, though it sprang from different causes: Selina disapproved of Lady Liz, who resented being disapproved of, especially by a governess. Bess confessed to Lady Bessborough that Selina always affected her like a north-east wind, which in the brightest sun has still some chill in it. Miss Trimmer tried to hide her feelings and was always scolding the Cavendish girls and Caro Ponsonby for their attitude towards her Ladyship; but it was no good, they detested her and only suppressed expression of their feelings in front of Caro St Jules who was, of course, Lady Liz's special protégée. Selina was fond, too, of Corisande de Gramont, though she was too frivolous and precociously flirtatious for Miss Trimmer's taste. Still, that was not her fault but her misfortune, being French.

They are all growing up fast: G. has had her hair up for over three years (though she still pulls it down and scratches her head wildly when writing a letter), and though Hary-o is now having trouble with her hair-pins, she is showing an interest in her appearance. 'I will give you a *description*,' she writes, 'as you would not think it was me unless I describe *my dress*; I must. It *was* a chip Hat with a wreath of grapes which looked very *small* and pretty, a white gown, gold chain and my Lilack cross.' She is also intrigued by why the grown-ups, who are so fond of Lady Holland (as Lady Webster had now become), should be embarrassed by her joining their juvenile party at Astley's circus. Selina had dropped hints of unbecoming behaviour in Lady Holland's past, but the shrewd child thought it foolish of Selina to strain at gnats when she daily swallowed camels.

Hart is settling down at Harrow and already plays the man, affecting to fear neither Dr Drury nor Mr Branby, though Selina still rules him with a rod of iron during the holidays.

Silly talk about whether G. will invite 'Mrs Trimmer-Adair' to Woburn when she is Duchess of Bedford has died down, and instead she blushes if anyone mentions the Carlisles, Castle Howard or, more particularly, Lord Morpeth. The girls tell their little secrets to Selina, for they have confidence in her discretion and judgment, even though they call her 'Raison Sévère' and 'Vent de Bise.'

Miss Trimmer is unhappy about her beloved Duchess, who has more and worse headaches than ever before and, sometimes, an unaccountable pain in her side. She remembered her early days at Devonshire House: how sometimes the Duchess had seemed jealous of the friendship with which Lady Spencer honoured her, and how once her Grace had sent a little note up to her bedroom: they had had a little disagreement and the tears had started to her eyes when she realized that the Duchess was, begging *her* pardon, assuring her of her undying love and respect and asking her to forgive and forget. 'All I can remember,' thought Selina, 'is how *good* she is—how good she has always been to me. If only her Grace had not to worry so over money....' For Selina knows that whenever there is a financial crisis it brings on one of those blinding pains that neither darkened rooms nor Bath waters can cure.

She had been with them to Ramsgate and witnessed the beginning of an extraordinary flirtation between those creatures of earth and air, William Lamb and Caroline Ponsonby, and another between Corisande and '*Mister* John Ponsonby.' She had chaperoned them while they dipped decorously in the sea; had been shocked by Miss Talbot tossing her little round body in the waves and by Lady Asgill showing her legs on horseback. She had accompanied them to breakfasts at Dandelion: to the theatre: had paled at the announcement of Fred Lamb's arrival, feeling she could not cope with 'un agneau de plus,' and in the evenings, 'when winds blow cold and loud and drear and Ladies 'gin to walk the Pier,' she had 'followed to and fro To watch each ill-designing beau.'

She had been with them to Bath, and remembered how they had had to put up in a poky, uncomfortable hotel where the Duchess had made light of every discomfort and treated the maids as though they were Princesses, whilst Lady Liz had whined and complained and asked for chicken and Bath waters for her dog. It had been at Bath that she had received the flattering and responsible offer to become sub-preceptress to little Princess Charlotte, only child of the Prince of Wales. She was glad that she had listened to the Duchess's assurance that she would be sadly missed at Devonshire House and that she had decided not to leave what had now become her real home.

She had watched her pupils at 'Juvenile Balls,' and smiled at the Court paid to the Duchess by the great Society ladies, who had formerly disapproved of her but who now found Devonshire House desirable, since it was open to the new generation and that the Marquess of Harlington was approaching manhood.

She had seen the Duchess's simple joy at her lovely new garden at Chiswick where there were to be flowers all the year round, and her silent unhappiness when the Duke, surely unthinkingly, had had it cleared away the following year. 'You will make another, dear Duchess,' comforted Selina. 'Oh no,' said the Duchess, shaking her still lovely head, 'the genius of Chiswick has quite gone from that place.' Instead of flowers, Hartington has installed an assortment of strange animals, which frighten the Duchess and the girls, and fat Mrs Brown now rules in Mrs Venables's place.

So much has changed in the fifteen years she has been with them—the girls have grown into young women and Hart is now six feet tall. Though the Duke stays out all night at Brooks's, they keep reasonable hours, occupying the evenings with music, charades or dancing. Lady Bessborough, handsome Lord Granville, whom the girls think conceited, sometimes Mr Sheridan and the Duchess sit in one corner playing chess, at which game the Duchess is apt to attack violently and then carry off one of her own men in triumph, while Selina sits quietly knotting a silk purse in another.

The lights are dimmer now: there are fewer candles flaring in the sconces. The mother-of-pearl counters and deadly fish are neatly stacked away by Selina in their tortoiseshell, velvet and ormolu case; no longer do they represent hundreds and thousands of guineas but modest sixpences and shillings.

The places at the dinner table are divided between the Duke's cronies, Fish Crawfurd, Mr Motteux, obsequiously eating his own superfluous presents of fish and game, and Monsieur Vigoreux, head of the family protected by Lady Spencer and the Duchess; and a horde of young men, those from Melbourne House making an uncommon noise. Fred, William and George Lamb eat, drink and laugh to excess; the two Fosters make preposterous puns and the Duncannon boys are gentle and well-mannered; sometimes young Althorp is there, and the Duchess shamelessly encourages his attentions to Hary-o, seeing in his taciturnity a love-stricken heart, whilst all the time he is reliving last week's hunt. Corisande coquets with them all, exaggerating her accent and asking 'Is it poss-sible? Is Hary-o med not to flirrt?'; while Caroline St Jules, with her sloping shoulders and deer-like eyes, languishes when George Lamb is near. Often Caroline Ponsonby is with them, and then the tempo quickens, the summer lightning plays and Hart is in heaven.

In the gardens the turtles roll about under the trees waiting till Mr Crowle and Lord Melbourne come to feast upon them, and in the porch there is a tinkling sound as the wind plays through the Pandean-pipes.

Every Twelfth Night they had drawn King and Queen, and once Miss Trimmer noticed that the Duchess and Lady Bessborough set aside two presents, such as they had given to their daughters. It did not concern her and she did not approve, but she could not help being stricken by the look of pain upon their faces. 'But Sin never brings happiness,' she thought primly, and then hated herself for a prig.

The years pass with the rapidity peculiar to large families. They are marked chiefly by domestic events: a great ball at Hardwick; Christmas at Chiswick; a report of dangerous footpads between London and Chelsea; young Lady Spencer upsetting the Duchess by refusing to attend a juvenile ball, pleading both mourning and that she was following Miss Hannah More's system. 'Really,' said the Duchess, 'Lavinia is always arrogating to herself some perfection or other. And she has not called for over a year.' It was very hard, especially as Lord Spencer and his sisters were devoted to each other. Then came G.'s coming-out ball and presentation, when she was marked by attention from the Queen, which delighted Georgiana who had been the black sheep of the Court for so many years. G. made friends with Miss Berry, that paragon of tedium, and the Duchess published her poem *On the Passage of St Gothard*, dedicated to her children and which had an incredible success, being translated into several languages.

Soon the Cavendishes and Howards were all rejoicing when G., at the age of seventeen, married Lord Morpeth, Carlisle's eldest son. Georgiana and Miss Trimmer were particularly happy, as they felt sure that their beloved 'eldest' would be fortunate with this quiet, attentive young man to care for her. They had watched them sitting together shyly on the tither-tother, silent with happiness and mutual trust, and when, just a year afterwards, G. had borne the first of her twelve children, Selina sighed contentedly and felt she was entering on the next stage of her career as honorary grandmother to the second generation of Cavendishes.

From time to time one of the young men comes to show off his uniform—it is his turn to fight Napoleon. They have been fighting first France and then Napoleon ever since Selina came to Piccadilly. She and her charges had watched the troops embarking from Margate for Holland, a depressing and recurrent sight, and the young people could not remember the time when England was at peace. War had become the accustomed background to their lives.

In 1802, during that short breathing-space called the Peace of Amiens, when the exhausted belligerents prepared themselves for the final titanic struggle, they had flocked to France, there to enjoy the same delights that had pleased their elders under a different régime. Many of the older generation went too; the Bessboroughs and Lady Elizabeth pointing out similarities and differences from their time to young Lord and Lady Morpeth and the two Carolines. Sheridan had infuriated Lady Liz by telling her that she went to Paris under pretext of seeing the Apollo Belvedere, but really to display all the tenderness of her nature. He said, with some truth, that he would bet anything that she would faint seven times running when she first saw Bonaparte if nothing else would attract his attention, and he and Mr Hare succeeded in thoroughly tormenting her. They were all bent upon seeing the Bogy Man of Europe, and Fox, staunch to his old principles, wrote to the Duchess that he liked Paris very much, and believed that she would like it too if she could rid herself of poignant recollections of the past. Georgiana, however, did not forget easily, and she made the excuse of the Duke's unwillingness to travel and her bad health reasons for remaining in England.

Indeed, her recurrent attacks of eye trouble were not only dreaded by her but also by her mother, sister and Lady Liz. Lady Bessborough wrote a full account of the first serious attack, and the operation which accompanied it, to Lord Granville Leveson Gower in August 1796. She said:

I have no future plans. I have no thought, no hope, no wish, but seeing my Dear, Dear Sister get well again, and I can know no peace or happiness till then. The anxiety of my mind has been so near distraction that you will not wonder at my not writing or writing so strangely. I scarcely ever quit her room for a moment. While I am with her I use every effort to keep up her Spirits and mine and to be of use to her, and appear calm and cheerful while my heart is breaking. My whole soul is fix'd on that one object, and when I quit her, body and mind sink at once, overcome by fatigue and anguish. After hearing what I did tonight I can bear any thing. If you could but see how well she bears the greatest tortures, tho' hopeless, you would admire and love her more than ever.... I scarce dare trust myself to hope after the despair of last night and the endless changes, yet they tell me I may. My heart beat so this morning when the Surgeons came into my room that I was oblig'd to sit down and drink something before I heard what they had to say. They swear to me that the dreadful mischief of last night has stopp'd, and that if it does not return, something like sight may be restor'd, and without much disfiguring, and that no more horrid operations will be perform'd. She, too, seems calmer and better, and the cruel disorder has done its worst and is turn'd. You can form no Idea of how bad and how shocking it has been. God grant this amendment may continue. I am almost dead.

Later in the day she wrote:

I could not leave her room for the post ... they [the doctors] are positive she is better. O, Dear Ld. G., how you would have pitied her, I am sure, if you could have known half what she has suffer'd and I have felt....

The apparent improvement did not last, for in November Georgiana had to undergo a further operation. She was already quite blind in one eye, and there were fears that she would lose the sight of the other. Lady Bessborough was sent for from Roehampton to be present 'through a dreadful operation, which she bore with wonderful courage, and I with wretched cowardice: but I trust it will have good effects.'

By dint of employing a secretary, various cumbersome appliances and using her remaining eye as little as possible, Georgiana was saved from total blindness, though her headaches were excruciating and frequent. In 1803, she was again taken suddenly and seriously ill, and once more Lady Bessborough hurried to her side. She never left the Duchess for a week, remaining the whole time in her room and sharing the duties of nurse with Lady Spencer. On September the 15th she wrote to Lord Granville from Devonshire House.

> ... I was sent for last night from Roe to my Sister, who has a return of those dreadful spasms.... No Medicine, not the strongest, nothing that can be given her, has yet taken effect. Six and thirty hours have already elapsed in the dreadful pain. I sat up with her last night. She was put into a warm bath and bled, which reliev'd her at the time so much that she slept from four till near seven leaning on my Arm and quite still. But today the pain is very bad again.... You know I can never love anything a *little*, therefore you may judge how I suffer at this moment.

The physician in charge was Sir Walter Farquhar, who appears to have mismanaged all his patients. This attack of illness was so severe that her life was feared for, and her friends, including the Prince of Wales, waited in anxious suspense. On September the 20th he wrote to Lady Bessborough, hoping, as he had not heard from her for several days, that the danger was past, and asking for news. 'God grant,' he cried, 'that the account may be a satisfactory one, for no one on this earth can wish it more than I do, as no one on this earth can love her more truly than I do.'

Though she recovered, the respite was but a short one. In March and again in June 1805 she was afflicted with further attacks. Lady Spencer wrote to Harriet Bessborough on June the 30th saying:

> I see plainly, my dear Harriet, by your letters that your sister is still very ill. I cannot learn from any of you whether the complaint is in the eyelid or in the ball of the eye, & whether there is not any danger of the eye sinking. As she cannot doubt the sincerity of my fervent feeling for any

distress of hers, I am less anxious to get to town, as I may add to her hurry of seeing people, but can in no way I fear lessen her sufferings....

The Duchess made but a poor recovery. She was in no state to regain health and spirits, for she was faced with the worst financial crisis of her life. The Duke had insisted that he must be informed, once and for all, of the full extent of her liabilities. Georgiana felt that her sister was the only person whom she could trust to impart the information to Canis, and he, in turn, wished Lady Bessborough to act as his agent. Lady Spencer knew the true state of affairs; the vicious circle of pain and debt, so closely intermingled, and the impossibility of unravelling the cause of her daughter's condition. At the end of July she wrote to Harriet Bessborough saying:

> You do not hint anything about your success in other matters which I fear are essential to your poor sister's peace of mind. I am truly unhappy about her—but if the change of air does not make an alteration, surely some effectual step should be taken, & would not Sir W. Farquhar be the properest person—in short, I know not what to say, my dearest Harriet, I plainly see I can do no good, but yet I think her life is almost at stake....

Two days afterwards she wrote:

> Your letter of today has been quite a cordial to me, my dearest Harriet. Oh that your good accounts may but continue, & above all may you succeed in getting something effectual done about her affairs; without that a momentary amendment is nothing....

Lady Spencer, as always, was right. There was neither full confession nor settlement of the debts, nor a permanent improvement in either Georgiana's health or peace of mind. The sands were running very low.

17

No Music at the Close

Georgiana never permitted her ill-health to dominate her. Indeed, those who loved her were more anxious and careful on her behalf than she was herself. Her letters treat each attack of pain as a passing inconvenience. It is always, 'I shall be better tomorrow,' never 'I fear I shall be ill.'

Her interests in the outside world were now few, unless they affected the many young people around her. She was only forty-eight and close to them in spirit. The trend of politics had sickened her: though she loathed despotism, yet she could only hate the war with France; but her love of freedom flamed in her horror of the Slave Trade, and she aided Fox in his efforts to abolish it. Almost the last note he ever sent her was to enlist her help as of old.

½past seven, H. of C. Pray speak to everybody you can to come down or we shall be lost on the Slave Trade. Morpeth, Ossulston, Ld. A[rchibald] H[amilton], Ld. H. Petty all away. Pray, pray send any body you see.

Yours C.J.F.

Loving England, and understanding that the sea was her safeguard and her glory, everything pertaining to the Navy was of especial interest to her, particularly as her brother, Spencer, was First Lord of the Admiralty, and Nelson, and his Emma, her close friends. She believed with Sheridan that 'if there is, indeed, a rot in the wooden walls of Old England, our decay cannot be far distant.' So it was with beating heart that she followed the many vicissitudes of England's fortune at sea. The riots at Portsmouth in 1796, Hoche's expedition to Bantry Bay and the mutiny of the long-tried, much-neglected sailors at the Nore, were matters which touched her closely. Lord Spencer had much of his mother in him; upright and single-hearted, he had inherited Lady Spencer's capability of judgment and had the strength to act upon his convictions. In December 1796, when England was waiting news of an invasion and the uprising of Ireland, Georgiana imparted some of her hopes and fears to thirteen-year-old G.

> I very much fear I shall not be able to come tomorrow—the accounts from Ireland are so various that your Papa does not like my leaving him in this anxious moment.
>
> There never was a deeper stake than mine—for tho' if any misfortune shd. happen in Ireland, we shd. be very much reduc'd in our circumstances, yet I trust all of us would cheerfully conform to any change it would please God to inflict. But besides this, yr. Dear Uncle Spencer's honour & happyness is at Stake—and bad success wd. fall (tho' undeservingly) on him. He has done his best, but the fleets not getting out as soon as he intended owing to weather, renders the manoeuvre truly critical.
>
> I am full of hope, & trust his active Virtues, & your Grandmama's prayers, united to those of all good people, will be accomplish'd—but the moment is too anxious to me & I am really a *wretch* today....
>
> An express is just come—nothing new but that they certainly are not landed & the Country is favourable—still the anxiety remains.

When after the many fluctuations of fortune, England received the double news of victory at Trafalgar and of Nelson's death, Devonshire House shared in the dismay which outweighed the rejoicing. The general sentiment was expressed by a turnpike-keeper who said to Georgiana's friend, Charles Ellis, 'Sir, have you heard the bad news? We have taken twenty ships from the enemy, but Lord Nelson is killed?'

Despite the great events in the world, Georgiana was more concerned in her children's future. Not only with her own three, but the others, especially the girls, whom she had taken into her home.

G. was firmly and contentedly established as the future mistress of Castle Howard. Yearly, with praiseworthy punctuality, she produced another baby, there were already four and the fifth was on its way. Morpeth was proving a good husband and father, and was making a creditable name for himself in politics. Though his parents, especially Lord Carlisle, were somewhat of a trial to dearest G., the Duchess had no fear that her daughter's strong sense of duty and piety would surmount such small difficulties.

Georgiana had no fears, either, for Caro St Jules: she was a gentle, pliable creature and Bess would, naturally, make it her business to secure for her a sheltered and happy life.

Corisande de Gramont was more of a problem: after many changes of heart, she had finally fixed her affections on the little person of Lord Ossulston, Lord Tankerville's heir. They appeared well suited; he adored her; they were both small and well-favoured; equally well-bred and both, if the truth be admitted, somewhat empty-headed. There was one great obstacle, however—Lord Tankerville would not countenance the marriage. He was an irascible, dictatorial old man, filled with a sense of the importance of his own family, and he refused to accept a dowerless daughter-in-law. Corise's émigré father, the Duc de Grammont, was quite unable to provide the sum demanded by Lord Tankerville and an impasse had been reached. Georgiana loved Corise as one of her own children, and it distressed her to see these two young people debarred from happiness. She determined that, despite her own financial straits, she would somehow provide Corise with a dowry, even if it meant that the girl would have to wait till after Georgiana's death to receive it. Somehow, the Duchess felt, she would not have to wait long.

Caroline Ponsonby had astonished her family by accepting William Lamb, who had loved her for years. Though their attachment had been regarded as unsuitable—for however fond Georgiana and her sister were of Lady Melbourne, they could not look upon her as an ideal mother-in-law for the temperamental Caro, and also William was but a comparatively poor younger son—yet his unswerving devotion and the sad death of his elder brother, Peniston, by which he became Lord Melbourne's heir, had removed the chief objections, and he and Caro had had their way.

Then there was Hary-o. Georgiana wished to see her second daughter safely and happily married, but all her plans had gone awry. First Duncannon, and then Althorp, had proved disappointments. She had hoped so much to see Hary-o married to one of her cousins, but it was not to be. Then Hary-o had had a decided penchant for Peter Burrell; but this had been scotched by an unfortunate incident, cruelly ridiculed and exaggerated in the papers. Georgiana sighed as she remembered how upset and distressed she, poor Hary-o and the entire family had been by the report in *The Morning Post* of Mr Andrew's ball, where owing to the heat the majority of the guests had retired, leaving Georgiana's party in possession. According to the newspaper, 'Her Grace had introduced *French Cotillions....* The grace and activity displayed by Lady Harriet Cavendish was unusually admired. Her ladyship's elegance of person attracted the eye, while her dazzling beauty overpowered the senses. The Goddess of Youth and Beauty seemed united in this lovely offspring of gentle Devon. An interesting scene took place between two lovers. From so much dancing the boards grew very slippery and this lovely nymph in one of her graceful turns, slipped, and would have come to the ground but for the timely assistance of the Hon. Peter Burrell, who, all assiduity to his intended partner for life, luckily caught her in his arms:

> Forbid it, Heav'n,' young Peter cry'd,
>   And clasp'd her to his breast,
> The wond'ring fair one turn'd to chide,
>   'Twas Peter's self that prest.

After this incident, Georgiana had decided she must let time take its course, and hoped fervently that Hary-o would soon find happiness elsewhere.

There remained one other child, the invisible Eliza Courtnay. When she thought of Eliza, it was always to the accompaniment of that nostalgic tune she and her sister used so often to sing—the words 'Que le jour me dure, passé loin de toi' would run through her head and she would sigh a little fearfully. Eliza's was the sorest problem and the one closest to Georgiana's heart. Charles Grey had said that he could do little for his daughter, and Georgiana was racked by anxiety as to her poor outcast child's future.

She had managed to provide an annual allowance, just enough to keep her, but what would happen when she was no longer there to pay it? She tried to set aside some money to create a trust, but found she was unable to succeed in this object. So she determined to appeal to Hart. It cost her all her strength and resolution to do so. In one blow she had to shatter his belief in her; she, whom he had always regarded as a saint far above all other women, now stood a self-confessed sinner before him. The mother and son gazed at each other as though seeing each other for the first time. She could not bear the misery in his face. 'How could you, dearest Em? How could you?' he cried. 'Remember,' she pleaded, 'that when I was but seventeen I was already a beauty, a toast and a Duchess and wholly neglected by my husband.' He left her silently, but after the first shock of disillusion, he knew that he had never loved her so well and vowed that he would never betray her trust in him.

Instinctively she felt reassured, and that she had been justified in her statement to her mother, that her three, out of Lady Spencer's thirteen grandchildren, though least in quantity, were the best in quality. She knew that they would always act in a manner which would reflect honour upon her memory.

Connected with, but apart from, these problems were her own unsolved difficulties. The last attempts in 1805 to clear her from debt had been, as ever, incomplete. Despite Canis's assurances, Harriet and Bess's good offices; despite Mr Coutts's, the Duke of Bedford's, her brother's and Mr Adair's efforts, she was still beset by fears and creditors. Sheridan, who had often handed her into her coach, literally sobbing over her losses at the card-table, had been unable to help her. She had kept Adair's letter, every word of which was engraven on her heart, but she had not been able to follow his advice. He had assured her how truly happy he was to think that some real settlement of her difficulties was about to take place, and had gone on to say:

Let me now avail myself of the priviledge of the sincerest friendship to implore you by every consideration you value in life to render this arrangement solid and effectual, and not a measure of mere palliation and delay. Excuse me if I should use too strong expressions in opening my heart to you on this subject, and remember it is not I alone who speak to you now, it is your fame, your quiet, and your happiness, it is every friend you have living, it is our common and ever lamented friend who is no more [the 5th Duke of Bedford] who invokes you from the grave to put an end once and for ever to that system which has caused you such endless anxiety and alarm. Count over, for god's sake, every debt you have, every thing which, although not strictly debt, has a tendency to produce debt in the future, and even those things which by bearing the appearance of obligation, might lead people to reasonable expectations of future favour, count up, I repeat it, all this mass of mischief as scrupulously and as exactly as if you were making up your account with Heaven, and lay the whole before those who are best capable of advising and of saving you. Remember that you are now drawing out your last stake; you are disposing of the fee simple of your resources; that you are, in a manner, at *your world's end*, beyond which there is no room even for hope to live in! Tenderness for your feelings when I have seen you agitated and suffering has often checked my utterance, or I would have told you before this the horrors I have anticipated on your account at times when sufferings of my own have kept me waking. I will but barely allude to a dreadful possibility which although, thank God, far removed from your present fears, is nevertheless in the hands of nature. This world without the Sun would be less dark and cheerless than your situation then! Could the friends you would then have remaining effectually aid you? ... *would* the wretches who have been preying on you for such a course of years, shew you the least mercy or forbearance? There have been moments, I give you my honour, when this idea has haunted me so as to deprive me of all the priviledges you have allowed me; and with reason, since a moment's reflection must shew you that it is no exaggerated picture of your condition.

If I have said one word too much, I again entreat you to forgive me; but neither the duties nor the feelings of friendship would suffer me to be silent, or to pass by this, which I pray to God may be the *last* occasion of my speaking to you on these matters which you were never made to hear about....

It had been useless.... Her ingrained fear of Canis, her belief in his possible ruin, and her deep sense of shame at the extent and depth of her folly, had prevented her from making a full confession which would have cleared her once and for ever.

Early in March 1806 she went to Court, where she caught a chill. She returned home, sick and shivering. The old pain in her side returned, redoubled in violence. She had had many of these attacks, and there was no cause for anxiety. The house was hushed, for, as always, illness had brought on one of those terrible headaches. Caroline Lamb wrote her a little poem, expressing her love and pity, which was read to her.

> *Gentle sleep, thy blessings shed—*
> *Soothe her weary soul to rest;*
> *Angels, guard her suffering head,*
> *Calm the troubles of her breast.*
>
> *'Tis for others' woes she weeps,*
> *By their sorrows quite opprest;*
> *Angels, guard her while she sleeps,*
> *She who blesses, should be blest.*

Lady Spencer guessed that Georgiana's illness did not arise from a wholly physical cause. On March the 14th she wrote anxiously to Harriet Bessborough:

I am most uncomfortable about your sister, my dear Harriet. Some horrible difficulty is hanging over her I conclude, & what can be done? The weather is very unfavourable for your convalescent party. I hope to hear you are all safe in town again for their sake as well as hers, for I conclude her illness is owing to the old & hopeless story of money difficulties. Burn this dab as soon as you have read it. I have not courage to enter upon any other subject....

Lady Bessborough was still at Roehampton; her sister's condition, though distressing, did not cause alarm. Georgiana was well enough to write to her mother, which occasioned Lady Spencer, on the 17th, to say:

I am sadly distressed, my dear Harriet, about your poor dear sister. I inclose her letter to me, to which. I have been under the cruel neccessity of saying the truth, that I have but 20£ in the banker's hands, which I had reserved for my journey back from hence, but I can manage without it, & have sent it to her. I dread however the effect of disappointment to her in her present weak state, & inclose therefore to you a Draft for the remaining 80£ dated the 3rd of April, which, as it is a little more than a fortnight from this day, is nearly as good as ready money, especially as my credit is so good. But you will easily understand the danger there is of my letting your dear sister know that I can do this, as it would then be constantly expected, & my credit would soon be lost, besides the real inconvenience it would put me to. Do not therefore, my dear Harriet, make use of this, if it can be avoided, but if her health be injured by it, use it without scruple—if not, send it back to me with the name torn off that I am sure it is not littered about or lost....

On March the 21st Georgiana was much worse and Lady Bessborough remained with her instead of returning to Roehampton. The next day Harriet wrote to the being she loved next to her sister, Granville Leveson Gower, then Ambassador at St Petersburg:

The events of a sick room can only be interesting to those who witness them, and have nothing else to tell you, as I rarely quit her room. Yesterday she was very ill, today much better, but tonight a shivering fit has come on again. I fear it will at best be very lingering! I am very anxious and absolutely pass my life at D. H.

The following day she was able to add better news to her letter:

23rd, Sunday. After sitting up the whole night I have not yet been able to find a moment when she was well enough for me to go home. It has been a sad day, but she is at length in a quiet sleep and I hope will have a good night. Dr Bailey sits up with her; he is now sitting opposite me with his night-cap on, and so uncouth a figure that nothing but her illness would prevent it being laughable. He is blunt and rough, but more encouraging than Farquhar. I am miserable at her suffering, but do not feel alarm'd; if I did I should scarcely be able to support it....

Indeed, indeed, she is better tonight, and Bailey says he thinks Farquhar takes alarm too easily.

Farquhar, for once, was right. For two days Georgiana was so ill that Harriet could not find time even to write to Granville or her son Willy, who was with him as his secretary. But on the night of the 25th, Fox was able to send better news to Russia.

My Dear Lord, I add these few lines to what I wrote this morning merely to tell you that I am just come from Devonshire House, where I had the satisfaction of hearing a far better account of the Dss. than we had before. The Physicians think there is now no danger, but those who love her cannot be easy till the fever has entirely quitted her....
Yrs. ever, C. J. Fox.

G., six months gone with child, Hartington, Hary-o and Bess, all waited anxiously for the expected improvement. They waited in vain, for on the 28th she became desperately ill, and at 3.30 in the morning of the 30th she died. Lady Spencer's draft had still three days to run. It would not be needed now.

They could none of them believe the truth. It was not she who lay lifeless and unanswering before their stricken eyes. The escutcheon was hung above the door, silent crowds stood before the house in Piccadilly, there was a constant stream of callers. No one was admitted. The house was a citadel of grief.

Barely conscious of her action, Harriet wrote once more to Granville.

You will know, Dear G., by the newspapers—I cannot write—if anything should happen to me ... Mrs Baker will send you a letter. God bless you—break it to Willy.

Anything so horrible, so killing, as her three days' agony no human being ever witness'd. I saw it all, held her thro' all her struggles, saw her expire, and since have again and again kiss'd her cold lips and press'd her lifeless body to my heart—and yet I am alive....

Georgiana was to be buried in the family vault at Derby. The little band of those most close to her, their differences forgotten and united in their love and sorrow, watched together till the last vestige was borne away, away from them, away from all that she held clear.

Then, tacitly, they agreed to go with Harriet Bessborough to Roehampton. Before they left, Fox insisted on seeing Harriet. He told her brokenly how he felt their loss, of what Georgiana had meant to him. Harriet listened with dry eyes. She was unable to speak one word.

It was a month before she could bring herself even to receive the Prince of Wales, who, too, was stunned by grief.

Every day she and Bess made a sad pilgrimage to Devonshire House. Georgiana's final mark of love and confidence in her friend had been to entrust all her papers to Bess, who asked Harriet to help her in the painful task of sorting them. Each day they drove into:

> ... that court, seeing her Windows, her room, all the places which from custom seem'd incorporated with her, and seeing at the same time the sad escutcheon and the deep mourning all around, which point out what has happen'd.

It was the same story at Chiswick:

> ... where I went with Bess to look for papers. I will not attempt telling you what I suffer'd, but that place more than any other, that place which seems almost her creation—the place where I have pass'd the happiest and the most miserable hours of my life—where every turn recalls to me all that I have lov'd best, where remorse and regret equally tear me, and bitter grief from seeing her almost present to me and losing her again.

Seven months afterwards, the Prince went to Chatsworth, and to Bess he wrote that:

> I confess to you it was almost too much for me, the recollection of several of the pieces of furniture which I had seen in her room and which I had so often sat upon in her room when conversing with her, quite overpowered me, for it is enough to have known her as we have never to be able to forget it. It is quite impossible to describe to you all that I have gone through of late, such a loss and such a calamity are almost beyond all sufferance, at least it is so to me.... I would, if I dared, call at

Devonshire House, but really I am not sufficiently stout to venture it as I could not expose myself in entering that house.

They all felt alike: life might go on, but it could never be quite the same again. Even Canis, when the task of sorting her papers and disentangling that unhappy web of her debts was finally accomplished, was moved to an unwonted cry of pity. 'Was that all?' he said. 'Why, oh why did she not tell me?'

At some time in her life she, who had written so many epitaphs for the deserving poor in her mother's village, had written her own. It was found among Lord Halifax's papers, so she must have given it to Charles Grey, humbly, yet in the hope that at last he would see her as she saw herself. She had written:

Beneath this stone
and in the small portion of the earth it covers
are consigned
The ashes of one—who in Society
held no inconsiderable rank.
She was once exalted in Situation
She was once lovely in person
Her heart was warm though weak
Her disposition friendly though incautious
And her understanding good though misguided & obscured
By her hastiness of decision & want of judgement.

It was to her a source of shame when she considered
That she had misused talents that might have been useful,
It was a source of sorrow when she reflected
That she had misapplied liberality & good-nature,
And it was the cause of poignant regret when she discovered
That she herself had destroyed the fairest prospect of happiness.
But if it was her misery to have offended her friends

It was her Pride & Glory
That she ever was beloved
And always forgiven.
Happy in her Parents, her Husband, her Children, her Sister
And her Friend,
She above all received

From her affectionate respectable & beloved Mother
Religious Principles
Which tho' she sometimes neglected she never renounced

And the sentiments inspired by the thoughts of Death were these—

Gratitude to her friends for their indulgence
And the hope
That her rememberance would be harboured
With affectionate kindness
And forgiving Love.

And to her God she offered
Her deep contrition
And the sorrows of her life
And her presumptuous hope
That the All-good long suffering and All-seeing Power
Who best would know the extent of her error
Would although dreadful in His judgements
Compassionate and appreciate
Her Repentance.

To this she added a short, conventional prayer. It was a long epitaph, both over- and under-written: she could have expressed it in five words,

'She was true to herself.'

If it was the warmth of her heart, the hastiness of her decision and her want of judgment that caused her weakness, it was because she so strongly had the defects of her greatest
quality—self-forgetfulness. Totally oblivious of her own interests, when she had smiled upon Canis and Bess; when she had raised money to pay her gambling debts and then given it away; when she had surrendered herself to Grey, her impulsiveness had prevented her from even considering the ultimate interests of others. It had never occurred to her that she might be harming her husband and her friend by her generosity, that it might recoil upon her children, that she impoverished, not only herself, but her husband by her charity, that in her love she gave more than she received. She believed that she herself had destroyed the fairest prospect of her happiness and never thought of blaming others; she accepted exile

and separation from her children as just punishments for the crimes of extravagance and frailty. The undisciplined giving of her soul had been her only sin, generosity her greatest fault. Subconsciously she had known, though her age had forgotten, that the integrity of life depends upon the practice of 'to thine own self be true.'

She could not know the reward that was to come too late: that the acquiescence, so foreign to her nature, towards the relationship between Canis and Bess would be redeemed by the principles she had absorbed from her mother and passed on to her children, who, though generous, ever regarded Lady Elizabeth as their mother's greatest enemy and betrayer. Though she had her Pride and Glory in being beloved, she could not know how her image would live with Hary-o night and day; how when G. was beset with despair, she would turn to her memory, praying to be made worthy of her; of how, on the night before he died, Hart would ask that his picture be hung next to hers.

She does not know that her hope has come true, and that her remembrance is harboured with forgiving Love.

LONDON,
    December the 8th, 1942.

Sources

Chatsworth MSS.

Castle Howard MSS.

Lord Granville Leveson Gower, Private Correspondence 1781-1821, edited by Castalia, Countess Granville (Murray, 1916).

Paxton and the Bachelor Duke, by Violet Markham (Hodder & Stoughton, 1935).

Sheridan, by Walter Sichel. 2 vols. (Constable, 1909).

The Westminster Election (1785).

Hary-o, edited by G. Leveson Gower and Iris Palmer (Murray, 1940).

Life of George IV, by P. Fitzgerald. 2 vols. (Tuisley Bros., 1881).

Town and Country Magazine various years.

Gentleman's Magazine various years.

The New Bath Guide, by Christopher Anstey (1766).

The Grand Whiggery, by Marjorie Villiers (Murray, 1939).

Anglo-Saxon Review (June and September 1899).

A Book for a Rainy Day, by John Thomas Smith (1845).

Nollekens and His Times, by John Thomas Smith (1828).

The Letters of Horace Walpole, 1798-1825.

The Two Duchesses, by Vere Foster (Blackie, 1898).

Lady Bessborough and her Family Circle, by Bessborough and Aspinall (Murray, 1940).

Farington Diaries, by Joseph Farington (Hutchinson, 1922).

The Diary of a Lady in Waiting, by Lady Charlotte Bury. 2 vols. (Lane, 1908).

The Age of Grey and Peel, by H. W. Carless Davies (Oxford University Press, 1929).

The Diary of the Rt. Hon. William Windham, 1784-1810, edited by Mrs H. Baring (Longmans, Green, 1866).

Historical and Posthumous Memoirs, 1772-1784, by Sir N. W. Wraxall, edited by H. B. Wheatley (Bickers, 1884).

Memorials and Correspondence of Charles James Fox, edited by Lord John Russell (1853-7).

Historical Manuscripts Commission (Castle Howard MSS.).

The Diary and Letters of Madame d'Arblay, 1778-1840.

The Works of the late Right Honourable Richard Brinsley Sheridan (1821).

Lord Grey of the Reform Bill, by G. M. Trevelyan (Longmans, Green, 1920).

The demolition of Devonshire House, February 1925.